DUBLIN'S FUTURE

New Visions for Ireland's Capital City

Edited by
Lorcan Sirr

The Liffey Press

Published by
The Liffey Press
Ashbrook House, 10 Main Street
Raheny, Dublin 5, Ireland
www.theliffeypress.com

© 2011 Individual contributors

A catalogue record of this book is
available from the British Library.

ISBN 978-1-908308-12-2

Relevant maps are covered by Ordnance Survey Licence AR0077411.

Printed in Spain by GraphyCems.

Contents

Acknowledgements

Firstly, thanks to my colleague, collaborator and sometime co-writer, Conor Skehan, for all the interesting and provocative discussions on our capital's future in Leuven and Dublin over the last few years. In a similar vein, thanks must also go to Dr. Brian Hughes, formerly of Dublin Institute of Technology, for his insights on the populations and statistics which will most likely make up a new city-state of Dublin by 2060. To the *Centre Culturel Irlandais* in Paris for accommodating me in the final stages of this book: *j'ai vraiment apprécié mon séjour à Paris*. This sojourn was kindly funded by a research grant from the Society of Chartered Surveyors Ireland, and was much appreciated. To Sarah Browne for the prod to get on with the book; and to Emma Sherry for her presence as a sounding board for ideas as the book progressed. Thanks also to David Givens of The Liffey Press for having the courage of my convictions. Finally, of course, to all the contributors who have submitted the chapters which make up this volume. You were a very easy, insightful and professional group of people to deal with, and for that I am extremely grateful.

Photographs are the editor's unless otherwise credited. Views expressed are those of the individual authors.

Prologue

Lorcan Sirr

This is a book about the future of Dublin. Its authors, styles, interests and of course visions are diverse and sometimes divergent. They represent the range of competing voices, dreams, influences and ideas that weave together in a constant battle of power, persuasion, aspiration and occasionally co-operation which en mass determine the future of any city. Each individual chapter, not only in content, but also in style, is a reflection of the way different people and groups perceive the future and how it may be determined.

Over the years of this book's gestation from first idea to publication, Ireland has changed and painfully so. Although Dublin remains Ireland's economic engine, there is always a danger that in times of desperation this engine, instead of being better tuned for enhanced performance gets neglected, if not ignored. In desperate times, cries for assistance come from many quarters, and political parties, ever mindful of retaining their share of the vote, are very susceptible to diverting resources away from 'super-tuning' the engine to other, no doubt worthy, but often far less productive, areas. And so, whereas the future of Ireland's capital city has always been an interesting topic for discussion (arguably entered into by only a few however), it is even more pertinent in times of shortage.

This book commenced life with six chapters, and ended up as you see it today. Its contributors are, in the main, relatively young people. This was not deliberate, it just happened that way: approaching one potential author to contribute a chapter often led to discussions about other already-decided and potential chapters, and then on to other potential authors. Finding contributors was a combination of networking and snowball research (or a very minor Delphi study). The smallness of Dublin was a distinct advantage in uncovering people who could not alone write about the future of Dublin, but people who also had something to say. Several will have travelled and lived abroad. All are well known in their specialist field. Each is interested in the future of their city. Their brief was simple: to write about the future of Dublin in the context of their expertise. In the spirit of a collaboration, with many differences making a coherent whole, how they did that was up to them, whether it was a narrative, polemic, stream of consciousness, or even interviews; their definition of Dublin, what geographical boundaries constituted their capital city, was also in their hands.

Finally, a word on the title. I have occasionally detected the unseen hand of the snake-oil salesman when I see the word 'vision' on reports and in titles. In the case of this book, I struggled to find a better title: it dawned on me as I asked different people to contribute their time, experience and energy to this project that in order for these people to write about their vision for a future Dublin they would have to think on, reflect, evaluate and describe their ideas; and so a vision which has a foundation based on this level of thought is a very positive thing. You may not recognise nor agree with every idea contained in *Dublin's Future* – in fact, I hope you don't; indeed the authors themselves might not agree with each other – but the experience, energy, hard work and reflection from the contributors that brought their ideas to these pages has provided a starting point from which we may legitimately begin to consider – not just on a big paper map, but more holistically – the future of Dublin.

Lorcan Sirr
Paris
August 2011

1

Cities, Futures, Illusion and Delusion

Lorcan Sirr
Introduction

Number one child

Cities are, for an increasing percentage of the population, globally and in Ireland, the places which house us, employ us, contain and entertain us. The ancient Greeks said that houses make a town, but it is the citizens who make a city, and so the city is what man has created for himself, nature being what he was originally given. Cities have a certain dynamic of their own, a social, economic, artistic and technological momentum which perpetuates itself against the best wishes of what man sometimes thinks he wants. What we end up with is a somewhat troubled relationship between cities and their inhabitants. But such troubled relationships are part of what creates reality, and so the fallibility and imperfection of a city is perhaps an indicator of the presence of a soul. It's when imperfection descends into dysfunction that trouble starts. Sometimes the most perfectly laid out cities on paper – perhaps overly-planned – are often the cities which have least attraction for mankind intent on seeking a place with a soul (to my mind, Los Angeles, for example). But it's not just cities in tension with their inhabitants: over two thousand years ago, Plato was writing about every city being in a natural state of war with every other city. Cities are still in tension with other cities, although we now refer to it as competition

1

rather than war. This competition is of course commercial in nature. For good or ill, commercial imperatives always have and still shape our cities – think of Manchester's mills or London's Canary Wharf – and if the physical structure of a city is a product of its functions, then what kind of cities will we have in the future? Commercial imperatives rarely have at their heart the genuine good of the citizenry, so a balance must be achieved between commercial reality and human necessity. Cities should be good at this though, as they have always also been repositories of culture and ideas, functions with the good of the citizen at their core. This is part of what they do. The arts in their multifarious forms have flourished in cities, providing respite from the commercial and social tensions of city life, whilst also symbolising the health of a city. A city with a vibrant arts and cultural movement is in the main a healthy – or at least interesting – city, as such movements require considerable human energy, and where there's energy, there's still life.

The presence of wealth in a city is not necessarily indicative of a city which has at its heart the benefit of its inhabitants. The idea that because there is money in the air, the city is in a healthy state has been repeatedly proven to be false. These days much wealth is not created through industry – mills and factories – but in offices at desktops with computers. If cities are the result of what goes on in them, then whilst wealth may be created like this, it doesn't automatically mean that a city that is pleasant to live and work in will also be created. If the functions within a city determine how that city looks and feels, then we must carefully consider what we want to be happening in that city commercially and socially. There is no right answer as to how to achieve a balance between two functions which can often be diametrically opposed, but that's no excuse for not trying. As Jane Jacobs noted over 50 years ago, 'cities are an immense laboratory of trial and error, failure and success, in city building and city design'.

Dublin is a city which has escaped much of the experimentation of many of the great urban thinkers of the last 150 years: Ebenezer Howard, Geddes, Mumford, Stein, Wright, and Bauer never got a significant foothold here. Le Corbusier with his vertical city to house people at 1,200 per acre leaving 95 per cent of the ground below open (wealthier inhabitants would have luxury housing with 85 per cent of their ground left open) failed to inspire local city fathers to any great extent in the early 20th century. Despite being the second city of the British Empire for many years, Dublin also escaped most of the costs (and some of the benefits) of the Industrial Revolution, the legacies of which can be seen in many cities across the north of England, and indeed in Belfast. The Industrial Revolution shaped many of these cities, and Dublin, having in the main skipped this economic period, is a city with little in the way of an industrially-shaped landscape, bar a significant numbers of bridges built in that era. It did have some industry, but it also could be argued that the Guinness plant was as industrial as Dublin got.[1] There are few mills, or factory chimneys looming on its horizon; its streets are not endless rows of terraced red-bricked housing for workers à la Bolton or Saltaire or Blackburn, romantically picturesque as an advertisement for Hovis bread as they may be. Yet despite not having given much to the world industrially, Dublin still managed to survive relatively gracefully and in some periods even flourish. It has mostly retained that balance between economic reality and human necessity. Much of this balance has been the result of strong links with the arts and culture movements which have made Dublin's name from Swift onwards, despite our sometime less than generous attitude towards these great artists. This balance of perspectives, interests and potential is the key to Dublin's survival as a city with a soul.

Conor Skehan (see chapter on Economics) and I write occasional newspaper articles together on various topics, mostly to do with planning for the future in various guises (economical, political, and so forth). For our literary efforts on the future of Dublin, a two-piece series which graced the pages of *The Irish Times* in 2008, just as things were starting to go severely wrong in Ireland, we were both praised and pilloried.[2] On the positive side, our ideas were welcomed by those who felt 'it was about time' that somebody had written honestly about Dublin and its importance; the negatives were of the mind that our pieces were distinctly anti-rural. Ignoring the fact that this artificial urban-rural debate has stymied Ireland for decades now, the truth was that what we were doing was somewhere in between: we weren't the first people to ever write about the future of Dublin, but we were quite strident in our belief that the future of Ireland lies with the future of Dublin. In no way was this being anti-rural Ireland; in fact, we were simply explaining the significance of the economic and demographic figures before us – the Dublin region gives more return per euro invested than any other part of Ireland and development would continue to occur on the east coast. The 2011 census is bearing this out. Indeed, research has consistently demonstrated the greater economic value of cities. It follows, therefore, that the more money invested in the economic engine of the land, the greater the output for sharing with the rest of the country, for building roads, for keeping hospitals open, for social welfare payments, for arts, for tourism development and so forth. This was perhaps an unpalatable truism for many people, especially politicians, and most of the most public of politicians at that time were from rural areas. In recessionary times, however, it remains truer than ever as rural regions lose their industries and employers at an alarming rate, and even greater pressure then falls on those more stable economic locations such as Dublin to provide what employment and opportunities they can, and to house, entertain and move around the economic migrants that come its way – as they should: it's what a capital city is for. But if Dublin is to properly play the role of a capital city, it should be treated as one. If we look after the capital, it will look after us. Like a precious family member, it should be cared for and indeed nurtured. Nurturing the city means not being afraid to be that pushy parent, to admit that this is our number one child, this is our hope for the future. To date, very few politicians have been willing to step up to that particular plate. During the 2011 general election, Gerard O'Neill[3] created

A 'Wordle' of political parties' manifestos for the General Election 2011.
Image courtesy of Gerard O'Neill.

a 'wordle' of the main political parties' manifestos: it says a lot about national priorities to see that the word 'Dublin' does not appear in the image at all.

The future(s)

It is quite sad that so few have championed Dublin to the nation; it is also very short-sighted. Aside from all the other value that goes along with having experts give their thoughts on Dublin's future, highlighting and discussing issues of interest and importance is a form of risk management. See Sinéad Shannon's chapter on ageing for example: ageing is something that happens to everybody and yet we consistently let it take us by surprise. So, facing up to the future, like ageing, and thinking about it in a considered way, is a means by which we can direct it to a certain extent, but also, and more importantly, by which we can be ready for it. Whatever it turns out to be.

Therein lies a significant point: prediction is pointless. Preparation for the future is, however, invaluable. This is not a book of predictions of what Dublin will look like. Instead, and more interesting, are a series of thoughts and visions on Dublin's futures. Such a process is not scientific, and nobody can be held to account (which in itself gives great freedom to authors to write unshackled from the binds of pinpoint, pedantic accuracy). What it is trying to do is take a look at the bigger picture, by breaking it down into many constituent parts, or as many as could fit in. The process of looking at the future is interdisciplinary, which brings a degree of holism to the practice. It also avoids that common error of simply thinking that the future of cities, and indeed the future of any- or everything, is based around money, economics and politics. It is not. It is based around its people and their interests, be they music, money, dance or heritage and everything in between. The time horizons are also invariably long, but that doesn't mean the future can be ignored. Preparation for the future – which is, ironically, something that never arrives – is essentially preparing ourselves for the present. And we all live in the present.

Dublin is, of course, a city, albeit it a very small one by international, or even European, standards. Merely having a cathedral no longer counts. It takes up a lot of land though for such a small population: the Dublin area occupies a land area the size of Los Angeles, a city of over 12 million people. Dublin has just over 1.6 million and just under 40 per cent of the population of the state; how that happened is and no doubt will be the subject of other books. As a city, however, Dublin has some common traits with other cities in Europe and globally, and is influenced by similar issues and dilemmas.

Some of the factors which will influence the future of cities are relatively obvious – technology (advances and regressions), energy and the flow of money, and the relationship between the three, are reliable forces of influence on most countries, and especially in areas where there are large urban conurbations. An additional aspect for Dublin will be access to clean water, not only for domestic use, but also for that of industry. The availability of clean water will be an increasingly large and important factor for industry and their location choices, which has significant and obvious implications for Dublin's economic well-being. Climate change and health and well-being are two other areas which it can be seen from some considerable distance will impact on the future of any city, including Dublin. Climate change matters whether or not it is a myth or reality, such is the extent to which it is embedded in our systems, our products and our behaviours. Climate change will, through regulation, taxation and peer pressure (local, national and international), be a major influence on how and where we live, on everything from the materials we use to construct our buildings to the aspect of their location. Considering waste and emissions, look at the number of ungainly multi-coloured bins householders have in back yards and front gardens – at which point the question arises as to why we pay for our waste to be collected, especially given the economies of scale in urban areas, instead of *being paid* for accumulating and sòrting this rubbish for the benefit of the private sector collectors who then use it to generate financial return: we are, quite literally, fuelling their profits.

With a rapidly ageing population (by 2060 more than one in five of the population will be over 65), and most of this ageing population on the east coast in and around the Dublin region, the health of Dublin's dwellers is of vital importance and will influence greatly our capital city. If done correctly – and it's easily done mainly through our planning system – planning Dublin for ageing has enormous and widespread knock-on benefits for everybody, not just the aged. For example, what the aged need is also just what young mothers with children need, and it also suits everyone in between (ramps, low ramp buses, ease of access and so forth). This means not merely the presence of, to take the most obvious example, medical services, but easy access to them, both financially and physically. This also means general medical care – non-emergency visits to the doctor and trips to the pharmacy – must be viable: such services need to be proximate and integrated into the community, not add-ons after the bookies, the take-away and the local Spar have been accommodated.[4] (To paraphrase Hemingway, it seems there is no quarter too poor to have at least one bookmaker's shop.) But of course, the aged want and need more than medical services: they want culture, entertainment, travel, exercise and everything else that normal citizens desire. In taking care of the aged in our city – if we do it – we are also taking care of the city, as we should because some day it will have to take care of us.

Other influencing factors are perhaps more subtle.

Firstly, cities *are* the future, globally and nationally. Ireland as a country needs to accept that the future is urban. That is not an antagonistic statement; read the census results for the last few decades and the trends towards greater urbanisation in Ireland (reflecting a global trend) reveal themselves. It is nearly 50 years ago that there were for the first time more people living in urban areas in Ireland than in rural areas. This particular Rubicon was crossed was back in the 1960s, but yet the reality of that and the implications of Ireland becoming an urban society centred on Dublin has not yet quite sunk in, especially politically. Acceptance of this fact should lead to proper planning for it and hopefully getting better value – economic and social – from it. We should be planning to use the economies of scale a large urban area provides, and not planning against it, especially by diluting our resources through the inappropriate attempt at balanced regional development: you can't balance a bowling ball with a handful of marbles.

Speed is an essential requirement of a successful city, and will increasingly be so. The pace and ease at which people can live, move around, do business, access information, communicate, and everything else which requires faster responses will be a more and more noticeable facet of the city of the future.

It is also quite likely that cities worldwide, including Dublin, will be characterised by increased instances of anger, division and polarisation, not just politically but throughout society, and especially with perceived injustices, be they security- (UK riots) or economy-based. As Robert Cohen wrote in the *International Herald Tribune*:

. . . the only people who walked away unscathed from the great financial binge that created this mess were those who were its main architects and greatest beneficiaries: the bankers and financiers and hedge-fund honchos pulling the strings of the universe. Justice assuages tempers; its absence enflames them.[5]

Ireland already has a large gap between the 'haves' and the 'have nots', and this may not decrease if left to its own devices and external influences (if we continue to think Boston rather than Berlin). Being a small city, Dublin may not feel the brunt of this divisiveness as much as other larger, more dense and complex conurbations, but in many areas, the middle ground may not be where people want to congregate any more, this middle space being increasingly characterised by conservatism, evasion, abrogation, inaction and inertia in the face of an ever more demanding and informed population. As we watch what were formerly radical political parties (then representing strong specific political philosophies) encroach ever more on the centre in order to catch that increasing middle-class vote, it is notable that the standardisation of ideologies has become a '*bland*ardisation' of ideologies. Once forthright beliefs have become diluted and dull, watered-down to appeal to the highest number of voters and the lowest common denominator. The parties from whom most was expected naturally disappoint the greatest. Increasing bureaucracy and the rise of the technocratic, corporate state push urban people to the margins of the ideological spectrum, and extremism finds fertile breeding grounds at the edges of society, where a lack of resources can sometimes make expression of discontent a disruptive and relatively crude affair.

Partly through increased interaction and accessibility, cities will also be increasingly influenced by each other for good and for ill. They will hopefully not, as Plato referred to earlier, go to war with each other, but they will be in an endless cycle of competition: Dublin is and will remain in this competition. That is by no means to suggest that Dublin will always win – and winning is less likely unless we begin to better use our urban resources – but yet Dublin cannot afford *not* to be part of this cycle: self-regarding protectionism is not an option. Cities are universal, and the competition intense. Activities thinking of relocating to Dublin will also be looking at other cities, so a well prepared city will be able to offer the best it can in order to attract and, just as importantly, retain these operations. Dublin's competitors are well-built and ruthless, and we should be careful not to send our player in under-nourished.

Somewhat surprisingly perhaps, will be a probable rise in the importance of ethical issues in and for cities. This does not mean that our banking community will suddenly develop a bad case of scruples, it may simply be that urban dwellers will have a greater awareness of their actions, their inactions, and the implications of both. Living in close proximity to one another brings home how much the way we live, and the way others around us live, impacts on us personally. Some of these ethical developments will evolve naturally from increased proximity and all that brings; other developments will be imposed upon us from outside, particularly institutions and organisations to which Ireland belongs, and from agreements to which it has signed up. These agreements are likely to proliferate in the international community of nations in decades to come, especially if they are connected to economic or monetary support. Issues such as ethnic and women's rights will still be issues, but perhaps regarded more as positive challenges than problems. Cities, with their diversity of activities and inhabitants (becoming more diverse with freedom of movement and ease of migration, as is easily seen in twenty-first century Dublin), are significant testing grounds for the ethical treatment of individuals.

Management and the management of cities will play an increasing role in cities, especially in areas such as housing. Naturally, the quality of this management is vital. In the longer term, this is where education comes in. Dublin will always need surveyors (building, planning and development, quantity and so forth), and architects and builders and engineers and planners. But increasingly the shift will be away from the *creation* of developments, to the *management* of developments, be they buildings, public spaces, water supply, bridges, and especially housing. In some respects, developing is the easy part – bringing an idea to fruition and then perhaps moving on – but it is the ongoing management of our city which requires commitment, understanding and skill. Some developments in Dublin emanate evidence of not being properly thought through, and as they deteriorate, they bring the city down too.

Parisian walkways

I have had the privilege and pleasure of writing some of this book in the centre of Paris. In my opinion, this is truly one of Europe's – if not the world's – greatest cities, so steeped in history and architectural grandeur that even the

Nazis refused to destroy it in their wake as they fled the oncoming American troops. The Germans had mined some of the main bridges, but Dietrich von Choltitz, the officer in command (a man who had left Sevastopol in ruins behind him), couldn't find it in him to destroy the city, and deliberately went against Hitler's orders. It is – in many ways – a grand city. It can be shockingly rude, but surprisingly polite; you can find great value and feel robbed in the space of 50 metres. The opening and closing hours of shops and restaurants are somewhere between bizarre and incomprehensible, especially during summer; the bureaucracy is Byzantine, shoulder shrugging endemic. Attempting to pay for goods in a department store requires a degree of patience which would be beyond Job: everybody in the queue in front of you has a question, a voucher, a complaint, a return, and only one person in four is actually handing over money. But with the right attitude, with wry detachment, it's all good.

Other aspects of the way Paris operates are perhaps more subtle and more complex (such as commercial lease structures and the manner in which the poor are housed),[6] but the ease of moving around the city above ground is a positive activity and one which crosses all ages and sectors of society. For such a large city, even ignoring the metro system, it 'moves' very well. Several years ago the Panthéon was like Piccadilly Circus with traffic circling around Soufflot's masterpiece like bumper cars at the funfair. Now it's verging on being an oasis of (relative) peace with far fewer vehicles, mostly tourist buses, in its environs. Instead of being suffocated by cars in an endless circular battle, tourists now come to take photographs (mostly of themselves), visit France's great and good in the Panthéon's crypt, get married in the local *marié* (town halls), and then go and spend money in the local bars and restaurants and shops. And these are not all tourist shops either: there are art supply shops, clothes shops, specialist publishers and bookshops, an independent cinema or two and so forth. Despite being one of Paris's greatest tourist destinations, this is no Knock.

And it's not just at the Panthéon. The humanisation of traffic flows has rebalanced the city centre away from the movement of motorised traffic and towards the movement of human traffic. At many traffic lights, the red light for cars coincides almost precisely with the green man for pedestrians waiting to cross.[7] An orange light means prepare to stop, not just three more cars; a red means stop, now. Similarly, a 'red man' means pedestrians had better be standing on the pavement. The ability to cross the road, albeit carefully, has been re-claimed it seems. Even a small adjustment to these traffic signals has changed getting around, not totally in favour of the pedestrian (who, remember, are the young, the old, the infirm, the don't-want-to-drive), but definitely towards giving a more equal priority to both. As a result, Paris is now getting an im-proved reputation as a city that is actually possible not only to walk, but also in which to cycle. Since 2007 it has had the *Vélib* (an amalgamation of 'velo' and 'liberté') bike scheme, which is similar to our own *dublinbikes*. Cycling down the Champs Elysée and around the Arc de Triomphe still requires nerve, but it can be done; crossing the city on a bicycle requires care, but not a police escort. Public buses in Paris have a second horn which is like the lightest bell on the LUAS, to warn pedestrians and cyclists in a non-aggressive way of their pres-ence.[8] Simple, but effective. In contrast, Dublin has a concept known as shared bicycle lanes, which may have looked good as an engineering solution, but in human terms – in everyday practice – is an oxymoron of the highest order: an 80 kilogram cyclist does not *share* anything with a 16,000 kilogram bus. Paris, by tweaking the balance away from pure engineering solutions to more 'hu-man-gineering' ones, has demonstrated the benefits of putting people, if not first, then at least on a par of sorts with other forms of traffic.

The next step for Paris, and perhaps too for Dublin, would require some-thing like a shift in driving culture, attained by several European countries (like Belgium, for example) by a legislative change whereby when a vehicle and a bicycle collide, the presumption of guilt automatically rests with vehicle un-less it can be proven otherwise. The result in cities, you can imagine, are drivers who don't take non-motorised traffic too lightly. The balance – and cities are all about balancing competing interests – is that police take traffic infringements by cyclists very seriously and are regularly (and rightly) seen handing out on-the-spot fines for a multitude of offences (except that of cycling up one-way streets, which is, very sensibly, permitted for cyclists). Once again, a gentle and fair appreciation of all interests works well.[9] Which one of our politicians would be brave enough to face down the insurance companies and motoring lobbies to promote this idea?

When writing a book like this in a city like this, comparisons like those above are going to happen. Some would argue that they are somewhat point-less; maybe, but some comparisons are also rather pointed. Paris is of course a

Interior of the Panthéon, Paris: peace inside and out

larger city than Dublin. From a pre-second world war city population of c.3 million people, it fell to 600,000 during the war years under von Choltitz, to finally recover to where it is today at about 2.2 million. It may be bigger, but Dublin and Paris are, however, both cities and cities generally have the similar requirements: to move people, to house people, to generate employment, to entertain, to keep the local economy going, to support the national economy, to maintain the streets and buildings, to keep the city safe, to welcome visitors, and to help those who can't help themselves; the similarities between Paris and Dublin outweigh the differences.

Leaving aside perhaps rather micro-observations (or are they?) like the presence of pedestrian crossings on nearly all roads (where have Dublin's disappeared to?), a commercial lease system which allows for an interesting mix of uses, shops sizes, and origin (indigenous and international) on most streets, and the relative cleanliness of the city, the underlying difference one senses in Paris is what might be termed the 'urban sentiment' that emanates from the works of the various *marié*. Although very far from perfect, one realises from the conservation, the development and especially from the ongoing maintenance that the people in charge, not only care deeply for their city, they actually *understand* cities.[10] This concept of urban empathy, this urban ethos, this comprehension of a city comes from a deep understanding, coupled with experience, of living in close proximity to others. It is this proximity which makes a city a complicated organism. Proximity involves a range of experiences and emotions on a daily basis: frustration, friendliness, competition, arguments, stress and complexity. Relaxing views and landscapes are few and far between. Relations are formed and broken; but a relationship which sours may mean still having to live next door – in close proximity – to your former friend. Moving, working, doing business in such close quarters requires an understanding of never really being alone. It is this proximity to others which means that urban voters tend to have different requirements to rural voters, particularly in local elections. Urban issues tend to be about making living together an easier process (bus lanes, speed ramps etc.). Research has also shown that urban dwellers in Ireland classify themselves as both 'carers' and being 'cared for' than their rural counterparts.[11] This is obviously not because rural dwellers care less – far from it – but because it is easier to be a carer in the city. Once again, it's about proximity and mobility.

This urban sentiment is not something I have often sensed in Dublin. Indeed, Ireland, and by extension Dublin, often appears as a place with northern latitude but southern attitude (I'm thinking of the wry acceptance of corruption over the years, the *laissez faire* admiration of 'cute hoorism', lax law enforcement and even the influence of the church).[12] Unfortunately, for whatever reason – background, education, training, habit – the feeling perpetuates that some of those senior people in charge of Dublin's future, be they central or local government, have little in the way of empathy for urban environments. If Dublin is to be properly managed, then it needs to be managed by people – from whatever walk of life – who understand that cities are for and of the people first and foremost. The management of this 'urban ballet', to update Jane Jacobs slightly, requires choreographers who know what it is to tread the boards.

Dublin-born and bred ministers for agriculture are few and far between, naturally enough – Charles Haughey and Alan Dukes were just two – but to date, over half of Dublin's city managers (and previously town clerks) have not come from the city of Dublin (Tipperary, Limerick, Kerry and Galway). Of these, almost all have or had commerce or accountancy backgrounds.[13] All town clerks and city managers also seem to have come through the public service promotion route. So, wouldn't it be interesting to have a city manager who was, for example, not an engineer or accountant/commerce person (perhaps from an arts background); who maybe hadn't come up through the ranks of the Irish local authority system; who came from a city – maybe Dublin, maybe not; or who wasn't even Irish? (The same criteria could also apply to other Dublin-relevant functions: why not have a non-Irish person running Dublin Bus, for example?) Perhaps more challenging, but also potentially more rewarding, would be to introduce the concept of integrated development not just at the coalface, but at the top – let's call it integrated achievement. Wouldn't it also be interesting to have the salaries of the senior management (CEOs etc.) involved in managing Dublin cut by say 40 per cent to be returned on achievement of a raft of targets set by government? These bonuses would only be payable, however, if all the bodies involved in the achievement of these targets manage to meet them – if one fails, no bonuses are paid to anyone. Take smart ticketing, a long-standing debacle at this stage in Dublin's transport history: the salaries of each of the CEOs (or equivalent) involved could be reduced by a percentage and returned in bonus form only when proper integrated smart ticketing happens across all the transport systems within a specific timescale. If one of the partners – LUAS, Dublin Bus, whoever – fails to deliver, or holds up the process, then none of those involved get their bonus. This principle of integrated achievement might be difficult to implement, but might also yield interesting results.

Illusion, delusion and a book

Back in Ireland, I find myself upstairs in Bewleys café on Grafton Street,

Well-worn 'no entry' sign on Dublin's Henry Street

where a cup of coffee steams on the table in front of me. Outside the window on the street below, my attention is easily attracted by the vast array of people passing, playing, pausing on the street below. There are students, foreigners, street entertainers (for many of whom the title is somewhat of an exaggeration), businessmen and women, friends, children, mothers, fathers, drunks, delivery men, the homeless, the helpless, drug addicts, policemen and priests. I see pick-pocketing, salesmanship, shopping, networking, catching up with friends and people-watching all happening beneath my window. This small area of tacky red cobble contains much of the future of the city in its behaviour and its people. It is both depressing and uplifting all at the same time. Much like Dublin itself really: this is a city which to me has always been a place of downs and ups, depression and hope. The soar in property prices was for some a time of hope (that they would continue to rise); the attendant economic 'boom' was one of hope (that it would continue); and hope was there too when things started to go wrong (that it was all a big mistake) and beyond (that it wasn't our fault); that we knew nothing (hope they believe us); and that we could fix it. It was all, of course, a grand delusion. And so Dublin exists in a constant state of hope and potential – states of illusions and sometimes delusion – which is healthy really.

Having returned to Dublin on two separate occasions from living abroad, I have noticed developments that would normally take decades, happen much, much faster. On my first return I witnessed what is referred to as 'the boom' (which is coincidentally the noise an exploding bomb makes); the second time back in Ireland I was witness to the collapse of this boom, the crater left after the explosion, sucking people guilty and innocent into the wet, inescapable mud of its economic and social no mans' land. What has been shocking is not that these events occur – they have, are and will occur the world over – but the speed with which they have happened. The word 'unprecedented', frequently used to describe these events, is an abrogation: an inappropriate, inaccurate, and unsubtle attempt to divert blame for the consequences than a description of the velocity of the occurrences. Never were events unprecedented, but their speed was phenomenal. Ireland in general, and Dublin in particular, was on a roller coaster zooming up to the crest of a slope, and like any memorable roller coaster, the dip on the way down has to be bigger and more breathtaking than the preceding incline. And so it is. We're strapped in, and all the waving and screaming to stop will have no effect.

Life in Dublin goes on of course. Clothes are bought, stolen or exchanged. Coffees are drunk, pastries guiltily savoured, big menu meals eaten in fast food chains, masses are said, Allah prayed to, pints are ordered, children continue to be born (we still have one of the highest birth rates in Europe – perhaps connected with the pints being ordered), families still have disagreements, people exist, work, fall in love, die and are buried, or increasingly, cremated. The mainstays of life proceed as usual. And that's the funny thing about the future – for all the unknowns, the essentials will remain the same. Recall photographs of Grafton Street in the 1950s; Sackville Street in the 1910s is still eminently recognisable as O'Connell Street over 100 years later. So, Dublin will change but still be Dublin, in appearance but also in its people. The physical future is pretty much the same as today, but different. Despite our recent building frenzy, Dublin remains and will remain a modest-sized city. It has been said that modesty is nothing more than the hope that others will discover by themselves how great you are, and in a way that sentiment suits Dublin very well.

But perhaps a more interesting aspect about the future is that, in many respects, it is ours to determine. What, for example, is there to stop Dublin becoming one of Europe's top cities to cycle in, or to age in? Nothing except ignorance of what is possible (a lack of vision which is increasingly unlikely), or a lack of will – a stubbornness that they way things have been done is the right way – from those with the power to make it happen.

So, given what has been written earlier about the future of cities, what would a future Dublin look like? Indeed, is there even only one future for Dublin? I'd like to be able to say 'if you don't want to know what happens, look away now', but it's not quite that easy. The future(s) of Dublin is a question I mulled over with Conor Skehan for several years both in Ireland and abroad. Other colleagues and peers had drawn up scenarios and plans for what Dublin could and will probably look like (often incorrectly and disgracefully dismissed by politicians), with population sizes[14] and location of settlements and employment, but in setting out to write about the future of Dublin I quickly discovered a complex web of influences and interests which interweave in overlaps and undercurrents. Beneath any grand paper schematic of a city (sometimes called the Development Plan) is the actual city itself with its people, its economy and its life, and the life of a city is a function of many competing interests each trying to find their way, their future, and directly or indirectly influencing the others. Some of these interests are quite niche, whereas others pervade almost all other areas; some are both. Realisation rapidly dawned that to dissect Dublin as it exists and put it back together in the form of its future required experience and ability that I didn't have. But I reckoned I could find people who had.

In setting down an initial plan for this book, first attempts at ideas of what are the constituent elements of a present and future Dublin merely reflected my own interests and capabilities. The chapters I had outlined were therefore predictable and represented a lack of experience of the vast array of different Dublins – surface-cultures and sub-cultures – out there. Reading Maurice Craig, Michael Fewer and Joseph Hone's *The New Neighbourhood of Dublin* I came across a sentence from the original 1949 manuscript by Hone and Craig, which encapsulated nicely what I now realised it was necessary to do. Like them, I wanted 'to combine a difference of treatment with a readjustment of perspective'. Studies of the 'future' of topics are frequently beset by their one-dimensionality in analysis and in topics, and so in treating Dublin differently, I sought various potential authors to cover different topics, to reflect that balance between economic reality and human necessity. However, as one after the other conversations lead to new ideas; my eyes were soon opened to the broad range of other topics and interests which were important in their own right and which were also important for the impact they had on the original topics I had planned. This book is therefore an attempt to address a wide range of interests and topics which together constitute the fabric – physical and social – of Dublin, with a perspective adjusted to take account of the present and moving into the future. No doubt there are areas and interests that have been overlooked (or excluded, for example, religion, death, sport), but what you hold in your hand is a comprehensive attempt to look at the future of Ireland's capital city from multiple angles.

As said before, all writers' views are their own and it is not expected that all readers will agree with everything that is enclosed between these covers. John Milton wrote in 1644: 'Where there is much desire to learn, there of necessity will be much arguing, much writing, many opinions; for opinions in good men is but knowledge in the making'; and so, if the words on these pages merely provoke thoughts and discussions, that is good. If they lead to ideas which are implemented for the good of the city and its future, then that is a positive outcome and the book will have worked.

Endnotes

[1] It is interesting to note that the Industrial Revolution in England also sparked a renewed soul search for what were perceived as lost the values and ideals of former times. Ireland too missed this 'revolution' and has been battling with its past ever since. The problem is, of course, that the past, like the future, is far more complex than is either comfortable or than we choose to remember it. Events that were history-making have therefore a tendency – especially in political hands – to become glossed, glorified, or simply misrepresented. In relation to significant events in Dublin's history, this type of revisionism does the city no favours.

[2] See Sirr, L. and Skehan, C. (2008) 'Planning for a future that is going to happen, not against it,' *The Irish Times*, 31 March; and Sirr, L. and Skehan, C. (2008) 'Proactive planning will make most of regional differences', *The Irish Times*, 1 April.

[3] See Gerard's excellent website www.turbulenceahead.com for more interesting comment and opinion.

[4] This ubiquitous triumvirate, coupled with some homogeneous residential accommodation, is in my experience what Dublin knows as 'mixed-use'. Mixed-use, of course, is much more interesting and useful than that: a school on the ground floor,

perhaps a library and doctor on the first and suitably-sized apartments on the rest occupied by a genuine mixture of society.

[5] Cohen, R. (2011) 'The Age of Outrage', in *International Herald Tribune*, 13–14 August, p. 6.

[6] Whilst in Paris, BBC Radio 4's Sunday programme broadcast an edition about being poor in that very city. They quoted one lady on benefits who, for €1,750 per month, lived with her two adult children on the fifth floor in 16 square metres, only 5 square metres of it classified as 'habitable space' by the police inspection.

[7] The system in Pamplona, Spain, is even more interesting: a countdown timer informs waiting pedestrians when the red man will go green; as they cross, the same countdown timer tells them how long the light will remain green, and as the time gets shorter the animated green man moves with increasing speed.

[8] Buses in Rennes, France, connect the two: the internal display screens in buses not only tell passengers what the next stops are, but also how many public bicycles are free at the nearest bicycle station.

[9] Lest it be thought I am some sort of 'cycling fundamentalist', I am not. I am, however, a 'movement fundamentalist' and someone who believes in the parity of the car and other forms of non-motorised transport. I drive and enjoy driving as much as anybody.

[10] This urban sentiment is also quite noticeable in other larger cities (New York, Barcelona); cities roughly the same size as Dublin (Stockholm, Bordeaux, Copenhagen, Helsinki); and even in much smaller places (Trieste, Ljubljana, Lille).

[11] See the Skehan and Sirr reference in Shannon's 'Ageing' Chapter 4 Bibliography.

[12] It's not good: as the late Professor Peter Mair said at the McGill Summer School in 2011: "That's the culture of the cute hoors, the strokes, you get away with it and getting away with it against the State is getting away with something which is not us and doesn't belong to us but belongs somewhere out there and it is not ours."

[13] Of the four Dublin-born town clerks and city managers, two were from a clerical background, one accountancy, and one engineering. See Dublin City Council's *Serving the City: The Dublin City Managers and Town Clerks 1230-2006* (2006) for more information.

[14] See, for example, Brian Hughes's doctoral work on the population of Dublin over the next 50 years: 'The Greater Dublin Area: Ireland's Potential City-State of the early 21st century', DIT, 2010.

2

The Aggregation of Knowledge

Ferdinand von Prondzynski
On Higher Education

Concentration and variety

In 1852 John Henry Newman, who was to become Rector of the Catholic University of Ireland, delivered a series of 'discourses' or lectures 'to the Catholics of Dublin' under the title 'The Idea of a University'. Newman's time in Ireland was not a particularly happy one, but he left a major footprint. The Catholic University eventually became University College Dublin (UCD), now Ireland's largest university, and his series of lectures were a few years later published as a book that has influenced higher education thinking throughout the western world.

Of course UCD was not the first, and is not the only, university in Dublin. Today's higher education landscape in the city is a rich one. There is Trinity College Dublin (TCD) – or to give it its correct title, the College of the Holy and Undivided Trinity, formally the sole college of the University of Dublin. TCD is now over 400 years old, and has over the years adapted from its original Protestant and Anglo-Irish character to become a leading mainstream institution. There is the Dublin Institute of Technology (DIT), some of whose constituent parts date back to the nineteenth century and which will soon occupy a purpose-built campus in Grangegorman in North Dublin; there is Dublin City University (DCU), of which the writer was President for ten years up to 2010, which is located on the campus of the former Albert College in Glasnevin and which was awarded university status in 1989; and there are the Institutes of Technology in Dun Laoghaire, Tallaght and Blanchardstown. In addition, there are various colleges of education (teacher training colleges), the most significant of which is St Patrick's College, Drumcondra, which is a college of DCU. There is the Royal College of Surgeons in Ireland (RCSI), an internationally known medical school. There are some private higher education colleges of increasing importance. Finally, there is the National College of Art and Design, which has a strategic link with UCD. Near Dublin we also find the National University of Ireland, Maynooth, and St Patrick's College (described as a seminary and Pontifical University) in the same location.

It can therefore easily be said that Dublin is a major centre of higher education, with a greater concentration and a greater variety of universities and colleges than many other cities in Europe. Its institutions are both traditional and modern, and they have genuine excellence across a wide array of disciplines and subject areas. Its universities and colleges have for much of their existence been over-subscribed, and host students from across the world. They have been and are centres of learning and scholarship, and more recently have been magnets for high value industry investment.

Nevertheless, despite this picture of vibrancy and success, Dublin's higher education institutions face a more uncertain future than many might have anticipated. They have experienced a loss of taxpayer funding and staffing over recent years, and have been the subject of some criticism from stakeholders. Furthermore, the vision of higher education put forward by John Henry Newman, of general scholarship rather than professional training, has become controversial in today's society, and in any case the academic profession is divided over how the sector should develop.

This is the backdrop against which I propose to look at some ways in which Dublin's higher education institutions may play a key role in the city's, and indeed the country's, future. Despite all the problems, I shall conclude that higher education in Dublin is alive and well, and I shall argue that the city needs to emphasise the importance of its universities and colleges to its own future.

The nature of education

I should perhaps state here that I am myself a product of Dublin's higher education. In the 1970s I was a law student in Trinity College Dublin. I had come to TCD from an unusual background. Having moved to Ireland when I was seven years old, my family returned some six years later to our native Germany, where I completed my schooling and then worked for two years in a German bank. However, I had decided that my future lay in another profession, and in another place, and so in 1974 I returned to Ireland to take up my studies in TCD.

My first impression was, if I am to be honest, that my studies would not kill me. I had eight lectures per week, and on average a further four tutorials. As far as I could see this meant that, with preparations and follow-up work, I was going to be occupied for maybe 20 hours each week. It did not take me long to conclude that this just wasn't filling my days, so I decided, with the relevant permissions, to fill up some of the remaining time by attending lectures in forestry (which was a private interest of mine) in UCD, thereby studying in both the then Dublin universities simultaneously. Amazingly, throughout my time as a student, no two lectures or classes from the two institutions ever clashed. In addition, I was also spending some time working on the family farm in County Westmeath.

There was something else I also had to get used to. I had finished school in Germany, and during the last two years in particular of my German education I had benefited from a strong liberal arts curriculum, studying philosophy and politics as well as the sciences. We were encouraged to engage in critical analysis and to develop our own thoughts. From this experience I arrived in Dublin and found myself sharing classrooms with graduates of the Leaving Certificate. The Leaving was, I believe, better in those days than it is now, but even then I was struck by the very mechanistic expectations of learning that most of my new friends had. Many of them wanted to know what it was they would be expected to remember. At the beginning, the idea of education was really one of exam-prediction; it was about being prepped for a test that would, if negotiated successfully, produce a qualification. It wasn't about learning in any deeper sense.

The college was very much aware that this was an issue, and I observed how during the first year students were gently coaxed away from rote learning towards something more analytical. In fairness, however, this was not the custom in every subject, and in two of them in particular I quickly discovered that having a view was something that was neither expected nor welcomed, nor recognised in marking; but they were the exception.

But in the intervening years higher education has become a much more serious business. As we know there are regular comments about the extent to which we have experienced grade inflation, in that examination results are now routinely much better than they used to be. But what is never factored in to these claims is how students' working habits have changed. Their contact hours are now much greater than they used to be, and the pressures on them to perform are much more intense. Back in the 1970s, a 2.2 grade was fine and dandy and would open whatever career door you wanted to step through. Nowadays, even a good 2.1 is often not enough. It is not surprising that students now work harder and are more tactical in their learning.

Furthermore, at least to some extent, both students and their lecturers are conscious of the need to make learning an intellectual experience, and an analytical approach is much more the norm than it used to be. But there are still contradictions and unresolved issues, and the most significant is one I am going to address next.

Higher education or training?

As I write this, we are still scraping around in the ashes of the 'Celtic Tiger' to see what, if anything, might be salvaged. What we sometimes forget these days is that the economic boom was, at least for a while, a genuine one, based on real economic growth and added value. What may also have been forgotten is that none of this could have happened without the universities. All of Ireland's colleges stepped up to the plate and educated thousands of young people whose skills were needed by the international companies scrambling to invest in Ireland. The Dublin universities, and I believe my own former university DCU in particular, made a massive contribution to this effort.

It was during this period, in particular the 1990s, that the link between what the universities did and what industry needed became much more explicit than had traditionally been the case. Massive student intakes were funded in areas like computing and electronic and software engineering because the Intels and the Microsofts and the Apples and the Hewlett Packards needed skilled graduates. The fact the universities, and indeed the institutes of technology, were able to keep this tap running sufficiently was a key reason for the success of the early Celtic Tiger, and to be fair, is a key reason why Ireland's exports have picked up now and the FDI sector of the economy is powering ahead again. The contribution of higher education cannot be over-stated in this bit of Ireland's story.

But one consequence of all this was that the universities and colleges had moved closer to being what might be called training grounds for industry, and students had become much more focused on which career outcomes they might secure with their studies. This had a powerful effect but also carried some risks: when the dot.com bubble burst early in the new millennium there was a sudden massive over-supply of graduates in particular disciplines, and a resulting sharp drop in intakes in those subjects, with resulting problems for the now over-staffed departments concerned. The same experience was repeated all over again in 2008 or so when the departments of architecture and civil engineering that had mushroomed in the preceding years suddenly found that the collapse of the construction industry was leaving them in dire straits.

So, were we all wrong? Should we have stuck with a liberal arts approach to higher education and kept the professions and trades at the door? In truth, few people really know the answer to this, except that the lessons from the past decade suggest a better balance needs to be struck between a professional and an intellectual orientation. Universities will need to get better at holding back the rush in pursuit of the current hot favourites and at taking a longer view. But on the other hand, we cannot retreat to the ivory tower. Society no longer accepts a claim of academic élitism and purity, and does expect universities and colleges to help further the national interest.

But in all of this, what was happening to research?

Research and the knowledge society and economy

On my first proud day as a Lecturer in Industrial Relations in September 1980, my Head of Department, the truly wonderful Charles McCarthy, pulled me aside and said that if I wanted to have a successful career, then what I needed to do, from the start, was to write and publish. He was of course absolutely right, and his advice guided me through the years that followed. But at the time the advice was unusual, and the practice even more so. The annual list of published output for my whole department probably did not exceed six items, and these were not evenly spread between staff. It was not what staff were necessarily expected, or at any rate certainly not required, to do. The research that did take place was done in what was the lecturer's spare time, was unfunded and not excessively recognised. Since in those days almost nobody became a professor, the scholarly output required for such preferment wasn't an issue for the overwhelming majority of staff.

What changed all this was the realisation, some time in the 1990s, that Ireland needed to become a genuine knowledge economy. Furthermore, it became obvious that a country boasting a knowledge economy had to be a centre of discovery and innovation, and could not just be a derivative society exploiting other people's inventions. This realisation struck just as the extraordinary Irish-American philanthropist, Chuck Feeney, was persuading the government that it needed to put in place serious research funding, which he was willing to support financially. As a result, in the late 1990s the government launched the Programme for Research in Third Level Institutions (PRTLI), which together with the subsequently established Science Foundation Ireland (SFI) transformed the landscape. Key players in this were the Chair of the Higher Education Authority, Don Thornhill, and the visionary American leading SFI, Bill Harris. As a result of their work and the work of others, serious money was made available for high value, collaborative and innovative research, and suddenly Ireland became a good bet as a location for global research and development.

The decisions taken on research during that period had a profound effect, and changed Ireland in more ways than might have been anticipated. Amidst all the bad and unfortunate stories towards the end of the Celtic Tiger boom, this was a story of real innovation and progress, and its positive effect is what now gives Ireland a prospect of real recovery. It has made the universities the guarantors of national relevance in the new world of high value industry.

But apart from securing Ireland's new strength as an R&D centre, the research effort also produced major insights in society more generally, and has created a body of knowledge that can address social, cultural and ethical issues.

So what of the future?

Dublin's higher education scene would now be unrecognisable to anyone transported here from the 1970s, and overwhelmingly the changes are good. But not everything is going right. Despite all the progress recorded above, society appears to be deeply suspicious of our universities and colleges. It is felt that academics are in an excessively protected environment; that students graduate without being sufficiently literate; that academic staff are over-paid; that the universities and colleges waste resources; that there is too much duplication of provision. Politicians claim that their postbags are full of complaints about the attention (or lack of it) that students receive from their lecturers. Industry representatives state that Irish graduates do not compare well with those from other countries.

And while all these gripes are being aired, academics in turn feel they are not sufficiently valued; that their institutions are managed in a bureaucratic way that neglects traditional intellectual and scholarly principles; that students are being pushed into seeing higher education as training rather than learning.

In short, while so much is going well, there is a crisis of confidence, made worse by dramatic funding and staffing reductions caused by the economic recession. In Dublin in particular, this has the capacity to unsettle future prospects.

In the world today, economic growth and prosperity depend in a major way on the aggregation of knowledge and innovation in particular locations. In the context of knowledge-intensive investment, companies in the biomedical sector, say, will seek out places that have both people and facilities relevant to them: medical schools, departments of pharmacy, or biotechnology, or bio-engineering, and so forth. They also favour the proximity of other companies in the same field, as this will increase the likelihood of appropriate facilities and services being locally available. This process is called 'clustering'. In some rare cases this may occur in more remote or rural areas, as happened in the North Carolina Research Triangle around Raleigh and Durham. But usually this takes place in and around major cities. While in Ireland there are places with high value investments around various parts of the country, in global terms the only real show in town is in Dublin. Dublin has a cluster of innovative and successful universities and colleges, and it has a growing high value industry base. This is where the engine room for the country's future growth can be found. And this is where universities and colleges must be supported and developed. Getting this right will bring countless benefits. Getting it wrong will spell disaster.

In this setting, therefore, Dublin cannot afford the ambivalent view of higher education that seems to have gained ground. Dublin must celebrate its universities and promote them, and must ensure that they are well integrated into planning and development. The sales pitch for international investment in Dublin must be built around the higher education sector.

Equally, the universities need to understand that they have a critical role as the city approaches its future. They must work with the city in seeking investment, but they must also play their part in promoting and facilitating entrepreneurship and new start-ups, particularly knowledge-intensive ones. At the same time, they must continue to educate students, so that they can become responsible citizens, innovators, and members of society with critical faculties and an ability to engage in lateral thinking. Universities and colleges are more important now than they have ever been in Dublin's history.

Conclusion

If John Henry Newman were to be transported to Dublin today, he might well find the universities as baffling as the city's transport system. But not all of his values have been lost in the development of higher education in the city. Universities still have the task of stimulating learning and the appreciation of knowledge. They are still places of scholarship and critical inquiry. Newman understood the changing challenges of society very well, and he might come to understand the role of universities in this new age.

At any rate, the idea of a university in the Dublin of our near future will be as important as Newman identified it to be in the 1850s. That much will not change.

Biographical note

Ferdinand von Prondzynski is the Principal and Vice-Chancellor of Robert Gordon University in Aberdeen, Scotland. He is known as a lawyer, a legal academic, a high profile public commentator and a university leader in Ireland and Scotland. A German-born Irish citizen, he is a former lecturer and Fellow at Trinity College, Dublin, and was later both a Professor and a Dean at the University of Hull, before serving as the high profile second President of Dublin City University (DCU) from 2000 to 2010. He has been Principal of Robert Gordon University since late March 2011. He is an authority on employment and commercial law and on certain EU and competition policy matters, and an active commentator on academic affairs and public policy.

3

. . . that was then, this is when?

Helen Carey
On Visual Arts

The Grand Tour

The Grand Tour – notions of the richness of European Art History and Culture being delicately but determinedly consumed by well-to-do Americans, a couple of generations at most away from the immigrant refugee from the poor castes of Europe, living the American dream. The map was romantic: London, Paris, Nice, Rome, Florence, Geneva (to restore the spirits), and wintering in Monte Carlo before returning to graduate in the New World. Or some such itinerary that makes for nice clean reading.

That was then in the nineteenth century, but in some ways, you could be forgiven for thinking that the Grand Tour and visual art understandings are variations on that theme today – a sort of finishing school that adds to some middle class dinner party conversations that will enhance the party, not unlike the soirées of Proust or Tolstoy. The talk among undergraduates and in the galleries and art centres of Dublin at specific times in the calendar are all of Venice and Berlin, of Stockholm and Shanghai. Surely a result of Celtic Tiger wealth, it must indicate most emphatically the Middling of the Classes in Ireland, buying into the baggage labels that could stand squarely with any well born culture hounds from the past.

And no harm, since actually seeing visual arts is part of what feeds the artists' imagination and what makes them understand who we are in this day and age, and most of this takes place off the Island. Remembering what working in the arts was like in Dublin in the 1980s, the magic formula 'Dublin-Paris-London' on the rare glamorous shop windows on Grafton Street when buses snaked down that way, was a world impossible to imagine, as we travelled to rare work on a manpower scheme to the National Gallery or to the Project Arts Centre, the two bright lights in Dublin that allowed you to dream.

No harm at all to realise Dublin had the potential to be seen to be as marvellous as those places in every respect. But not if it makes the artists of the twenty-first century replicate nineteenth century patterns. Artists must always travel and never again feel cut off and isolated, and perhaps the task is to see where our young artists are going, to direct what they are looking for. This is where educational guidance and strategy, as well as arts agencies, must imagine new worlds for Ireland.

The state we live in

And so to the time those young artists live in. In Dublin, 2011, artists and curators in visual arts cannot make a living from their training and their 'profession' without a subsidiary 'real job', which means that the society in general has not yet given the artist the respect that being considered to be 'at work' when making art allows. Questions around tax exemptions in my opinion come up here, as it sets the artist apart, and is that something that Artists want, when that 'apart' hurts their standing, and potentially their earning capacity itself, so saving nothing in the end? Of course if Artists earn little from their work, they will not be taxed, but like all freelancers, if you do make more, deduct your expenses and contribute – what's wrong with that? Before the indignation reaches fever pitch at this suggestion, of course Artists pay tax in their other work, and pay VAT where it is due. Of course they do, but is it possible that there is a false economy of tax exemption for full-time artists who do not make much money from their art, one which both restricts growth of opportunity and puts them outside supports like Social Welfare or Social Insurance? This is a society issue now more than ever, when ideas around public purse and culture are in jeopardy, and anything that keeps art outside of the normal growth that pertains to any part of our social living should be thoroughly investigated, anything to prevent the restrictions on full time artists having clear careers. No uninformed decisions are desirable, just a clear analysis of the benefit of this exemption when considered in the round, both moral and financial.

The art apparatus

So we have the two parts of the art world in Dublin, more pronounced than in other Irish cities because more Institutions are based in Dublin – the artist and the institution, joining together to present to the Audience. Another question for mid-twenty-first century visual arts is how possible is it to imagine that around the family breakfast table in Dublin on Saturday, or as part of the chat of 'what did you do today/where are you going', is the breathless 'guess what I saw in Dublin Contemporary ...' with the sense in the city that something's on, something's happening, coming from the visual arts, involving younger people as well as older. It may be too much to imagine excitement to run to All Ireland matches, or soccer and rugby internationals, but even a fraction closer would be great.

There is no doubt that the Dublin-based National Gallery is such a treasure, no doubt that the Dublin Municipal Gallery the Hugh Lane provides such a sanctuary on Parnell Square, no doubt that those other Dublin-based institutions, Irish Museum of Modern Art (IMMA) and the Royal Hibernian Academy (RHA), can bear comparison structurally with many of their counterparts world-wide. There are well documented issues related to building and the collections, related to revenue, but another is, crucially, who goes there? For sure, visitors to Ireland discover we too have Monets and Manets, that the Irish can indeed paint – sometimes naming five Irish painters was in the league of naming five famous Belgians, but not anymore with Nathaniel Hone, Jack Yeats, William Orpen, Evie Hone, Mainie Jellett and Sean Scully widely known. The history of art in modern Ireland is as fascinating a picture as you will find anywhere, as the 2011 exhibition 'The Moderns' triumphantly demonstrated. The staff and direction of these institutions provide Dublin with first class, well-maintained facilities and collections within their given resources. The issues continue, however, around who is the audience and how can it be developed, when most galleries are freely open to the public and although some large exhibitions need to generate some income, the entrance price is very low. Where young vitality is absent or only periodically present, there is a sadness, a potential unrealised.

Some other Dublin arts institutions are Temple Bar Gallery & Studios, and the Project Arts Centre – publicly funded and a rich heritage synonymous with bravery and courage, in prime position to be a rich source of visual art for Dubliners. And they are both figuring out who they should be for twenty-first century visual arts; how they can attract a greater audience; whether going into the galleries can be a highlight instead of a trial; and whether artists' working conditions can move apace – the hangover from the Celtic Tiger that a sense of entitlement pervaded even our publicly funded cultural frontline will make this a difficult job. Commercial galleries are growing in Dublin: as with other commercial areas, there is an in-built stratification that is distasteful but that can perhaps be re-visited in these economically challenging times, because in the end they are business. It would be marvellous to feel that Enterprise Ireland or Business Development Grants, especially in developing collectors abroad – can I call these exports? – might recognise that this is a growth area and could create the loyalties and return market, which by definition are their holy grail. There are art fairs and events that seek to create an exchange or marketplace for art in Ireland – the problems are the sledgehammer with which these are planned and organised, with little development in-between. Any such development would of course mean that entry price, exhibitor price and outlay would increase, and unlike other market-driven sectors, there is little understanding of informed 'speculate to accumulate' when it come to the art market in Ireland. Unlike in the sporting life, studying form and going just has not found its equivalent.

In 2011, looking at the art institutions that characterise any visual arts Grand Tour of Dublin, it is an interesting notion to ponder, that if change is happening in society generally, what are the shifts that are noticeable now that mean we can predict the shape of the visual arts future in Dublin, or is it just too ingrained in us to think of art as the plaything of the middle classes for Dublin, prevented from coming of age and having a growing place for art in daily life? In asking the question, 'What is to be Done?' a radical proposition for Dublin would be a most exciting proposition.

What is likely to be done

Emotions associated with art are superlative – exciting, gorgeous, generous, dramatic, sanctuary, riveting, incredible, bewildering, perplexing, demanding, horrendous, very bad, very good . . . and in the future, there will be other words to be attached not yet in our vocabulary.

31

For the current generation of 14-year-old Dubliners, what superlatives will they demand of their visual art, and how will they see it? This is no less a question than asking what is the more mature legacy of the Celtic Tiger, and with the pace of change in the 2000s, hostages to fortune about what will happen would be foolish indeed to predict. But what would be good? What would reflect a positive outcome from the years of excess? It is invidious to compare, but America post-depression and post-war produced some of the greatest boundary breaking artists, with Rothko and Pollack finding new ways to paint. One of the excitements about now might be to nurse the prospect of some new way, which of course cannot be recognised right now. Inhabiting art works, experimentation with places and spaces, presentation of the invisible and calling it art, ideas around technology and how that enormous energy can be harnessed into an object – the idea of the temporary and the disappearing, imagined by Joseph Beuys, find their echo in social truths – what it seems to be is possibly not what it is, and the transient is not less valuable than the permanent, savour the day and hour.

Without the looming shadow of conservative Catholicism behind every dream and desire, the 14-year-olds will, to borrow a phrase, inherit the earth. As mentioned previously, the peppering of the artists' year with the Grand Tour destinations exhibits a confidence that is welcome, but is now unbridled and essentially unstable. This is unsurprising when you think of it, arising as it did out of the Celtic Tiger. For the early teenagers, however, they have no hint of a world which is morally out of reach; but crucially, they will have a greater stability around how to achieve sustainability. Their parents have become wiser and will ground the confidence. And this is the test, their legacy to their children is that confidence to understand about ambition and how hard it is to make their own ambitions come true, but how possible it is.

The increasing pressure on public funds means that, inevitably, privately funded culture will fill the vacuum. The challenge is to make sure that that private funding comes with a civic pride and a desire to enrich the public domain. This must also mean that there is a freedom for artists that is not bounded by 'acceptable forms' of expression or subject. This must mean the growth of philanthropy in Dublin as well an interest in the well-being of artists, knowledge of the negotiating spaces, as well as a keen sense of conviction. It would be uncomfortable of course – control would be abdicated, as the artist must constantly seek to be out of step. Being two steps ahead in any day is what gives the artist their searching energy. In times when hopefully peace is widespread in Ireland, history should take its place alongside contemporary influences. Visual arts do not have to live with a constantly re-visited legacy such as theatre and literature; while the relatively niche area that visual arts occupies in Ireland is often a source of insecurity, the upside is that visual artists are not living with ghosts constantly at their shoulders, as in theatre, literature and music.

Who will make the decisions around the institutional framework, the matrix for visual arts to renew? Perhaps now in 2011 is a time of changing of the guard at museums. Perhaps new blood will be injected into the museums' structure in Dublin. If not, it is likely that the centre of gravity for the future will move away from the institutions, with less money for collections, fewer options for staff development, and fewer new structures. The challenge to recruitment and to training that is urgent, but alongside an imperative to be relevant – this is a question of nothing less than survival for all institutions. The challenges presented to the institutional firmament as well as the broader arts matrix are to envisage new ways of seeing, new forms to show art, moving away from stability and a security, which is the challenge for the overall society of our times. Although the new arrival, Dublin Contemporary 2011, aspires to be a repeating exhibition, marking every five years, are we seeing an attempt to create another form claiming another tired territory, in the style of institutions from the twentieth century?

What is most sure, and Dublin Contemporary knows this more than most, is that the restlessness and the sophistication of the young artist and the young audience will pass judgement very quickly on any innovation now, and this has to be one of the most exciting aspects of how visual art functions – if it replicates a format we have seen before, leaving no room to mutate, the really smart thinkers will go elsewhere. Already pop-up structures, reading groups and other ephemeral formats imagine things differently, in tune with the shifting times.

Artists' working conditions, along with display of their work, demonstrate the cut and thrust of the times we live in. The strait-lacing of the controlled conditions that are found off-site and outside the gallery, being shoe-horned into becoming replacement white cubes with decision-making around labelling, lighting, backdrops, invigilation conditions, insurance, the rise of the art fair and the celebrity circuit and huge money – all legacies of the 1980s/'90s which fed the 2000s for eight years. Now is the beginning of an anarchy around what is acceptable in display, with the associated and deliberate decision-making process intact. What this might mean is that Dublin's public domain as a gallery might reach a maturity which is about surprise and yet also about sure-footedness.

What it might also mean is that the gallery might need to re-invent itself, yet again, watching how real estate reflects possibility and beginning to think about mixed usages, about the life of a city after artists move in. In previous recessions, depressed city areas became possible areas of artistic endeavours as rents plummeted. With the difficulties of value, with the Dublin-based National Asset Management Agency (NAMA), market management, and rent complexities, the inner city is not yielding to medium-term interim usages. The proliferation of 'pop-up, one-term-only' limited licence areas for artistic intervention means that the artistic offer of regeneration is kamikaze. This has long term consequences for the use of artists as tools for regeneration, something economic action plans for Dublin incorporate in their thinking. The instrumentalisation of art for regeneration purposes carries problems for art and its potential to be compromised in these circumstance; however, policies about integrating art has informed most regeneration projects and, in a cyclically changing environment, was a dependable collaboration. Now it is argued that the cycle is not the problem; it is the structure that is dysfunctional. This means art has two options: either become a nomadic intervention or become a means of exploring how to change the structure. This is where visual artists need to combine their expertise in education and training, to include formal environmental, economic, architectural – whatever – into their training, and crucially, the architects and engineers need to combine practical art into their own training, and perhaps art history also. In this way, seeing art as apart begins to diminish, and its inclusion within is managed with a pedagogic base. It means looking at the separateness of the arts education from the other academic faculties, with questions around combination study possibilities.

This might be two generations away, but poets and painters of the future, along with all the people of Dublin and Ireland, expect sophisticated planning and informed decisions. Perhaps the sort planning of the past can be consigned to the past.

A fantasy perhaps

The word that perhaps ideally could be applied to a fantasy for a Dublin visual arts scene in thirty years' time is an old fashioned word but one, if ever thought to be applicable, would indicate intense and profound change manifest: it is 'collegiate'. The germs are there, mostly in the younger community, who see information sharing and talking to each other as another real forum of Artistic endeavour, becoming an art form in itself. The portents to shake off the last twenty years in Dublin are good – the competitive nature of being in the art world of the boom years was exhausting at best.

The real problems of scale that arise for artists living in a small artistic community in a small island include the number of opportunities that arise, the circulation of influences which can become narrow and safe, and the competitive character of the communities that are intent on surviving.

The artists of the Celtic Tiger period for Dublin included separate clusters. Those who were part of the ethos of the boom, saw their expectations rise and move into the new and unexpected notion that artists could survive on what they earned. This was as exciting for art as it was for any other sector, and has brought the disappointment of the burst bubble as much as for other sectors. Other artists continued to warn against the rising issues around depending on capitalism, as well as notice the 'ungenerous' character of what was happening, with minority groups marginalised, immigrants treated as apart and an abandoning of value in living apart from monetary value. This applied to the arts sector as much as any other sector and, of course, applied to many countries, not just Ireland. It does seem that, apart from periodic stabs at exhibitions to make these points, those artists were not listened to, and the market place dictated what value meant. In a recent craft makers' discussion, it was clear that for makers, the monetary rewards of the art world which had excluded craft in the 2000s, was a source of bewilderment and resentment. Money counted, and of course still does. But in the early 2000s, it counted too much.

In thinking about where the visual arts will be in Dublin in thirty years' time, it must be the case that the experience of younger artists at the hands of established artists now will play a part in decisions made, and early indications are that it is more generous. Against a backdrop of shifted expectations, the framework for younger artists to continue to work must also be different to that of the last twenty years. So for policy makers, the anticipation of what that framework can be, bearing in mind what one might like it to be is challenging: how much dependence will there be on private means to support a public culture, if it is accepted that public culture is a 'good' worth having?

Something already absent from this essay is any clear and determined engagement between artists from Dublin and Belfast. The overwhelming energy that the Berlin of the twenty-first century gives to all artists drawing on its recent history and the divided city it was is easy to understand. What is less easy to understand in the Irish context is the lack of real engagement drawn from Belfast into the Dublin artistic context of today. Bringing some of the energy from Belfast into the Republic as well as understanding the nature of the process that city embodies is surely one of the most riveting challenges for all artists – but significantly, that relationship is as complex as ever.

Another fantastic notion lies in the possibilities around philanthropy. The tradition of Victorian philanthropic industrialists created the bedrock of the marvellous collections and galleries of the United Kingdom. Dublin and Ireland, not having had the extraordinary nineteenth century industrial boom and with the added layer of colonisation, has not had the conditions in which philanthropy could flourish. Did our version of a boom create a potential for philanthropy? There certainly are indications that foundations and trusts supporting not-for-profit establishments are becoming part of the picture, with legacy building and enduring contributions in mind. The competition with health and education causes is intense, and the approval of Irish society for artistic support in cash terms continues to be hard won. So it seems that in order for philanthropy to flourish in Dublin and Ireland, the conditions within which it can operate must be strategically determined. Certainly ideas around charitable giving are being examined by the Arts Council and other government bodies, and in the sector, ways of managing engagement through website campaigns is strong. However, there are other necessary pre-conditions if philanthropy is to flourish, for example, the encouragement of strategic long-term engagement with a narrative through collections by individuals as well as by organisations and companies acquiring art, seeing their acquisition as part of a bigger story.

Deutschbank's extraordinary German collection is based on commitment to supporting and developing German art over many years post-war, and so strong today, when priorities demanded brave decisions. The bank's gallery in

Frankfurt is now a dense and valuable statement of confidence in their visual art. Jena in the former East Germany chose to spend money on art to build up the fabric of their city at a time when jobs and housing were crisis issues. Jena now has a thriving cultural life and although not without problems, it does have a proud city collection of great moral – and monetary - value, in the city that Goethe, Schiller and many Romantics knew and lived in. It provides a valid place for Jena on a route that includes the Bauhaus, Weimar and Romantics, coming down from Berlin, through Leipzig, Dresden on the way to Weimar. This is a superb tourist route, and Jena's addition is because of its place in the German historical and contemporary art story.

Another individual collector I can think of, collecting below the radar for many years, acquired the quiet painters of the Camden Town School, of the St. Ives School, of the Suffolk school of painting, and suddenly has filled in all the gaps between the well known, established names of that period that include Hepworth and Nicholson, making his collection invaluable in the story of British art. There are many quiet collectors in Ireland but it is an activity that is almost carried out in secret: this activity should be encouraged to be more wide spread and logical, so that in thirty years, ideas of quality and depth make sense in collecting, and philanthropy has a context in which to thrive. The idea is that a public policy approach encourages a private collection through tax advantage, public recognition and a branding of the activity as a 'public good'. Just one idea.

It is widely understood to have been throughout our history that Irish strategy to bring its illustrations, its art abroad, has already an honourable tradition in the Pre-Christian symbolisms that found their way throughout the Mediterranean and North Africa, the early Christian Golden Age, with its illustrated manuscripts, and even in later times, the architecture of churches built in Africa by Irish modernist architects. Another fantastic development will be the confidence with which Dublin artists, in thirty years, will build on the global potential to exhibit and place their work. As young artists make their way around the globe, they realise they have lots to say to peers in these countries and that their concerns have a lot in common. In thirty years, the building up of these networks is crucial, to arrive at the point where proactive interest in the Dublin arts scene sees collectors, curators, museum directors, writers, thinkers, artists across genres and decision makers eager to see the

Irish artistic response. In order to see this network chart new worlds, a new Grand Tour route should be envisaged: not an Anglophone world, but one which embraces language and difference as nourishment.

Engagement by the audience in our fantasy visual arts idyll – what would be thrilling is if the audience engagement with the visual arts was as full as for sport. A respected art historian told me that the flowering of Weimar Culture in the fraught inter-war years in Germany resulted from the profound engagement of the people in their cultural cathedrals – going to a museum or to a concert provided solace to a population recovering from World War I as a default – places of normality and sanctuary in times of crisis. For us, the Irish, we go to sport in increasing numbers, and flourish. While visual art can probably never rival sport in sheer numbers, it would be fantastic to see the engagement as passionate and as energetic. How can this be achieved? Visual art must become integrated into the everyday, it must reject the language that has set it apart, and it must be more fun, and not at all pompous. It must allow young artists to experiment without incurring disapproval or insecurity, and for established artists to champion and develop these artists. It must embrace the tools of the age, the technologies, as legitimate artistic tools of our age without dismissal, and people must be allowed to suspend their conservative and conventional understanding of visual art. The State must enable art to play its full part. An understanding which runs across sectors is the value placed on experience and evidence. One of the last defences against changes is where decision making stays in the same structure and with the same people. Bulgarian political scientist Emilia Zankina, following intensive field-based research into the post-Iron Curtain Bulgarian political participants, concluded that unless there is wholesale root and branch replacement of the decision-making élite, most change remains at a superficial level. When we think of Lech Walesa in Poland and Vaclav Havel in the Czech Republic, coming to power following revolutions, the understanding of what real radical change means is clear – how long will Ireland have to wait before a Taoiseach – not a President – is an artist, or how long will it take until Dublin's City Manager claims an arts training background? If the education system embraces new hybrids, perhaps it will be sooner rather than later.

Not a 'small ask'. Nothing more is being asked in any other sector, in any other business, in any other educational pathway, at this time. All this is eminently possible, crucially underwritten entirely by the collegiality and the maturity of the Dublin artistic community – that might be a utopian future, but it is a place to imagine at this time. Perhaps in thirty years it will seem like a given that the visual arts really will be at the heart of the Dublin culture.

Biographical note

Helen Carey is an independent curator and project manager, who is based in Dublin. She was formerly the inaugural Director of the Centre Culturel Irlandais, Paris, Executive Director of Galway Arts Centre, and Public Art Project Manager for the landmark award-winning Millennium project At Bristol. Her current projects include development of an exhibition for the centenary of Dublin's Lockout 1913, public art commissions for Kilkenny, and member of a think tank looking at artistic action in post-colonial Ireland, with the Fire Station Artists' Studios, Dublin.

4

A City to Age In

Sinéad Shannon
On Ageing

Ageing is better than the alternative

Almost every writer from Socrates to Oscar Wilde has had something to say about ageing. Every one desires to live long, but no one would be old, wrote Jonathon Swift. Some of them reflect on the losses and problems of age, while others advise that 'ageing' is a state of mind and that we should focus on the gains we have made throughout our lives rather than the losses we experience in later life. I have been asked to consider in this chapter what it is to be an older person in Dublin at the moment, and to imagine how it might be. I have been asked to write on this subject, not as an older person, but because I have spent the last few years reading and researching issues relating to ageing on behalf of the Ageing Well Network, a network of people concerned to make Ireland one of the best places in the world in which to grow old. This chapter does not reflect the views of the Ageing Well Network; it simply presents my personal views, informed by research carried out in Ireland and internationally.

Ageing is a subject that many people do not like to consider, although as the old saying goes it is better than the alternative. Like many people, I spent my youth believing that old age would somehow pass me by or that if I must age, I would somehow manage to avoid the negative effects of ageing. Pension planning, getting plenty of sleep and having a healthy diet was something I would worry about later.

Multi-million euro cosmetic industries tap into this desire to avoid ageing and I, like many others, happily keep them in profit. Invariably, however, it is the negative effects of ageing that we wish to avoid. We don't wish to be pushed aside when we reach a certain age, our lifetime's experience ignored. We don't wish to suffer ill-health or experience ageist attitudes when we seek help for those health problems. We don't wish to become a burden on our loved ones and lose our independence or autonomy in making decisions about our lives.

The Dublin of the future is likely to be one in which most people will live longer, healthier lives. All predictions are that the prosperity and medical advances which have contributed to our growing longevity will continue to extend our lives and that the number and proportion of older people in Dublin will continue to grow. This is an advance that is often presented as a negative and seen as a danger to society, and while it is important to recognise the need to plan for a different future we should not regard longevity as a threat. But whether the future of this larger group of older people is happy and fulfilled will depend on a range of factors both individual and societal. Whether Dublin as a city will meet their needs will depend largely on how we, as individuals and as a society, plan and adapt now for the changes to come in the future.

Increasing numbers of older people

Since 1960 Ireland's population has grown strongly and the most recent census shows a widening gap between births and deaths as the number of births increase and the number of deaths reduces. Our life expectancy is increasing and is expected to continue increasing. According to the 2006 census there were 467,900 people over 65 in Ireland, an increase of 54,000 since 1996. Of these 111,804 (24 per cent) were living in Dublin city and its suburbs. The predictions are that over the next twenty years the proportion of older people in our population will increase to more than double the current level and that that the numbers aged 85 years and over will rise from 48,000 to over 100,000.

As a proportion of the overall population, the number of those aged 75 and over is projected to increase from five per cent to ten per cent by 2031, and the number of people aged 60-74 is also expected to rise sharply. On current projections, the proportion of older people is expected to continue rising to 20 per cent by 2036 and to between 20-25 per cent of the population by 2041. It is predicted that there will be over 1 million people aged over 65 years in 2036 (an increase of almost 250 per cent over the 2006 figure) and between 1.3 and 1.4 million by 2041. The greatest increase is expected to be in the over-80 age group, where numbers are expected to quadruple from 110,000 in 2006 to about 440,000 in 2041.[1]

The new generation of older people will not only be a larger proportion of the overall population, but they will also have very different expectations for their later years. While for many of the current generation of older people education was not widely available or was too expensive, like the 'baby boomer' generation in the US, many of Ireland's next generation of older people are well-educated, well-travelled, computer users who have spent their adult years contributing to their families, workplaces and communities. I believe that they will expect to continue contributing in new ways as they age, that they will hope that there will be new social roles available to them that provide them with enjoyable and fulfilling lives rather than retreat from society.

What do older people need?

While most people do not plan where they will live as older people, their fervent wish is that they will be able to continue to live in their own homes as they age and avoid being 'put into a home' if their health and faculties fade. In thinking about later life – and the majority prefer not to until it becomes unavoidable – most people hope that their health will remain good, allowing them to maintain their independence; that they will remain mentally engaged and cognitively healthy; that their pensions, if they have pensions, will provide them with enough income to sustain them throughout their years in retirement; and that they will be able to stay connected to their friends and family.

Research in both the UK and US asked older people to identify the things that most contribute to a positive experience of ageing. Their findings were similar. In the UK the research highlighted seven areas of importance: comfortable and secure homes; adequate income; safe neighbourhoods; the ability to get out and about; friendships and the opportunity for learning and leisure; the ability to keep active and healthy and access to good, relevant information. The US research focused on a smaller number of key indicators: active participation in the community; the ability to remain independent and to receive community support to remain socially connected and avoid isolation.

The built environment is a key influence on older people's health and quality of life. The World Health Organisation (WHO) looked at ways that a city can adapt its structures and services to be accessible to, and inclusive, of older people and others with different needs and capacities. Through consultation with groups in 33 cities throughout the world they identified eight key areas: outdoor spaces and buildings; transport; housing; social participation; respect and social inclusion; civic participation and employment and communication and information. The Dublin of the future should be one in which the key needs of older people will be a priority for local authorities, service providers and communities.

The importance of location

Other than the 'summer holiday dreamers' who spend their working years planning their idyllic retirement home in some sunny part of the world, most people do not specifically plan where they will live as older people. Recent Irish research has found that if you're over 40, the chances are about 80 per cent that the house you currently live in is the one in which you will spend your last days. The same research also found that quality of life was compromised for 22 per cent of older people by the location of their home, and by the standard of their housing for a further 13 per cent.[2]

The lives of some older people can be enhanced by the location of their home, often more by chance rather than by design. Take one older person that I know, for example, I will call him George. He is 83 and lives alone in the house he has lived in most of his adult life. His health, although starting to cause him some problems, remains fairly good and most days he walks along the seafront near his home in south Dublin. He never married so, according to the statistics, he is at greater risk of spending his final years in a nursing home, but because his niece lives nearby and calls in to check on him most days, he has been able to stay living alone in his own home. He likes to walk to the nearby laundry every week to clean his clothes but if it is too heavy he has a number of people he can ask for a lift. He visits the local library regularly and sometimes attends talks on local history organised by the librarian.

His community has changed quite a lot over the years, many of his friends have moved away or died and his neighbours are now mostly families with young children, but they all look out for him and regularly drop in when they are on their way to the shops to check if he needs anything. He stays in touch with his former teacher colleagues through the Retired Teachers Association and likes to remain involved with the big issues of the day. He travels across the city to attend any of the big public meetings organised by the Association about issues such as the pensions of future retired teachers.

Although not perfect, Dublin offers many advantages for those who are getting older. In many parts of the city there is a good sense of community and people like George can benefit from the large population base which offers the potential for plenty of friends and neighbours to provide regular social contact. Though in need of some improvement, the transport system does allow him as a non-driver to get to where he wants to go, for no cost if using the public transport system with a free travel pass. A range of interesting activities can provide continued mental stimulation, either within the locality or within a distance easily reached by public transport. Essential services such as shops, banks and health services are often within walking distance, and many communities also have libraries and parks or other outdoor amenities such as the seafront near George's home.

George is obviously one of the lucky ones and a combination of factors has enabled him to remain living independently. As a retired teacher his pension income is good and he lives in good quality housing. The fact that his niece and neighbours help allows him to remain independent, and the fact that he has been able to maintain good social connections all contribute to allowing him to enjoy good health and well-being into his later life.

Many others are not so lucky; their sole source of income may be the state pension; they may suffer ill-health or live in areas where anti-social behaviour makes them feel unsafe when they go out in their locality. It is important to recognise that, while there are many advantages in city living, not everyone enjoys them equally.

A more age-friendly Dublin

While there are many features of urban life that make it more suited to older people, there are also many that need to change. In this section I will give evidence of a number of either current or potential problems for older people – problems that could be solved by creating a more age-friendly Dublin.

Low density suburban development, for example, can make life more difficult for older people. Some of the newer suburbs do not have any footpaths or often they are not completed for some time after the housing. Older suburbs may have poorly maintained footpaths or bad lighting that can cause falls and make people less confident about getting out and about. The National Disability Survey (2006) found that many older people had difficulty walking for as long as 15 minutes. Those with physical impairments were more likely to experience difficulty walking even a short distance if they lived in areas where the streets were poorly lit or footpaths were narrow or uneven.

Retailing and banking can often be concentrated in large shopping centres and suburban design tends to be based on the assumption that everyone has access to a car and public transport options to these centres can be limited. While many older people do have a car, they eventually lose or give up their driving licence because of concerns about their eyesight or reaction times.

In some areas parks and public places are not always accessible or safe for older people and the lack of convenient public toilets can be a problem for people who suffer from incontinence.

Older people have a much greater risk of becoming pedestrian fatalities than the general population. According to a recent Irish study based on Road Safety Authority statistics, over 15 per cent of all those involved in accidents as a pedestrian are aged over 65. They are also the age group with the highest level of involvement in accidents as pedestrians. Of those, 21 per cent are killed while only 2 per cent of those in the 25-34 age-group are killed.[3] In the EU, pedestrians aged 65 or more accounted for 45 per cent of all pedestrian fatalities, but only 15 per cent of the population.

A safer Dublin

Safety is another key factor that contributes to a better late life and older people who live in an unsafe environment or areas with multiple physical barriers are less likely to go out, and therefore are more prone to isolation, depression, reduced fitness and increased mobility problems. All age groups need to feel safe in their own homes and neighbourhoods. However, there is some evidence that older people are more fearful for their own safety – a fear which is linked to their potential vulnerability.

Despite the fact that older people are less likely to be the victims of crime – 1.7 per cent compared to 4.6 per cent in the general population – they feel less safe. In a comparison of perceptions of safety among people in different age groups,[4] 12 per cent of people aged 65 and over feel unsafe alone at home after dark. A higher proportion of older people felt crime was a serious problem – 63 per cent among older people but only 46 per cent among all age groups. Older people also feel less safe walking alone after dark – 52 per cent of those aged over 65 felt either unsafe compared to only 26.4 per cent for all age groups.[5]

Healthy later life

For most people the biggest concern about aging is that their health will fail, resulting in loss of their independence and autonomy. At present, a majority of older people feel that their health is quite good, and 67.6 per cent of those aged between 65 and 74 state that they are in good or very good health. This compares very favourably with our European neighbours and is considerably higher than the EU average of 40.2 per cent.[6] This holds true for all age groups and 45 per cent of those aged over 85 report that their health is either good or very good. The number of healthy life years at age 65 is 10.3 years for females and 9.4 years for men, both of which are above the EU average of 8.2 for men and 8.3 for women.[7]

However a rise in the prevalence of chronic diseases, including heart disease, arthritis, congestive heart failure and diabetes, was recorded in older people during the past two decades in the US and in many OECD countries.[8] Total cancer incidence has also been rising, mainly because of population ageing, but survival rates have generally increased. While there has been an increase in age-related diseases it is not fully known how these trends are linked to the level of disability. It is not yet known whether more older people will experience what Professor James Fries of Stanford University School of Medicine described as 'the compression of morbidity',[9] which suggests that if the age at which disease or disability develops can be postponed, then the increase in longevity would result in an increase in the number of healthy years.

Living independently at home

As people grow older they spend relatively more time in their homes. Research has found that on average, very old people tend to spend 80 per cent of their time at home.[10] They may often have lived for large parts of their lives in the same house. One German study found that the people aged 70-85 years spent an average of 31.6 years in the same home and 50.3 years in the same town.[11] Irish people have strong views on the importance of being supported to remain in their homes for as long as possible.

The 2008 Eurobarometer report found that most Irish people were in favour of using public budgets for support services allowing older people to stay longer in their homes – 76 per cent felt that this was very important and 22 per cent felt it was fairly important. This was significantly higher than the EU average of 61 per cent who felt that this was very important. When asked about their preferences for moving house during retirement only 31 per cent of Irish people would consider moving to a smaller house in the same location (compared to almost 60 per cent of Danish people or 57 per cent of Dutch people). Only 4.5 per cent of Irish people would consider moving to sheltered housing, compared to 40 per cent of Slovenians or 24 per cent of Austrians.[12]

However many older people and their families are often forced, in a crisis situation, to come to terms with the fact that their homes, perhaps because of size, location or structure, are not suitable for growing levels of frailty and physical impairment. Most housing has not been designed with older age in mind, and the arrangements of the home can often prevent or hinder them in managing the activities of daily life. Basic household maintenance of a property can also be difficult for those on low incomes. If older people are to stay in their own homes as they age, adapting or modifying the house can help them to continue living independently.

Injury in the home is very common and accounts for around a third of injuries in all age groups and more than half of injuries for people aged 75 and over.[13] For older people with some loss of function caused by age, the placement of sinks and baths, or heavy doors and lack of handrails, can become a barrier to their independent living. Homes with proper design with fewer physical barriers can ensure that the environment accommodates to the older person allowing them to be more self-reliant and independent.

Adapting the city for those with different needs

There are many ways to address the problems and tackle the barriers to ageing well in one's own environment. Good, safe conditions for walking are clearly an important part of making Dublin more suited to the needs of older people. Improving the city's physical infrastructure such as footpaths and public lighting could slow or reverse the process of 'disablement' for those at greatest risk of losing their freedom of movement outdoors.

Providing pedestrian-only areas offers potential for creating more attractive and safer environments for all people in the community. The design of villages and towns in many parts of continental Europe could offer an example, where social and commercial activity in the village or town is centred on a pedestrianised, enclosed square or area where people can meet in cafés or on the street, without cars or other traffic presenting a danger. Other options to promote greater mobility and safety for older people in the future Dublin could include bollards or other barriers to prevent parked cars from blocking footpaths which should be wide enough to accommodate all users safely.

Crossing the road at complex intersections with a high volume of traffic, a regular feature of city traffic, can be a real challenge for older people, especially on streets without central islands. Many older people express concern about the short time programmed to allow them to cross. Road engineers have to balance the needs of the pedestrian and the car user and are often reluctant to introduce 'across the board' increases in signal times because of the possible disruptions to traffic flow. However in other countries new technology allows the green signal to match the time required by pedestrians to cross the road by tracking pedestrian movements through use of infrared detectors or other devices.

This type of crossing, known as a "PUFFIN" crossing (Pedestrian User Friendly INtelligent), was first introduced in the UK. When they evaluated its success they found that all pedestrians, regardless of age, took longer to cross the road, which suggests that all users benefited from a reduction in the stress associated with timed crossings. Older pedestrians' crossing time increased the most, a sign that they received most benefit from the change. In my Dublin of the future, technological changes such as the PUFFIN system or microwave pedestrian detectors, which can either extend the red signal for vehicles or advance the pedestrian green signal if a pedestrian is detected, would be introduced to benefit older road users.

To increase the perception of safety among older people in the Dublin of the future local Gardaí could create a register of the older people at risk, living alone or in isolated situations, who would wish to be visited regularly by a Community Garda. Overall safety could also be increased by involving older people in the local Community Alert/Neighbourhood Watch schemes, where they can be the 'eyes and ears' of the community, particularly during the daytime when many younger adults are out at work.

Homes of the future

Living in the same house for many years can be a positive as it allows an older person to compensate for or alleviate the symptoms of some age-related conditions. For example, the familiarity with the interior of a house that develops over a lifetime living in the same home can play a significant part in helping to compensate for vision problems and unfamiliar environments are known to be unsettling for dementia sufferers.

Staying in one's own community also allows local friendships and ties in the community to be maintained. The ideal future would be one in which innovative ways of providing services, which help people to stay at home, are put in place as a priority. This would leave nursing home places for those who prefer them or who need constant nursing care that cannot be provided in the home.

The design and construction of most housing tends to be based on standardised heights and widths. Because older people, in general, tend to be less flexible, shorter and not as strong as younger people, housing areas and features which do not take account of these differences can make it more difficult for an older person to stay living independently. The ideal in the future would be that all housing would be based on the concept of 'universal design', that is, housing that can be modified as required, at minimum cost, to suit the changing needs of residents irrespective of age, level of mobility or health.

In homes which are built to 'universal design' standards, features that are generally standard building products or features would be placed differently or omitted: standard electrical products would be placed higher than usual above the floor, wider doors would be used as standard, and steps at entrances could be eliminated to make housing more universally usable.

Some of the more common universal design features focus on ensuring ease of access to the house such as no-step entry; thresholds flush with the floor, making it easy for a wheelchair to get through a doorway; one-story living which is barrier-free; doorways that are 32-36 inches wide to let wheelchairs pass through; wider hallways (36-42 inches) and extra floor space. Other features provide greater levels of security for everyone such as floors and baths with non-slip surfaces or handrails on steps and grab bars in bathrooms; good lighting which helps people with poor vision; and lever door handles and rocker light switches help those with poor hand strength.

Technology to support independent living

Technology offers ways of supporting older people to live independently in their own homes and to do so for longer. Despite the fact that a 'smart home' equipped with technology which can monitor health conditions could make a significant difference to helping people to continue living independently in their own homes, there is only very limited access to these technologies at the moment. In a city such as Dublin and its surrounding areas, in which several world leading technology firms are based, it seems only logical that the future will be one in which our homes will be equipped with the best of monitoring and smart home technologies.

The benefits of smart home technologies have been proven by research and have shown that they can reduce GP visits, the use of Accident and Emergency and other hospital admissions. Those with heart failure can gain great benefits from tele-monitoring. Often these patients experience a significant deterioration, such as an increase in weight or other symptoms, over a period of days and weeks before presenting to medical attention and requiring hospitalisation. A system of frequent monitoring could alert their doctor to the early signs and symptoms, providing time to intervene before they become severely ill and require hospitalisation.

Supportive technologies can be grouped into those which help people perform tasks that they may find difficult, such as video entry systems or medication reminder units, and those which respond to people and help them to manage risks or raise alarms, such as unburned gas detectors or panic buttons/pendants. Another category is that of activity recognition and assistance. Smart Homes monitor the activities of the user within their home and based on this information the environment can be modified or activity assistance provided to the person within their own home. Some prevent health problems, such as falls, by monitoring for physiological symptoms, or monitoring activity through room occupancy monitors. Another widely used technological solution is the blood glucose meter which can record vital sign-based information. In conjunction with other activity-related information this can provide a broader overview of the status of the person within their own environment.

In both Norway and Finland national legislation governs the provision of assistive technology and municipalities are responsible for providing the technological devices. These assistive technologies are generally provided free or on loan and are funded by tax revenues and state grants. In Norway, each municipality has Technical Aid Centres (TACs) which purchase, install and re-circulate the technologies to other users when they are no longer needed.

Because successful ageing also depends on the psychological health of an older person, technologies that provide social connectedness would be an important component of any home-based care system. These technologies might include computer-based products designed to assess cognitive decline or help older users enhance memory; or perhaps entertainment systems that offer both physical and mental stimulation; or maybe even complex systems that provide important reminders to older people with memory loss.

As far back as 1966 a computer programme was developed which mimicked the role of a therapist – it was called Eliza and it was proposed as a device that could be used with older people who were socially isolated.[14] A more recent product was the robot developed by Sony, called the QRIO, which is an autonomous wireless robot designed to live with people in their homes. The QRIO recognizes individuals by their faces and speech and talks with them, remembering specific individuals and previous conversations. Its seven microphones allow it to determine sources of sounds and can turn toward the sound. QRIO also walks around and adapts to changes in the environment such as when a person or object moves. It is thought that it could be programmed to fetch things and help people with reducing abilities.

While such a development might seem overly futuristic, any technology which can improve the quality of life and independence of an older person should be considered for its potential benefits, and in a city with greater numbers of older people such technologies may become an important part of the mix of supports we will all need and use in the future.

Healthier lives

Increased longevity is largely a result of improvements in health care, lifestyles and diet. Health is a very important determinant of quality of life and well-being. If we want to ensure that the increases in chronic and age-related disease mentioned above do not result in increased disability, we will need to focus on finding ways to delay, reduce and mitigate the major health problems of old age. There are more and more areas in which research has led to knowledge about how we can reduce health risk.

For example, falls are more common in older people with poor balance; decreased strength and mobility are important risk factors. They are not an inevitable consequence of ageing and there is good evidence that interventions that improve balance and strength can reduce the risk of falls amongst older people. As another example injuries are an important cause of morbidity, disability and mortality among older people, impacting the quality of life and representing an increasingly large proportion of the health expenditure. Despite the fact that almost half of the injuries are now preventable, efforts to reduce the injury among older people have so far been limited. Mental stimulation using cognitively challenging activities can be a way of improving brain plasticity, which can maintain or improve cognitive functioning.

There is lots of evidence that physical exercise can play an important role in maintaining virtually all aspects of health and physical functioning as people age; it increases strength and is associated with lower incidence of cardiovascular disease, osteoporosis and bone loss. It can reduce the risk of falls, lower blood pressure for those suffering from hypertension, and reduce the risk of stroke. Exercise can even reduce the risk of depression and it is thought that it may decrease the chances of developing dementia. In fact, exercise has been described as the 'best preventive medicine for old age', significantly reducing the risk of dependency in old age.[15]

Ideally, the future Dublin should focus on providing information and knowledge to promote good health and extending the number of healthy, disability-free years Dublin people enjoy. Given the preventative health benefits of exercise, the Dublin of the future could ensure affordable and easy access to facilities which allow older people to exercise regularly and in comfort.

Conclusion

As people live longer, the focus for the future must be on ensuring the extra years of life are happy and fulfilled. Happy people tend to be psychologically and physically healthier than their less happy counterparts, with stronger immune systems and higher resistance to pain. The good news is that Irish people in general consistently report that they have a high level of life satisfaction.

While not responsible for the individual happiness of older people, policymakers in Dublin of the future could recognise the importance that societal and environmental factors, such as housing, transport or access to exercise facilities, can play in improving general well-being and quality of life. Furthermore, through the provision of assistive technologies, older people can be supported to live independently in their own homes for longer, which, according to all reports, is the desire of almost all older people.

Endntoes

[1] CSO (2007) *Ageing in Ireland*, Dublin: Government Publications Office.

[2] Skehan, C. and Sirr, L. (2011) 'Ageing in the Right Place', paper given to the Planning for Age Conference, June 21, Dublin.

[3] Martin, A.J., Hand, E.B., Trace, F., O'Neill, D. (2010) 'Pedestrian Fatalities and Injuries Involving Irish Older People', in *Gerontology* 2010; 56: 266-271.

[4] CSO (2007) *Ageing in Ireland*, Dublin: Government Publications Office.

[5] CSO (2006) *Census 2006*, Dublin: Government Publications Office.

[6] Eurostat (2009) Health status: indicators from the Statistics on Income and Living Conditions Surveys - EU-SILC Online Database, available at: http://ec.europa.eu/health/archive/ph_information/dissemination/echi/echi_30a2_en.pdf.

[7] Eurostat online database – data from October 2010, available at: http://epp.eurostat.ec.europa.eu/statistics_explained/index.php/Healthy_life_years_statistics.

[8] Crimmins, E.M. (2004) 'Trends in the health of the elderly', in *Annual Review of Public Health*, 25, 79–98.

[9] Fries, James F. (2005) *The Milbank Quarterly* Volume 83, Issue 4, December, pages 801–823.

[10] Baltes P.B., Staudinger U.M. and Lindenberger U. (1999) 'Lifespan Psychology: Theory and Application to Intellectual Functioning', in *Annual Review of Psychology*, 50, 471-507.

[11] Motel, A., Künemund, H. and Bode, C. (2000) 'Wohnen und Wohnumfeld älterer Menschen' [Housing and living arrangements of older adults] in Frank Oswald and Hans-Werner Wahl (2005) *Dimensions of the Meaning of Home in Later Life.*

[12] Eurobarometer (2008). *Eurobarometer Survey*, Brussels: European Union.

[13] Lyons, R.A., John, A., Brophy, S., Jones, S.J., Johansen, A., Kemp, A., Lannon, S., Patterson, J., Rolfe, B.A., Sander, L.V., Weightman, A. (2009) 'Modification of the home environment for the reduction of Injuries', in *Cochrane Database of Systematic Reviews* 2011, Issue 2, Art. No.:CD003600. DOI: 10.1002/14651858.CD003600.pub3.

[14] Kendall, G. (2001) 'Eliza', online, available at: www.cs.nott.ac.uk/~gxk/courses/g5aiai/002history/eliza.htm.

[15] Swedish National Institute for Public Health (2007) *Healthy Ageing – A challenge for Europe*, Stockholm.

Biographical note

Sinéad Shannon has a background in communications and spent over ten years working in public relations, publishing and magazine editing. Following completion of an M.Sc in Social Research she changed career to focus on social policy research and has worked on research projects for Dublin Simon, TCD (the Trinity Immigration Initiative) and the Children's Research Centre before joining the Ageing Well Network as Research Manager. Sinéad has a BA in European Studies (University of Limerick, 1987), MA in Mass Communications (University of Leicester, 1999) and an MSc in Applied Social Research (TCD, 2007).

5

Better Compromises

Ciaran Fallon
On Movement

From Dhaka to QWERTY

Cities exist to facilitate interaction with others. We live in cities to improve our access to other people and to engage in some form or other of social exchange. Hospitals, business centres, universities, theatres, sports stadiums, shopping centres and the other big things of cities represent the aggregated needs, interests and desires of a city's people. Cities are particularly good at supporting specialism and synergy. They allow people with shared needs, interests and desires to come together to exchange, collaborate and create. Proximity provides opportunities, advantages, pleasures and frustrations and increasingly it demonstrates that the benefits of cities spill over into the wider economy.

Movement within cities is the integration of the daily activities of many people with diverse interests and needs. Systems of movement can be as advanced as the Shanghai Maglev train or as simple as a Dutch bike. They can have the order of the Tokyo subway system or the chaos of the streets of Dhaka and everything in between. Movement is about people and the organisation of movement is about the organisation of people. It is about time, space, money, resources, risks and pleasures – the very stuff of social life. While it is often portrayed as a technical process – and modern urban transportation is increasingly technologically complex – at its core it is a social process with all the value judgements, compromises, trade-offs, imbalances, controversies and messiness that this entails. The organisation of urban movement is fundamentally and irreducibly social and political. However this is ignored in Dublin's current institutional arrangements and in the long term it will hold us back as a city.

Dublin has a history of invasions, colonisations, rebellions and various social and cultural upheavals and our story can be read all around us. When we move through the historical inner city we trace paths that have been laid down over generations. These imprints of our past are an undervalued cultural asset. In important parts of our city we have allowed the movement function of streets to overwhelm their place function. Streets carry traffic and below their surfaces they carry power, water, waste, drainage and communications networks. They are conduits of movement and circulation but they are also important parts of our public realm and their social, cultural and amenity value to citizens and visitors needs to be recognised more. Our historic streets, lanes, squares and public places are an important part of our city's unique image and identity.

Social change seems to follow a branching model and once a particular route is taken it is often very difficult to get back on an alternative rejected path. Even if there is widespread dissatisfaction with a particular situation or set of arrangements they can endure because maintaining them involves less cost, effort and hassle then creating new ones. Some situations and arrangements persist because we cannot even conceive of alternatives or because we regard as unrealistic alternatives that can be imagined. The layout of the QWERTY keyboard I am writing on now famously comes from a typewriter sales pitch by the Remington Corporation in the 1870s. There are many more ergonomically efficient ways to layout a keyboard but the signature of history has locked in QWERTY and billions of us live with it daily.

Likewise the movement options we have in cities are highly circumscribed. While theoretically there is an abundance of choice, in reality options are limited by settlement patterns, the fixedness of the built environment and by prior transport commitments. While mobility is to a degree a personal choice, it is sometimes helpful to think in terms of systems which variously enable or frustrate different forms of travel. Most obviously, it is not possible to take a tram if track has not been laid. Cycling and walking have quite modest demands and will eke out an existence under most conditions but they are made much easier by good bike lanes, decent footpaths and pedestrian crossing.

Cars require not only roads but also parking spaces at origins and destinations, signalising systems to regulate interaction at junctions and a refuelling network. In addition to these infrastructural requirements a 'car system' needs a developed legal framework, methods of financing and insuring vehicles and systems for testing drivers. While we take it for granted today, this 'car system' that took over half a century to develop is now deeply embedded and our commitment to it affects the viability of alternatives.

How did we get here?

The roots of Dublin can be traced to two distinct Gaelic settlements, 'Dubhlinn' and 'Áth Cliath', and some of our inner city streets can be traced right back to the ancient routes which linked these to each other and to surrounding settlements. Dubhlinn was situated around where Aungier Street is today and modern Camden Street follows the ancient route or *slí* that led from Dubhlinn south towards the uplands. From this time, through the medieval period and up to the eighteenth century, routes were established along the lines of slí creating an early network of urban streets and walkways within the city walls and extending beyond the walls into the south east.

In the eighteenth century the Georgian estates were developed and a new type of wide and uniform street appeared in the city. The Liffey Quays began to assume their modern form as properties were reversed to face the water and bridges were built to span the river. The four city bridges from this period that still serve us today are testaments to the skills of their builders and remind us of the long reach of time upon our movement patterns, as Noel Brady's chapter in this volume attests. Perhaps as defining and influential were the construction of the Royal and Grand Canals which arc the city north and south enclosing what we now consider to be the historic inner core.

The early eighteenth century also saw the introduction of regular public transport services in Ireland with the first one recorded being a stagecoach service from Dublin to Kilkenny which began operating in 1718. The simple horse-drawn cart was refined into an enclosed and upholstered coach first in Hungary and then quickly adopted by the wealthy across Europe. While many desired the comfort, few could afford to own their own coach or maintain a team of horses and coach hire services developed in response. By the 1600s, coaches were travelling along defined routes in Britain making regular stops at stations along the way. These stations were called stages and so the coaches became stagecoaches. In eighteenth century Ireland stagecoaches generally carried four passengers inside and one outside and intercity journey times were measured in days. The Dublin to Belfast service inaugurated in 1742 took two days in summer and three days in winter to complete.

The nineteenth century saw more intense bridge building with eight of today's twenty bridges across the Liffey completed. Other major developments along the waterside included the development of the docks and their associated streets to the east of the city. As the century drew to a close Dublin was very compact with most of the city's population living and working within the inner core area bounded by the Grand and Royal Canals. Population densities were high and for most ordinary people work was within walking distance and with supplementary horse power where necessary.

Horse-drawn rail systems were widely used for pulling heavy loads in mines and quarries, and in 1832 the first rail-based passenger system was introduced in New York. Introducing the first tram rails to the streets of Dublin proved highly controversial and suffered several false starts. Early attempts to lay rail tracks on the public street were abandoned following strong public opposition from other road users. Finally a recessed rail system similar to the modern LUAS system was adopted and in 1872 the first horse-drawn tram service running from College Green to Rathgar began.

The following decades saw an expansion of horse-drawn tram services throughout the city by three rival companies. In 1880 these companies merged to form the Dublin United Tramways Company which had 137 tramcars, nearly 1,000 horses and over fifty kilometres of routes across the city. Other independent companies added services to outlying towns including Lucan, Dalkey and Blessington and popular beauty spots such as Phoulaphouca in County Wicklow. Horses pulled in teams of two for up to ten kilometres before being rested and replaced by a fresh team. Each tram was expected to have a team of ten but in fact this was rarely achieved. Horses were usually worked for three years before being sold off and were highly prized by farmers and draymen.

Horse-powered transit may seem quaint at a distance but it was not without its problems. Movement of large numbers of people within confined city spaces always entails risk: writing in nineteenth century Paris, Baudelaire describes 'crossing the boulevard in a great hurry in the midst of moving chaos, with death galloping at me from every side'. Accidents were common and the sound of scores of horses' hooves clattering along cobbled streets created such a din that one New York-based commentator described it as the 'Age of Noise'.

However the main drawback was the titanic problem of waste. Each horse deposited 7-15 kilogrammes of dung and upwards of 7 litres of urine daily on the impermeable surfaced streets of Dublin. Rolling fly populations congregated at dung heaps creating engines of disease and malodour was pervasive. When it rained pedestrians were forced to navigate foul slurry streams and when it was dry the dung was pulverised into a dust by hooves which irritated lungs and settled in deposits everywhere. By the end of the century Dubliners were ready – more than ready – for change and it came in the form of a noiseless and odourless marvel.

The first electric tram service was introduced in 1894 by the Southern District Tramways Company, which was then an independent company operating in the south city suburbs. This company subsequently merged with the Dublin United Tramways Company and the new entity resolved to phase out all of its horses in favour of electric traction and the last horse drawn tram in the city travelled from Northumberland Road to Sandymount on 13 January 1901.

Dublin began the twentieth century as a compact but unsanitary city and ended it a more hygienic sprawl. Dense inner-city settlement patterns persisted until after independence in 1921, at which time city dwellers began to be re-housed in more spacious homes in new outlying suburbs and the share of population living in the city centre began to decline. This hollowing out of the city centre accelerated mid-century as the private car became more affordable and the trend has only recently been reversed.

In the early years of the century the Dublin United Tramways Company thrived and expanded its electric tram network to where it saw potential for profit. By 1917 a route numbering system was introduced starting with route 1 serving Ringsend in the south east and fanning out radially in a clockwise direction until route 31 to Howth in the north east was reached.

From the 1890s, European companies such as Daimler, Benz, Peugeot, Renault and Fiat were developing early automobiles but the First World War saw dramatic improvements in the reliability of internal combustion engines, and in the early 1920s private operators using diesel engine buses began competing with the electric tram services in Dublin. In the so-called 'bus war' that followed, the Dublin United Tramway Company fought by acquiring its own fleet of diesel engine buses and its timetable of 1927 lists 25 tram routes and 15 bus routes.

In 1933 legislation was enacted which gave Dublin United Tramway Company the power to compulsorily acquire all independent operators within its operational area effectively wiping out competition in Dublin. In 1938 the company announced its intention to phase out electric trams in favour of more flexible diesel-powered buses and in July 1949 the last electric trams left from Nelson's Pillar on O'Connell Street. Reportedly there were chaotic scenes as a force of 60 Gardaí attempted to prevent souvenir hunters stripping the last tram of every conceivable fitting.

In the early 1950s, to the delight of the city's many cyclists, the extensive network of tram tracks were stripped from the streets of Dublin as part of a relief project for the city's long-term unemployed. The Hill of Howth tramway which did not connect to the city system continued to run until 1959 before finally closing. The next tram would not run in Dublin until June 2004 when the LUAS Green Line opened on the old Harcourt train line.

In 1945 a new national transport authority, Córas Iompair Éireann, was formed and absorbed Dublin's public transport infrastructure. In the 1950s cars began to become affordable and planners across the developed world imagined a future of suburban car-based living. The 1949 Ford brochure described their latest models as 'living rooms on wheels' and linked the appeal of freedom and independence with that of modern home living. The modern home was a place of comfort, convenience and entertainment and driving too was like taking your front room for a spin.

In the 1960s plans for new stand-alone towns in Tallaght, Clondalkin and Blanchardstown were developed and in the following forty years major growth in population took place in and around these towns. CIÉ entered this period with rising losses including those sustained by the bus service in Dublin as a result of increasing private car ownership. More cars in the city meant less bus users, more road congestion and higher bus operating costs, and a review of services noted that nearly half of Dublin City bus routes were operating at a loss. Writing in *The Irish Times* at the time, the late Garret Fitzgerald observed that Irish cities were becoming congested because no system had been devised for charging car users for the cost of the space they used in driving through and parking on the city streets.

Cars made longer commutes viable, and with wider affordability and increasing ownership major settlements developed around Swords in the north and Dundrum and Sandyford in the south; county boundaries in the west blurred as development in Lucan spread to Maynooth and Celbridge in County Kildare. The continuous developed area, which we might call metropolitan Dublin, is surrounded by a mainly rural hinterland which spreads from Drogheda in the north, to Arklow in the south, and to Newbridge in the west. In the boom decade from 1996 to 2006, the housing growth rate in this hinterland area was three times higher than that of the Dublin metropolitan area. In many cases employment, schools, shops and services were limited or absent in these expanded hinterland areas, and with no public transport and road systems and trip distances that discouraged walking and cycling, the car was often the only viable travel choice. This recent episode of poor transport and spatial planning has locked-in car use patterns which will have a profound effect on movement in and around Dublin for decades to come.

Where we are now?

The key drivers of transport demand are economic activity and population growth, and as the current recession gripped in 2007 all transport activity in Ireland reduced. By 2006 the population of the greater Dublin area had increased by 18 per cent on the previous ten-year period and accounted for 39 per cent of the State's population. It was estimated that over 4.5 million journeys were made by people in the greater Dublin area on a typical weekday. Forecasts estimate that by 2030 the population of greater Dublin will grow to around 2.3 million and best estimates suggest that the number of trips per weekday in the greater Dublin area will exceed 6 million.

Within the inner canals core, nearly three-quarters of trips to work are less than 5 kilometres in length and about half of trips are walked or cycled. A further 28 per cent of trips to work are done by bus and tram and less than one-fifth of inner city dwellers travel to work by car. Look at the residential streets of Portobello or Stoneybatter on a weekday morning and see how few parked cars move. In the doughnut between the inner city and the M50, trip to work distances are still relatively low and more than half are less than five

One of Dublin's 5,000 cycling commuters

kilometres in length. However cycling and walking journeys are much rarer and account for only about one-fifth of trips. The majority of trips are carried out by private car (58 per cent) followed by public transport (24 per cent). In the metropolitan suburbs outside the M50, journey-to-work distances begin to stretch but still over one-third are less than 5 kilometres. However private car transport is now very dominant (73 per cent) with public transport following (18 per cent) and walking and cycling trips five times lower than the inner city dwellers (9 per cent). Most people who live in the recently populated surrounding hinterland travel over 10 kilometres to work and nearly 80 per cent use their car to travel to work.

The busiest time to travel is not surprisingly the weekday morning peak period from 7.00 am to 10.00 am at which time over 82 per cent of trips are commutes to work or study. The evening peak spreads over a longer period and is less intense, even though it includes an additional mix of shopping and recreational trips. Roughly 200,000 people enter the city centre each weekday morning. Around half come on public transport, 70,000 in cars, 17,000 walking, 5,000 by bike and the rest by taxi, motorcycle or commercial vehicle. Simple space constraints limit the number of vehicles that can move within the city at any time and these limits were regularly reached during the recent boom. The economic downturn has given some respite but we operate close to congestion limits and will quickly exceed them again as soon as recovery begins.

Private car transport makes massive demands on limited public space. Nine out of ten cars which arrive in Dublin every morning carry a single occupant. A modest-sized car takes up about 12 square meters of street and if that car is moving it needs a couple of car lengths ahead and behind and increases its demand to 60 or more square meters. Cars also occupy space when they are not being used. A car parking space is about the same size as a typical office cubicle and driving a car to work essentially doubles the amount of space needed for a worker. There are many good reasons why we should try to find alternatives to car transport in our city, but the most basic is scarcity of available space.

Dispersed settlement leads to longer journeys and a logical approach to managing movement is to encourage people to live closer together. There is a very strong inverse connection between density and car usage. Across a broad range of cities, as density doubles, the share of the population that takes the car to work drops by 6.6 per cent. But if we want more people to choose to live in our city we must find ways of making city life more attractive. A consequence of increased living density is a reduction in private space, and if a city is to have appeal as a place to live the loss of private space must be compensated with other advantages and one of these must be access to decent public spaces.

Where are we going?

Surface space in cities is a valuable commodity which the Victorians understood when they began building London's underground system 150 years ago. Of course, London was then the centre of an empire and is now firmly established as one of the world's megacities, but more recently cities with closer similarity to Dublin have also followed this subterranean approach. The Danish city of Copenhagen, which has a corresponding population and standing to Dublin, completed its first metro lines ten years ago. Its system carries 50 million passengers per year and this massive movement capacity frees up space at surface level for vehicles, excellent walking and cycling facilities and great public spaces.

Dublin has two metro projects under ministerial consideration at the moment, but with the country's difficult financial situation it is unlikely that they will be started any time soon. It is more likely that the near future will see modest extensions to the tram system – probably a link between the two existing lines and an extension of a tram service into the northwest of the city – and improvements in the bus service.

Buses will probably serve as the backbone to the city's public transport system in the coming decades but the capacity of the incumbent to meet this challenge is debatable. Dublin Bus persists with obscure and unresponsive route and timetabling systems, adopts technology late and often demonstrates a blasé approach towards its customers. Modern bus services are transforming cities around the world and the coming years are an opportunity for Dublin Bus to fulfil its potential and deliver a high quality service to the people of Dublin. A failure to do so must lead to the introduction of alternative service providers.

After a long period of decline, cycling is on the increase again. Dublin is very well suited to cycling. The city is quite flat, our climate is not too hot or cold, and despite the recent sprawl many trips are less than five kilometres – a distance that can be comfortably covered by most people in 25 minutes by bike. However our cycling infrastructure remains quite basic compared to German, Dutch or Danish facilities which limits the number of people who will choose to take the bike. Cycling is a cheap, clean and efficient way of moving large numbers of people over relatively short distances and we could increase its market share dramatically if we improve conditions and enhance the experience of cycling in Dublin.

Persuading drivers to give up their cars in favour of cycling and public transport will always be an uphill struggle. Some believe that rising fuel prices will change patterns but decades of commitment to a private car transport system has created a spatial and infrastructural lock-in which will not easily be changed. Cars are a symbol of late twentieth century individualism and consumerism and they are so much more than just transport. They allow us to control our immediate environment and pass through public space in a semi-private way. The car allows us to make individual choices about departure time, personal entertainment and even ambient temperature and fragrance. Car time is increasingly work time or 'me' time. The combination of convenience, functionality and emotional allure mean that the car, or something like it, will probably be a feature of Dublin and all developed cities well into the middle of this century – but with perhaps some differences.

The dublinbikes public bike hire system (see photograph below) has revealed something about the potential for collaborative use of transport infrastructure in Dublin. For a small joining fee members can automatically rent simple city bicycles from a network of stations around the city. The system has been an extraordinary success with each bicycle being used by an average of ten different people each day making these the hardest working bicycles in any public bike hire scheme. This, coupled with extraordinary low levels of vandalism, has been the basis of dublinbike's claim to being the world's most successful public bike hire scheme.

A dublinbikes bicycle station

Car-sharing schemes have followed and sophisticated electronically-based pay-by-use services are now available in Dublin. Again, for a small joining fee people can share the fixed costs of car ownership. Major car manufacturers are eyeing developments outside the traditional ownership model with interest. Outside Ireland, several have experimented with car-sharing schemes and with the provision pay-per-use car services rather than traditional sales. Both approaches could herald the late redemption of the resource-consuming, sell-n-scrap car industry as this new business model would tend to reward vehicle fleets on the basis of efficiency, durability and endurance.

Emerging technologies may mean we might get more 'auto' from automobiles. Cruise control has been available for decades but more recently automatic breaking and lane departure systems based on radar, infra-red and camera-sensing technology have arrived. A wireless standard has already been developed for communications between vehicles and is giving promising results on the test track. The first traffic signals in Dublin were installed at the intersection of Clare Street and Merrion Square in 1938 and today there are over 500 signalised junctions in the city alone. In the future vehicles may communicate their position and intended course to each other and to traffic control systems allowing higher levels of coordination.

Anyone who has ever had to push-start a car will know the immense energy required to get over a tonne of metal and glass moving and this massive expenditure of energy is repeated and repeated in stop-start urban driving. Future systems may minimise energy loss by reducing stops and restarts and instead gently slowing and speeding vehicles at coordinated intersections. 'Stop avoidance' has always been the strategy of momentum-loving cyclists and could feature in the future of urban motoring. Human-powered vehicles have always aimed to minimise weight and this is taken to its extreme in elite bicycle racing. Some of the lessons from this world may in the future be adopted by car manufacturers as ultra lightweight materials begin to be incorporated. Smart city cars have been on the market for some time now but ultra light 'quadracycles' are emerging with half the weight of a conventional city car and the energy efficiency of a motorcycle.

The city car as we know it today does appear to have lost sight of the original design brief. Using a five-seated, steel-framed, high-powered machine to move one person over short distances at relatively low speed might seem absurd in the near future.

Conclusion

Futures are heavily circumscribed and some of the key determinants are public finances, embedded traditions, the power and conserving effect of economic interests and the relative fixity of the built environment. The challenges associated with moving people and things under, over and across dense urban space have been around for a long time and in some senses nothing is really new except scale. When thinking about the future there is always a risk of epochal hubris – of believing that for some reason you are standing at some auspicious crossroads rather than at just another point on a long road. However right now we are pressing up against some spatial, environmental and public health limits which could tip us into a new way of thinking about movement.

There are also some interesting trends emerging. In 2009, for the first time in our history, the numbers of cars in Ireland went down rather than up and after a long period of decline the population of Dublin city centre increased. Now myself, and around 116,000 others, call the area within the canals 'home'.

The last two decades has also seen the establishment of two new mobility systems – 'networked computing' and 'mobile computing'. These technologies are increasingly diffused throughout the entire realm of human activity by growing miniaturisation and portability and they are ushering in new environments, social practices and economic entities that are laying down the path dependence patterns whose consequences will shape mobility for the twenty-first century.

Nothing approaches the car when it comes to comfort and convenience, but it is clear that the future transport needs of the city cannot be based upon the private car. Our streets only become useful for vehicle movement when they are not overused. The traffic problem essentially reflects the difficulty in sating the demand for anything that is desirable and free. Roads are expensive to build and maintain and we should charge on the basis of use. However people have a right to movement and when this right is infringed people suffer multiple exclusions and any road-charging system must be fair and equitable.

Road-charging in London was brought in by a directly elected mayor without a public referendum. Stand-alone referendums on road-charging in two other UK cities were resoundingly defeated. Technological solutions are coming onstream which will allow sophisticated tariff-charging and variable zone-setting but at some level all of these systems link individual movement with central databases which have implications for privacy. The need for some form of road-charging system is apparent, but the political challenges of this project are considerable.

Human ingenuity and our love of personal mobility will throw up some interesting urban solutions in the decades ahead and we need to have the flexibility to respond and adapt. Surface space in a historical city such as Dublin is extremely limited and as soon as it is economically feasible we should commit resources to tunnelling. Underground mass transit along routes with high commuting demand and a small bore network for city centre freight delivery would free up street space for other more interesting uses.

Transport planning and spatial planning are inexorably linked and any separation of the two is a hindrance. While population in the city centre is on the increase, Dublin still has the tidal ebb and flow of a suburban city and it needs more of the steady pulse of a living city. Density reduces commuting distance, supports efficient public transport and facilitates dynamic street life. Dublin has roughly the same population as Copenhagen but is more spread out producing a 30 per cent lower population density. In the coming decades we should steer towards increased density by making the city a great place to live and raise a family.

Most fundamentally, Dublin desperately needs a directly elected mayor. History has left us with a weak local government system in Ireland and leadership often ends up coming from unelected officials. At the core of planning are value judgements and these should rightly come from someone with a democratic mandate to provide leadership and vision. It is simply not appropriate for even the most competent, hard-working and high-minded public servants to lead in this area and I suspect that this is privately acknowledged. Without a mandate to lead, public servants inevitably tend to self-censor, low-ball and minimise confrontation. Consultation is extensive, compromise is relentless, decisions are too often timid and progress is slow. Conflict is an inevitable and healthy part of the change process and it cannot be avoided. City leadership was and always will be fundamentally and irreducibly political and the sooner we acknowledge this the sooner we can make the real changes that we need.

A good transport vision need not be a particularly complicated one. Gil Peñalosa's vision for Bogota as an '8:80' transport city has a beautiful simplicity. He challenges public servants to deliver a city that can be negotiated by anyone aged 8 to 80.[1] It is a simple vision from which good things flow. It affects the way bus routes are organised, footpaths and cycle lanes provided, junctions are configured and travel information is presented.

For most Dubliners the local authority collects the rubbish, fills the pot-holes and adjudicates on planning applications, and most people could not tell you who is the current Lord Mayor or what their duties and responsibilities are – they are in fact very few. This is not meant to denigrate the office or the commitment and hard work of those who have held it – in spite of the office's limitations some have made major contributions – but it could be so much better. A directly elected mayor with a substantial term of office could provide real leadership and enliven debate about the future city. He or she could ask publicly why is it we still do not have an integrated ticketing system, or why do the LUAS lines still not connect, or why do we think shared bus and bicycle lanes are a good idea? Dublin is a good place to live but with strong political leadership it could be really great.

Endnote

[1] See also Sinéad Shannon's chapter on Ageing in this volume.

Biographical note

Ciarán Fallon grew up in Lucan and emigrated to London at the tail end of the last recession. He returned to Dublin in 1999 and was elected to Dun Laoghaire-Rathdown County Council in 2004 where he served as a councillor until 2008. He holds an engineering degree from DIT and a PhD in sociology from UCD. He currently works for Dublin City Council's roads and traffic department as cycling coordinator. He lives in the city centre with his wife and daughter and enjoys running in the Phoenix Park with his dog.

6

On with the Show

Paul Donnelly
On Theatre and Performing Arts

Dublin's policy and practice

Dublin has a rich cultural heritage and while music, visual arts and literature will be covered elsewhere in this volume, the cultural impact of theatre and the performing arts merits a specific examination. The history of theatre and performing arts and Dublin as a place are bound up with one another, dating back to 1662 with the opening of Smock Alley Theatre. With the sheer number of other venues, institutions, companies and practitioners from 1662 to the present day, the wealth of tradition and history Dublin possesses inspires those who will continue this rich history. Taking a look at present circumstances in Dublin's theatre and performing arts, there are clear directions which this future may take.

A political debate began in 2009 on the feasibility of re-locating the Abbey Theatre to the General Post Office building. Proponents argued that our national theatre belongs on O'Connell Street; that we should place culture at the heart of our capital. Besides, that building on Lower Abbey Street is too restrictive and you can't enjoy a performance when you feel the rumble from the adjacent Luas line. Those opposed argued that it is nigh on treason to even consider going two for one on our national landmarks; if the GPO is fair game, we might as well throw Newgrange, Croke Park and the Cliffs of Moher into the mix. Why not compromise and build a new theatre in George's

Dock? A feasibility study was carried out at the request of the government with these possibilities in mind. Published in May 2011, one of the foremost statements of the report was that the Abbey theatre – as it currently stands – 'is inadequate for the requirements of a National Theatre of the twenty-first century'.[1] An initial estimate for the Abbey re-location project landed in the region of €300 million. However, the report recommended against proceeding any further with the site at George's Dock and raised a number of concerns about re-locating to the GPO. In June 2011, the Minister for Arts, Heritage and the Gaeltacht, Jimmy Deenihan, announced that the re-location to the GPO complex would not go ahead.

Taking this debate as occurring between 2008 and 2011, a number of interesting comparisons can be drawn. Between 2008 and 2010, state funding for the Abbey fell from €10 million to €7.25 million, but this was only the beginning. In 2009, the Arts Council stated a need to 're-examine the current approach to funding the production and presentation of theatre'. This re-examination became necessary as a result of annual reductions in the Arts Council's budget, meaning that available resources were not only insufficient for those who received funding but also could not provide for potential new artists and practitioners. Following a process of discussion around the document, the Arts Council published its new policy in March of 2010, *Supporting the Production and Presentation of Theatre: A New Approach*. Chief among the objectives of this new approach was the creation of a well-resourced theatre infrastructure: 'the infrastructure should be built around a sustainable number of production companies, venues, festivals and resource organisations'. These words notified practitioners of an imminent cull for production companies, altering creative directions for many practitioners in the performing arts whose work at the present time gave way to planning for the long term. Practitioners mobilised, the National Campaign for the Arts was formed and TD's were petitioned en masse to preserve the funding levels of the creative sector. Yet, whether it was practitioner facing a TD or a company meeting a government committee, the funding cuts came at the top and worked their way down.

Claiming there is a gap between policy and practice in the performing arts is hardly a new argument, but there is a chasm between policy and practice in the previous comparison. It was possible, on a macro level, to entertain the idea of a new national theatre at a cost of €300 million at the same time as funding cuts needed to be implemented on a micro level in the creative sector. Admittedly, a theatre as a long-term asset should be considered as separate to issues of annual funding; the true disappointment is that funding cuts became a reality and a new Abbey Theatre remained a long term pipe-dream. Of course, a gap between policy and practice should not be surprising. Policy makers and performing arts practitioners are inherently different; policy makers attempt to prepare for current and future circumstances, in either a reactive or proactive way, while practitioners create work to respond to or challenge circumstances that are ever-present. And yet, these distinct practices must seek a shared middle ground. The Arts Council's response to the reduced budget was to modify its support into six types: Core funding, Project funding, Shared administrative resources, Touring, Artists' supports and Development initiatives.

In the strategic overview for 2011–2013, the Arts Council aims 'to plan and provide in good times and bad and we will make all our decisions with the long-term good of the arts as our principal goal'. Such policies can be entertained on paper, but the truth of the matter is that – particularly in the performing arts – it is impossible to please everyone. Practitioners in Dublin have had time to adjust to these modified strands of funding. Though there has been lengthy debate over the production hub model as a long-term fit, many companies and venues are content to engage in short-term creative partnerships and projects in order to present their work. While some companies and practitioners have struggled, there are those who have thrived, establishing themselves as important players in the development of Dublin's future performing arts. Theatre Forum and the National Campaign for the Arts (NCFA) have become unifying forces for arts practitioners on an administrative level as the re-adjustment in the creative arts continues.

Dublin's performing spaces

Central to the performing arts is a sense of place within the city. An audience can make certain assumptions about what they will see by the venue alone. For a traditional literary theatre, there is the Abbey or the Gate. For experimental theatre and dance, there is the Project Arts Centre and for musical theatre, the Grand Canal. These are simple assumptions, but they act as a definition of each venue, something the venues may even struggle against. Indeed, ideas are bound in the architecture of Dublin's performing arts. The Gaiety is known for its pantomime each Christmas, The New Theatre is an outlet for new writing and The Ark produces theatre for children and young people. Tourists are as likely to attend the Abbey Theatre because it is the place where J.M. Synge's *The Playboy of the Western World* caused a riot as they are because of the show being presented at the time.

These assumptions may be simplistic, but they are the perceptions that can become bound in architecture and Dublin's performance buildings all have preconceived labels and tags attached to them. And yet, there is an assurance in becoming a trademark venue, in terms of retaining an audience. Consistently delivering on an artistic form allows the audience to engage with the venue as much as the performance they come to see. In this way, venues around the city have developed a rapport with their audiences and become sites of memory. A key consideration is the role of the venue as a home to work. Through combinations like Wayne Jordan and the Abbey Theatre, or work developed at the Project by members of Project Catalyst, practitioners gain an intimate understanding of the space and its capabilities. In some respects, this approach is to be encouraged. Dublin's practitioners often dwell in long periods of freelance work or no work at all. Partnerships between practitioner and venue lead to far more interesting examinations of the work in relation to the space it is presented in.

Another point of architecture which is worth noting is the sheer scale of space that the performing arts occupy in Dublin City. To give a brief rather than exhaustive detail, active venues around the city include but are not limited to: the Abbey (and Peacock), the Gate, Project Arts Centre (the Cube and Space Upstairs), The Ark, The New Theatre, Smock Alley, Bewley's Cafe Theatre, Samuel Beckett Theatre (and Players), Grand Canal Theatre, the Lir, the Gaiety, the Teachers' Club and the Back Loft to name but a few. These venues are accompanied by The Lab and Dance House rehearsal spaces on Foley Street and other functioning spaces such as the Pearse Centre, City Arts, Theatre Exchange and the Irish Theatre Institute. In addition to venues and spaces, there are other important professional institutions such as Theatre Forum, Dance Ireland and the Arts Council. It is also worth noting that companies based in Dublin hold administrative offices (some with small rehearsal spaces) and storage spaces around the city. Needless to say, all of this accounts for a large quantity of space in the city that belongs to the performing arts. Imagine the value of the land on which these spaces stand? This scale of architecture, whether owned or rented, reflects the worth of performing arts within Dublin. Given the diversity of spaces and locations, if all performing arts practitioners ceased operations in the morning, a substantial chunk of Dublin would be missing.

Unfortunately, the assessment of Dublin's venues cannot be entirely positive, especially if one considers the quality of venues from a dance practitioner's perspective. Presented to the Arts Council in 2010, the summary report *Giving Body to Dance* prepared by Maureen Mackin and Nicola Curry is scathing of the reduced and unfit for purpose spaces for dance practitioners in Dublin and throughout Ireland. Particularly in dance, the element of space is vital. Groups such as CoisCéim, Ballet Ireland and Irish Modern Dance Theatre are highly active around the city, despite the fact that the facilities they have to rely on are technically deemed inadequate. Creating work for an expansive space is complicated when all one has to create in is a back loft or transformed office. Added to a shortage of space, the quality of the space is also of paramount importance. Rehearsal areas without sprung floors, mirrors, air conditioning or working speaker systems limit the work a practitioner of dance is capable of. The Arts Council conceded that 'dance development has been somewhat limited by a shortage of essential infrastructural supports' in their publication *An Integrated Dance Strategy 2010–2012*. Quality of space is far more important to dance as a performing art than quantity. If one takes these inadequacies of space into account, the quality of work that Ireland's dance practitioners produce is all the more impressive. The disappointment for dance in Dublin and indeed on a national scale is that improvements of quality and quantity of space are perpetually long-term plans. Under these circumstances, it should not be surprising that performances across the arts are, with increasing frequency, taking place outside of traditional venues.

Some of the most interesting contemporary work in Dublin has been work that engages directly with the city, often on a site-specific basis, but not necessarily so. Fishamble's *The End of the Road* brought its audience around its protagonist's sites of memory, including Fishamble Street and Temple Bar. Beyond this approach, many productions take sites of memory as theatrical devices. Anú Productions presented *World's End Lane*, an exploration of the history of Monto, Dublin's notorious red light district of old, in a confined space in The Lab on Foley Street. The Company gave us *As You Are Now So*

Once Were We, a contemporary examination of Dublin in the manner of Leopold Bloom's experiential exploration from *Ulysses* but presented (using a lot
of cardboard) in the Project's Space Upstairs. Playgroup's *Berlin Love Tour*
brought the audience on a walking tour of Berlin projected on to Dublin, teas-
ing out the inconsistencies of sites or spaces and the memories we associate
with them. As much as this work was a trend of 2010, new productions continue to engage with Dublin (*World's End Lane* and *Laundry* by Anú Productions are two parts of a four part series). Site-specific takes on a new meaning
with these practitioners – taking a site in any part of the city and creating a
new connection between performer and audience and space without that site
needing to be present for the performance. This style of performance shows
that practitioners have an ongoing curiosity and willingness to interact with
Dublin as a place, taking specific sites as a launch pad from which the wider
geographical expanse can be considered.

In terms of wider geography, the performing arts in the capital city have
an exalted position as the production hub for Ireland, in the Republic at least.
Companies aim to perform their work in Dublin and reviewers for national
papers rarely go outside the capital. Casting directors are based in Dublin;
performers of all kinds make their homes in Dublin; and much of Arts Council funding naturally remains in Dublin with a majority of the practitioners.
As much as there was a move for political decentralisation, Dublin persists as
our cultural centre. Creative practitioners in Cork, Galway, Kilkenny, Kildare
and Limerick are not to be overlooked for the work they do in their respective
regions, but the diminishing tag of 'regional' is applied to any work outside the
capital. Admittedly, the performing arts are Dublin-centric and a combination of factors are to blame, chief among those the fact that many companies do not have the funds or logistical setup required to tour and regional
audiences trend in established patterns of attendance. It is not simply a case
of inclination on either side; organisation and timing are crucial. Efforts and
experiments continue to bring about networks that can ensure ease of rotation
for touring work. At present, NOMAD Theatre Network in Ireland's north
midlands and Strollers Touring Network (some ten theatre/arts centres across
Ireland) comprise a program of venues which are not traditionally in receipt
of such high-quality touring work. Around the country, venues like Galway
Town Hall Theatre and The Everyman Palace in Cork are creating openings

for touring companies to expand their audiences. Through the touring funding strand, Arts Council policy is actively encouraging work to tour, particularly following recent successes touring work abroad in the UK and in the United States through Culture Ireland's 'Imagine Ireland' showcase.

Dublin's festivals

Festivals form an integral part of Dublin's performing arts structure. After all, it would be an empty practice to list venues and encourage touring nationally and internationally if there was no effort to host international productions here. Dublin's major performing arts festivals – Dublin Dance Festival, Absolut Fringe Festival and Dublin Theatre Festival – succeed in promoting Irish work while also presenting international work. This balance is important for the future of Dublin's performing arts in a few ways.

Any injection of culture to contrast with our own leads to interesting experimentation with, defence or advance of our culture by our practitioners in the aftermath. Arts practice can become insular over time but being made aware of alternative possibilities and forms is necessary to avoid stagnation. A company like Pan Pan might seem unique or be misunderstood in Ireland, yet witnessing the work of groups like Forced Entertainment and Gob Squad allows us to appreciate Pan Pan's talents for what they truly are. In this respect, these festivals also serve to locate the work of Dublin's practitioners in an international context, allowing for recognition of work of quality through an international perspective. For instance, the Irish reputation for literary theatre would not be as well known without first placing it alongside international work of a similar style. Indeed, the strength of Dublin's three major festivals is in the broad variety of performance style that each festival caters to. Dance, experimental dance, experimental theatre, musical theatre, circus and acrobatics, street theatre, musical theatre, devised work and literary theatre all find an outlet in a specific festival. Between May and October, Dublin is a performing arts city.

Of course, important work takes place away from venues and performance spaces at the same time. Performers, directors, choreographers and producers all take advantage of the networking potential these festivals offer. All three festivals strongly encourage professional interaction and networking, short-term interactions which can lead to long-term artistic pursuits. Important initiatives are also a major addition to these festivals. The Irish Theatre Institute hosts its International Theatre Exchange, a networking event for practitioners with other international practitioners and venues during the Dublin Theatre Festival, while the Fringe plays host to the Information Toolbox. Also in the theatre festival, The Next Stage initiative gives those selected for the programme exclusive access to shows and practitioners involved in the festival, as well as a number of workshops and talks. The Dance Festival regularly programmes top international performers, expanding the cultural palette for dance in Dublin. Curatorial decisions such as these encourage positive development of artists and practitioners, both here and abroad, challenging their practices so that they may advance to a higher standard.

As a capital city, Dublin fulfils the need for performing arts that go beyond our own local culture. The insular perspective of Irish culture is broken down in both directions with international participation in Dublin's three major festivals and our own companies touring abroad.

Dublin's audiences

All too often, audiences are the last aspect of performing arts to be considered. However, the old cliché of 'build it and they will come' is losing relevance in terms of the performing arts. Practitioners have as much of a responsibility to their audience as they do to their creative practice. More than this, how audiences relate to performances is advancing to a point where productions can place audiences as co-creators.

One of the most intriguing developments in the performing arts in recent times has been the crowd funding website Fund-it. As an initiative created by Business to Arts, Fund-it supports greater individual contributions to creative practitioners. This approach is intended to strengthen the bond between a creator and their audience and to offer potentially wider-ranging, long-term relationships. As a result of this website, work that may never have seen the stage for financial reasons is directly engaging with the potential audience in order to gather the necessary funding. In a sense, the initiative for work to be created through Fund-it is with the audiences who are willing to support a performance. This responsibility for creation brings new thinking to the relationship between practitioners and their audiences. Of course, the present limitation of the Fund-it website is that most of the visible support for production comes from within the arts community or from families and friends of the producers. As the website grows, the long-term expectation would be engagement with a broad array of funders, open rather than closed.

Another important shift in the audience–practitioner relationship has been the rise of social media. It has become standard practice to create an online presence for performing arts companies and individuals. Practitioners maintain numerous social media outlets in order to generate further content for audiences around the central artistic practice or production. Facebook and Twitter accounts are used to give status updates on works in rehearsal and even to promote ticket sales or competitions. Lines between theatre and cinema are blurred by production trailers on YouTube, and active blogs on individual or company websites ensure that the production is not the only method of engagement the contemporary practitioner has with their audience. In many respects, it is a preferred method of promotion, what Phillip McMahon labelled 'paperless promotion' for companies and venues alike. On the other hand, presence on social media is not a one-way transaction for the practitioner's benefit; it also offers the audience a level of access beyond the performance. The audience now witnesses the process of a production and not simply the end product. Social media forms an indirect 'market research': potential audience response to rehearsal images or comments on whether they liked the show or not can all be taken into account by the practitioner. Again, this creates a bond between audience and practitioner, often before a performance even takes place. This is indicative of the wider shift in the audience–practitioner relationship, wherein the practitioner acknowledges the need for an audience. In the same line of thought, the responsibility of an audience to the work has also increased; the stakes are much higher. Whether or not there is an extension of ownership in this exchange is debateable.

Perhaps the more interesting result of this new dynamic is the displacement of the critic. Prior to social media as we know it now, a newspaper critic or reviewer acted as the intermediary between practitioner and audience. This granted enormous power to the critic. Historically, names such as George Bernard Shaw, Max Beerbohm and Kenneth Tynan, among others, could decide the success or failure of a production with their reviews. From a practitioner's point of view, this process had enormous flaws given the reliance on one individual and so, with contemporary media as it is, the move away from a critic preserving high theatre to the audience sustaining a popular theatre is inevitable. The role of a critic/reviewer now is chiefly a responsibility to posterity. This is perhaps best reflected by reviewers such as Fintan O'Toole or Peter Crawley who, while still reviewing individual productions, muse upon the performing arts in a broader context; see, for example, O'Toole's *Power Plays* documentary and Crawley's numerous feature articles for *Irish Theatre Magazine*. Practitioners still appreciate the thoughts of such reviewers, as well as actively pursuing exposure through RTÉ's *Arena* and *The View*. However, if the direct line to an audience is preferred, the reviewer's impact on the success or failure of a production is limited.

Dublin's practitioners

In a time of ongoing struggle for funding, many practitioners of theatre and dance would refrain from considering a future beyond six to twelve months. Artists are forced to consider their futures in a more immediate sense, to live day to day, in the present. These are terms that artists cannot avoid and yet their work is intended to transcend the present, as works of ideas and themes, not simply responses or reactions to the present moment.

Let it not be forgotten that, behind their work, practitioners in the performing arts are real people with real world problems. Many made the same mistakes as their peers during the past decade, spending where saving would have been safer, signing for mortgages that were ill-advised at best and ignoring the potential fall waiting in the future. As has been mentioned, practitioners also faced potential job losses and reductions of income. Now that this period of turbulence has ceased, whether permanently or temporarily, the performing arts sector is working to restore itself. The initiative that is perhaps central to the future of independent practitioners in this country is the Business to Arts program, ensuring that artistic experiment can go hand in hand with shrewd management and production values. Production companies have learned that overdependence on one source of income is poor long-term management. With the ongoing work of the Arts Council and the Business to Arts initiative, a broad and sustainable approach to private funding for the creative arts that complements public funding will bring practitioners out of the unsound financial practices of old.

Yet, there is an element of paradox in the contemporary Dublin practitioner. The boom years and excess are blamed for reducing the amount of funding presently available to practitioners nationwide, but at the same time, the boom years are responsible for the infusion of confidence and bravado with which work is now produced. After all, the proliferation of individual production companies probably has as much basis in commercial interests as it does in artistic autonomy. Dublin's practitioners have first-hand experience of the swell which placed national self-confidence at an all-time high. On the back of this, practitioners increased the stakes, took risks and made brave choices across the board. In the present slump, while there is an understandable self-examination process of the morality of the past decade, this confident identity has not been knocked out entirely. One only has to look at practitioners in THISISPOPBABY, The Company, Irish Modern Dance Company, Fishamble and many more to see that belief in the artistic creation is unwavering. Not every practitioner or company can claim to have stood by their artistic identity throughout this turbulent period, nor should they be criticised for choices taken to ensure survival. The point is that practitioners have not all balked in fear at funding cuts (reflected by Theatre Forum's most recent conference title, 'On with the Show') and to some extent, the confidence inherited over the last decade is behind this. However, practitioners must now work to ensure that this confidence never displaces sensible management.

In terms of the creative practice, practitioners have been placed in a compromising situation by reduced funding. A problem for many in a difficult financial position is that their work often gets forced into commercial territory. Add to this that some practitioners must go freelance to get work at all and the end product is a small percentage of work for which the creative art is the main motivation. Production hubs and partnerships are perceived as the alternative to individual companies but this idea is utopian – the reality is that arts practitioners want to create their own work on their own terms and always have. Nevertheless, compromise is a present necessity and production hubs are being identified as the means of progress. Collaboration and partnerships are succeeding in delivering short-term, even once off productions. If long-term artistic practice is to be secured, the options are production hubs or securing greater funding for individual production companies.

Dublin's future

Two important qualities must be constant in the development of Dublin's future, progress and conservation. It is a simple formula based on balance: progress should not be at the cost of tradition and conservation should not halt progress.

It may be from the comfort of distance from the harsh realities implied by the changes in Arts Council policy, but it should be observed that there is a great deal of sense and indeed logic behind them. The company model is corporate in its conception and places the bottom line firmly in financial and not artistic territory. What we see from a proliferation of performing arts companies is separation and fragmentation along financial lines rather than remarkably individual artistic goals. In fact, the competition aspect inherent in this corporate atmosphere inevitably leads to numbers of companies producing work simultaneously, saturating the market at given periods and exhausting their audiences. This, in economic terminology, leads to diminishing returns on productions. Consumption is greatly informed by habit and the more often an audience member does not see your productions, the more likely they are to continue to ignore your work. For this reason, the production hub model has a particular sensibility to it. Resources are shared, productions are limited and in turn so is supply. By reducing the supply, the demand increases and ensures a reasonable return. All this talk of economics may seem out of place, but it is worth pointing out that the individual company setup is further out of place, representing the wider commercial mindset of the last decade in the performing arts. Production hubs can take a share of the market at the same time as ensuring there are enough opportunities for practitioners to develop and present their work at a high standard. At present, partnerships are helping to ease practitioners into the idea of operating through production hubs but this must be a transition and not a substitute.

The guarantee of performing arts in Dublin's future is that there will be a new national theatre. As the Government's feasibility study indicated, the new theatre is a project design, which means that the main complication is finalising a location for that design. One can only hope that there will not be additional issues with financing and potential objections. In the case of the National Theatre in London, a site was chosen in 1948 and a foundation stone was laid in 1951. However, construction stalled while London County Council made arrangements to cover half the cost following the government's claims that it could not afford a national theatre. As a result of these disputes, the first theatre in the building (the Olivier) did not open until 1976 with the rest of the complex completed by 1977. It took 25 years from the foundation stone being laid – 28 if one takes the site allocation as the starting point – until the opening of the National Theatre in London. One can only hope that the pursuit of a new national theatre in Dublin will not encounter similar difficulties, and that the case of London's National Theatre can be taken as merely a cautionary tale.

If sense prevails, this essential development can advance to an arrangement between any combination of the Abbey Theatre, the Gaiety School and The Lir to deliver a national academy for the performing arts. The Lir offers itself as Ireland's national academy of dramatic arts and that is a starting point. Of course, there is greater potential to be realised. Dublin's future theatre and performing arts depends upon foresight at this time in terms of education. A national academy dedicated to the wide array of creative arts can see Dublin become an international creative hub. This will pave the way for all manner of collaborative work as well as challenges and defences of specific forms, but perhaps more crucial than that, Irish work that is aware of its international value.

The National Campaign for the Arts is currently leading the way in unifying practitioners under a common goal despite the multitude of variation across artistic forms. An important element of their work is removing the simplistic approach of vilifying those who would not fund the arts and instead working towards reasoning with potential funders and funding sources. In association with Business to Arts and the Arts Council, these groups will be responsible for the sustainability of the creative arts in Dublin and Ireland as a whole. Dublin's creative future will be with rounded practitioners, naturally devoted to their artistic practice but with the necessary knowledge to equate this practice with appropriate production and administration values.

Venues will advance the relationships and networks that are available to them both at home and abroad. Networking with other venues is a means of progress, and a means of exploration for the body of work Dublin produces. National networks for touring need to be established in order for work to reach wider audiences. This process would be most effective through a production hub model, creating links with venues and touring experts that are available to any group hoping to tour their work. Specifically by venues and spaces, long-term investments must be considered in order for rehearsal and performance spaces to grow in quality as well as quantity.

Audience and practitioner will have direct access to one another as association through social media grows. For the audience, this can ensure their input is taken into consideration, while the practitioner can develop tangible relationships with an audience beyond the short-term engagement of a performance. Reviewers can and should still campaign for the highest standards in the performing arts, but the transition from engaging with work in the present to examining work as a moment in cultural history will be equally effective in reminding practitioners of their responsibility to Dublin's cultural tradition.

All in all, the future of Dublin's performing arts rests in a balance between practitioners, policy, audiences, progress, conservation and the city itself. A new national theatre will remain a part of literary tradition, production companies may be replaced by production hubs but the high quality and individuality of output will be constant and practitioners may advance their administrative skills, but the art will always be their priority. Smock Alley Theatre first opened in 1662 and even though it has been a church and a tourist office since then, it will re-open in 2011 following a lengthy refurbishment. Whether this is conservation in restoring the venue or progress in making it a twenty-first century performance space, Smock Alley is perhaps the perfect metaphor of Dublin's performing arts. That is to say, no matter how turbulent its history has been, it is persistent. Dublin's performing arts, if nothing else, will persist long into the future.

References

Arts Council (2009) *Examining New Ways to Fund the Production and Presentation of Theatre: Discussion*: Dublin: The Arts Council.

Arts Council (2010) *An Integrated Dance Strategy 2010–2012*: Dublin: The Arts Council.

Arts Council (2010) *Supporting the Production and Presentation of Theatre: A New Approach* Dublin: The Arts Council.

Arts Council (2010) *Developing the Arts in Ireland: Arts Council Strategic Overview 2011-2013*: Dublin: The Arts Council.

Department of Arts, Sport and Tourism (2010) *Location of the Abbey Theatre - Amharclann Na Mainistreach - in the GPO Complex Feasibility Study*: Dublin: Government Publications. (See http://www.arts-sport-tourism.gov.ie/pdfs for documents and publications from the Department of Arts, Sport and Tourism.)

Mackin, M. and Curry, N. (2010) *Giving Body to Dance: Review of Building-based Sance Infrastructure in Ireland: Summary Report*, Dublin: The Arts Council. (See http://www.artscouncil.ie/en/publications.aspx for all Arts Council documents and publications.)

Endnotes

[1] Department of Arts, Sport and Tourism (2011) *Location of the Abbey Theatre - Amharclann Na Mainistreach - in the GPO Complex Feasibility Study*, p. 9.

[2] See www.fundit.ie.

[3] See www.businesstoarts.ie.

[4] Providing for a main Abbey Theatre stage and auditorium for an audience of up to 650; the Peacock Theatre stage with seating accommodation for an audience of 350; a Studio Theatre with seating accommodation for an audience of 150; and an Exhibition Space, a Restaurant, Bar and Cafe. This is a total of 13,174 square metres of net accommodation, or 20,104 square metres gross.

Biographical note

A graduate of the Masters in Drama and Theatre Studies in NUI Galway, Paul Donnelly is currently a PhD Research Student in the Department of English, Media and Theatre Studies in NUI Maynooth. His research interests include entrances and exits, performance spaces and contemporary performance. As well as working on research, Paul is a playwright. He received the 2010 Jerome Hynes Memorial Award in NUI Galway for his one act play I Go To Kill *and is currently working on an adaptation of Eugene Ionesco's novel* The Hermit.

7

Alternative Spaces

Seán Mac Erlaine
On Music

Particular spaces

When asked to write about music in Dublin and its future, I had no interest in trying to see whether someone in Dublin is going to invent a new scale or whether 'the lost chord' will be uncovered in a Dublin suburb in fifteen year's time! So, rather than talking about the fabric of music itself or suggesting who might be making great music in the future, perhaps the means of production, where people play and these social factors are the stuff of real importance and where significant change is taking place and will continue for people making music and their audiences. I talked with the organisers of three alternative art spaces where music, among other things, is presented. These alternative spaces are, for me, a really good example of a new avenue for music performance (though not all music may suit this arrangement) and they represent a very positive development in terms of bypassing the dominant licensed venue model, which doesn't always serve the music as well as it could. I choose these particular spaces because I believe they each represent a new working model of how music is being performed today in Dublin, and they raise questions as to whether this model may become more and more favoured into the future and what implications that scenario holds. I talked with Jack Phelan and Erin Michelle from Hello Operator, in Dublin's North Inner City; Miranda Driscoll and Feargal Ward from The Joinery, in Arbour Hill,

Dublin 7; and Ian Oliver and Monika Sapielak from the Centre for Creative Practices in the heart of Dublin's traditional Georgian business district in Dublin 2. Although the interviews were recorded on three separate occasions in the three spaces, the texts were treated as an audio collage (as many similar topics were touched upon) and transcribed into the format below.

History

Seán: Although there is a long history to artist-run spaces in Dublin, it seems that over the last four years or so, more and more independent alternative spaces have appeared in Dublin. There are a couple of myths surrounding their formation: the first is to see these as a result of the property crash, with artists snapping up cheap warehouse spaces. The other temptation has been to lump these spaces together under a common banner, implying a movement of sorts. But your spaces debunk these ideas, don't they?

Miranda: We started up 2008, early 2008, so pre-recession. So no, it wasn't as a response to the recession. But it was a response to challenging the accepted norms for progress for the artist after graduation and into their career. So, as a non-commercial space it takes out the representation of the artist by a gallery. In a place like this, artists can get stuck into showing their own work and not wait around to be shown by somebody else.

It started for us when we were looking for a place to work in and we came across this building. And then, in terms of the music we were just approached by an improvising musician initially and then very quickly we saw that musicians, even more so than visual artists, were really excited about places that were challenging the traditional venue approach. Other than that there isn't an agenda or sense of being part of a movement of artists setting up spaces.

Ian: We started the Centre for Creative Practice (CFCP) in September 2009. I had been working for the Irish Writers Centre and had been taking music photographs for a number of years for independent bands right through to RTÉ performing groups and most stops in between. When the funding was cut to the Writers Centre, we (with my partner Monika) decided we were going to start somewhere that was basically geared towards literature, maybe with a mix of genres but mostly to do with courses and education.

It soon became very apparent that courses weren't necessarily going to be the way that we were going to pay the rent let alone pay ourselves, which we still don't do, but we do pay the rent these days! So we started looking at events and what sort of things we could do and being friends with some musicians, music became part of that while literature took a back step. So music, visual arts, photography and film became very important.

Seán: Can you give an outline of how the economics of running a space works out? Do you receive funding or how do you cover costs?

Ian: Basically we get seven grand from outside sources, which is two grand from Dublin City Council, five grand from the Arts Council which has to go on our programme – we are not allowed to use it for core costs. But, for instance, if you bring a quartet over from the UK you are looking at a grand straight away, so it doesn't go very far. And that's not just towards music, it's towards visual art, it's toward photography, film, everything. So, one of the big problems is funding. It's difficult because, ok we don't get paid but we want the artists to get paid. And guys doing stuff for nothing: it's not helping creativity at all in any particular genre. Y'know there're very, very few full-time musicians in Ireland, most of them do something else other than making music.

Monika: So we are 98 per cent independent, of course we do get a little bit of funding but it's just really a handshake.

Erin: We did apply a few times for funding, but have never gotten any. But in a way it's a good thing, it has forced us to have our own survival strategy. And you know, if next month things don't work out, they don't work out! And we are prepared to walk away from it and do something else. We try to balance it so that a commercial TV shoot can in effect subsidise somebody else being here banging on glasses or whatever.

Jack: We see it first as a performance space and the rental thing as secondly, but it's not always that way around money wise. As long as it's going well and we are enjoying it and bringing something unusual and exciting to the city then it's great. If not – gone – we'll do something else. The few collective approach things we have been to have seemed pretty fruitless because you end up realising that the reason you started up a space like that was not to be part of something else! And periodically people represent it that way, or someone thinks that it would be a good idea to have a collective of everyone . . .

Music in visual spaces

Seán: Every visual artist has to have a studio: it's an amazing tradition they have developed compared to musicians. Shouldn't musicians all have their own studios as well? So far, to my knowledge, there has been no group of musicians who have organised and created a performance space, like you guys have or the general visual art community has for generations now in this town. So although none of these spaces have been set up by musicians, we are fortunate that you are all interested in hosting live music but us musicians are really all piggybacking on you guys.

Miranda: Right, I have never thought about it like that actually. I guess most visual artists would strive to have a separate space to work in that's not their house and perhaps that comes from having a space in art college. But I don't know why musicians don't do this, why is that?

Seán: I would put it down to a cultural inertia! But maybe in the future musicians in Dublin might now be more inclined to do this themselves, to have a performance space. It seems like a really important thing.

Ian: I wonder if it's because musicians have this feeling that, well, we are always poor for a start so spending money on a space is not seen as feasible and if I got a piano or something that needs moving I might need to carry it around because I am playing a gig and actually I've got a bedroom, that'll do. Also the majority of music gigs will take place in pubs, whereas art exhibitions tend not to take place in pubs. So if a musician is looking for a space he'd almost be looking for a space in a pub.

Jack: When we set up our first space, Red Space, in 2007, we did see it as a place where the bands who needed the rehearsal room there could also perform there. So we could run gigs there but we called it a gallery, or a very flexible gallery that could function as anything, but it really was more of a performance space.

Seán: So how did musicians react to it? Did people respond to it?

Jack: Yeah, we did a really great job on the room with the resources that we had. It was very well sound-proofed and had a nice size. But we found that the bands that would be interested and need a sound-proof room would be loud bands. They tended to be indie rock and if at certain points in the year we were desperate to get bands in to fill up a slot to cover some of the rent we started not caring about what kind of music they were playing. And of course it became tough then as property prices began falling and some bands took the attitude that they shouldn't need to pay a certain price for a rehearsal space.

Erin: But at the same time, there was more and more interest in the performances rather than rehearsals, happening in that room, so that was what was getting attention and people seemed to be interested in this. So then when we moved to Hello Operator we just said, y'know, we're not going to call it a gallery. First and foremost it's not for exhibitions necessarily, although we still do visual work – there's art work on the walls but it's not the first purpose of the space now.

Curating the space

Seán: So there's an interesting thing that came up there: you said you weren't into the music that some groups were playing. Is there a curatorial role then? Do you vet what happens?

Erin: Yeah, people do come to us with proposals and we turn them away. There is definitely a sort of thing that we really want to support. So things that can't happen in a nightclub or . . .

Jack: It's not very well defined. I mean there's nowhere where we have a document that says 'we will accept the following . . .'! You see, this space tends to dictate a lot of that for us which is really nice because we were very attracted to it when we saw it first. It acts like an amazing passive filter because people who want do something that wouldn't suit here tend not to like it when they see it. They come up here and say 'hmm, no, it's not quite right' and then we go 'phew!' They will usually make the decision themselves. Or when people see it and say 'oh, it has to happen here', then we tend to really like the idea in the first

Posters from events at the Centre for Creative Practice
(photographs: (left) studio 1500, San Francisco (middle, right) CfCP)

place. So with a place like this which demands a certain thing really, in a way, it makes things very easy. It curates for us.

Erin: We always meet and talk with everyone who wants to use the space to find out what their ideas are and how do you want to use the space. I definitely think that personal thing is important and we put a lot of ourselves into whatever happens here, if something is on we are always here.

Ian: Yes, we do put on our own stuff. There is a room for hire, but there is also a way that we curate stuff as well. Because we think that Dublin possibly needs it, or needs a space like it.

Seán: In The Joinery will certain bands say 'we wanna play here' and you'll say 'it's not right for you ...'?

Miranda: Yes, yes we do and more so now. At the beginning it was easy, people were emailing us all the time wanting to play, we'd listen to their music and simply say yes or no. It was really simple. I would have to say, at this point, that I have learnt so much about music over the last few years and that I really didn't have any ideas about music before then. So I am learning as I go along. I think if the music is more suited to a more traditional venue they would be better off just going and playing in Whelan's.

So we definitely try to find more unorthodox stuff, the more 'out there' at times the better! It keeps us on our toes a little bit. But now since the start of this year, we have started inviting musicians to play. There is still a bit of both, but it's mostly us scouting around more now. The only curatorial role, and I would use that term carefully, that we play would be that we might invite someone and then think of putting them alongside somebody else – what happens if we put them together and maybe that's an influence from the gallery space. So that's been fun. Often with a cross of mediums as well. So we feel a bit braver about having more input now.

Feargal: We have a call for submissions out now, trying to unearth new musicians and sound artists that might think that their stuff is a bit too abstract or obscure or bedroom-ridden to try it out here. So we are just trying to break into that, perhaps with people who haven't performed in front of an audience before. So they have to submit and we listen to their work and see. It's interesting to see what we might unearth with that.

Seán: Does that mean you see yourselves as having a developmental role? Are you interested in influencing things? It sounds like you are giving people a chance or a helping hand.

Feargal: Yes, but also to get something back, I think it's a flow and return thing though. We want to see people in here doing stuff that we haven't seen because we can work that into what's happening in the front of the gallery. That has already happened loads with musicians here; I work on documentary films and musicians who have played here have ended up sound tracking these films. And the same editor has used these musicians for bigger feature films . . . we are creative people so the idea of just being a facilitator or a developer – I wouldn't have much interest in that. So the flow and return thing has been really good.

Leaving the bar behind

Seán: Experience has shown musicians that when performing in an unsubsidised licensed room, at the end of the night the bottom line is always the barman's till. So it seems to me that, working in these kinds of spaces, there's much more flexibility and sensitivity to musicians; there's an element of the musicians, the venue and the audience all being on the same side of the fence. These spaces provide a safe place for performance which is unique in a non-subsidised environment where the promoter (quite often the performers themselves) is freed from the proprietor's concerns about selling alcohol. The vast majority of Dublin's music venues rely on alcohol sales as an important part of the economic equation to make the space work financially.

Ian: Yeah, we're not interested in what goes into the bar till because we don't have a bar. And if people want to come, they come because they want to listen.

Seán: Leaving simple economics aside, there are so many other complexities with traditional performance spaces, that's why so many musicians are interested in playing in a room like this. If you don't have the make-or-break factor of having to deal with the barman's till at the end of the night and you can work with people like yourselves instead, you have a much more sympathetic and symbiotic interaction.

Miranda: Yes, and at the end of it you are dealing with a person, not an institution or a place or a bar. And although it's BYOB [bring your own beer] here, in three and a half years we have never had any drunken scenes. Once you take the bar out and people throwing money behind a bar the night becomes about what's happening in the room. That's the only reason people will be here. And the people who are performing really feel and sense that from the audience that is here.

Seán: For me, it's inspiring that this model is now changing. The local Dublin music scene is just at the start of working with this new model of no bar, no institution, an informal space whose raison d'être (at that moment during the gig) is to act as a listening space. With low overheads, a DIY approach and, in the main, voluntary workers these spaces aren't blown about by the ill winds of national bankruptcy. The music continues regardless. But it does rely on the generosity and the spirit of the people to make it happen. It already has changed for certain groups of musicians and into the future this path will become more popular, it's also the cheapest way of putting a performance on and, yet, sometimes the most rewarding for makers and listeners alike.

Feargal: I think the best thing about The Joinery or any of the other spaces is taking the performance out of its 'comfortable home'. Yet, it's funny because I don't think music has a comfortable home in the traditional venues or in the bars. The bar, the drink, the night out, the loudness . . . music in a lot of venues is secondary, it's almost like it's relegated to something over to one side. But with small intimate spaces with no P.A., the idea is that everyone is coming here to listen to music.

Miranda: I have become quite intolerant when I go to a gig now in a established venue. It's quite you know . . . it's shit! If everyone's talking over the music, and then combined with the lack of intimacy . . .

Seán: It's a paradox, isn't it that people can pay twenty euro into a gig and then talk their way through it, but if it's a donation affair or a five euro hit, people can be absolutely respectful to the performers and listen to every note.

Feargal: Absolutely. I think that this kind of space or set up is a more natural home for music. It seems to work on so many levels. We've had thousands of people through here for gigs of all kinds, and we have never had a drunken person. But in town, you can easily pick a venue where you'll regularly have at least ten people screaming, fighting, drunk . . . There's a weird kind of self-regulation here when you take away all those systems – bar, pub, ticket, exchange, vend – people really get it. They seem to relax, they don't shout and they just drink what they want.

Miranda: It's also to do with the way the space seems like an extension of someone's place. It generates a natural sense of respect.

Seán: It seems to me that the whole sense of the ritual of music is much easier to pick apart and to look at in a space like this than a venue with a high stage, a sound man waiting for you to start and a large P.A. It's easier to build a community around the music in an honest way. Obviously you can do great things in a big purpose built room with good lighting too, it's just a different thing. It has been a very rewarding thing for all the musicians I have ever seen playing here. And that's true because otherwise we wouldn't keep coming back – we are not in it for the money!

Location

Seán: The Centre for Contemporary Practice is located in Dublin 2's Georgian business district; Hello Operator is in Rutland Place, an alley way off Parnell Square; and The Joinery is in Arbour Hill. How much does the location affect what happens in the space?

Musicians at the Centre for Creative Practice (photograph: CfCP)

Ian: I think in some respects the location picked us more than anything else in particular. It's wouldn't be, geographically, my ideal location, it's a very business-y area, here just off Baggot Street. During the weekend and the evening footfall outside the front door is practically nil. This time of day it's pretty busy but who wants to go to a gig at three o'clock in the afternoon? That is an issue, if we were in Temple Bar, for instance, that's an ideal location.

Jack: The location has affected us both good and bad. If this space as is was on the southside you could get a hell of a lot more business in terms of rental. Where we are tucked down an alley way, there is zero visibility and probably negative footfall!

Erin: But, in a way that's nice because there's that air of the undiscovered. People are thinking, 'Where am I going? Should I even be going down here?' And I like that. When they come in the door they are still not sure what is going to be inside and that's why people get upstairs and say, 'oh wow, it's clean!' And that's a progression – it's a second generation space after Red Space. I think the building that you're in and its location is really important and has a huge effect on your outlook and what you do.

Miranda: The Joinery is not in the city and there's a bit of an effort to get here, but there is a sense of community here and we have both lived here in the area on and off for years. We have got to know a lot of people who live around here and a lot of the artists and musicians who live locally have played in here.

Feargal: You can leave the front door open when a gig is on and that's really nice, a couple of hundred metres down the road we would need to have security guys on the door, it changes so quickly in Dublin. It's a bit of an oasis here, it's a unique little pocket.

Seán: It will be interesting to see if more of these spaces open more centrally to see how that would work. Or would it work at all I wonder?

Feargal: Well anything that's off the mainstream should be off the main road. I mean by having it on Dame Street, how would it work?

Who plays here and who listens?

Seán: Which musicians uses these spaces? And who comes out to listen to them?

Ian: We didn't want just to be a white box gallery, we wanted people to come in and interact with the space, so hence we have beanbags on the floor rather than chairs and it's great for doing smaller intimate events. We do lots of experimental music, electro-acoustic stuff, contemporary classical. The one thing we tend to shy away from is rock and indie, purely because the space isn't set up for it, we don't have a licence, although we have no problem with people bringing their own booze but it's not really the way the space needs to develop. There are so many spaces catering for that in town.

Seán: What about the idea of Dublin today with recording industry expiring and the industry now getting more and more involved with live music. So we see the resurrection of bands who haven't done anything for twenty years playing in Dublin. With this kind of a commercial push does this resurgence in attending live music trickle down to spaces like these? And are musicians more interested now in getting out there and playing instead of sitting in their bedrooms and producing tracks?

Jack: I am a little out of touch to be honest, but being here is great because the music comes to us. And I have really become very interested in improv music and hybrid-jazz-electro-whatever and since we have been involved in the space we have come across the best that Dublin has to offer. But I do get the feeling that among more mainstream-tending bands and musicians that they are more and more aware that you need to have a great live act. So I think a good bit of that does trickle down to electronic music for instance where you have to think about your live show and I think that's a good thing.

Erin: But from the point of view of, say, a band who are trying to make the next big leap, I don't think the space like Hello Operator appeals to them. They want to play commercial venues and have posters all around town and do a certain thing which is not really the way we work. But then we do get audiences in who might not know what they are going to see . . .

Seán: Or what they just saw! Because, yes, it's not a big room, there's space for forty to fifty seats, maybe seventy standing. So that eliminates a lot of people's ambitions!

Jack: It does seem that the people who play here, either tend towards smaller spaces or else it's used for people's side projects. This space is informal and friendly and so people feel free to try out works-in-progress.

Erin: And because we try to make it fair. So if it's a gig where we don't really know how the audience will be, it will be a split on the door. So they're not paying to rent a venue up front and all the pressure that that brings.

Miranda: For me, the interesting thing is the cross-over between visual art and music now, whereas before they were very separate. There's an equal emphasis on both here, they work very differently and there's a lot more work involved, for us, in the gallery stuff. So with funding, there's a real problem there with the separation of these practices. The Arts Council model is an old fashioned model; I am really interested in where the two meet. People coming to gigs are exposed to the gallery and vice versa, and we have found that some interesting collaborations have taken place between sound artists, visual artists and musicians because of that. I don't think that happened so much before. Previously the gallery was seen as a pristine white space and having musicians there was a really strange idea.

Monika: What we try to do is mix audiences. Not to have a place where people only come to see an exhibition, no, just the opposite: people come to a concert and see the exhibition. People who come to an exhibition might stay for the gig. I think it keeps the place alive, because when you look at many galleries and venues, they suffer because for quite a substantial part of their opening hours they are empty. That's what we are trying to avoid in any possible way.

Seán: Talking about performing in a small space like this, in front of say fifty people, there is something for the audience and also for the musicians in terms of the amount of contact you can have. When you stop playing, put down your guitar, you are standing right in front of your audience. There's no backstage thing and the musicians are forced to present the music in a very honest manner. And I think that experience is an important thing, and I think it's going to become more and more important in the future. At this point, our lives are being channelled through the internet and basic human interaction is becoming a less common thing. Same goes for experiencing music up close and in the flesh. These spaces overcome this tendency and I can see this standing to them in the future.

Miranda: Pretty much all the gigs in The Joinery are busy now. It will be interesting to see what happens with our current call for submissions and if people are really emerging.

Seán: So it's interesting that people are coming here because it's The Joinery, sometimes without knowing what the music will be like.

Miranda: Yes, I think that's happening much more. And a lot of that audience comes from the visual side of things.

Feargal: Yeah, I think having an almost radical diversity in the programming, rather than having three noise acts and getting the noise crowd, that gets a bit insular, you can get a good mix.

Miranda: And now, here, there isn't that risk on paying twenty quid to see the music and expensive drinks, so people will come out and just see what's on.

Seán: And for people who don't drink, there's much less pressure there too. You're welcome to just show up, sit there and listen.

The space shapes the music

Seán: Do you think the listening attitude changes the nature of the music practice itself?

Ian: I think it gives the musicians a bit more confidence. It might be a bit scary to start off with because, 'oh shit, these people have actually come to listen to us,' there's no distraction. But I think that the musicians themselves think, 'we actually have an audience'.

Seán: I am interested to see if the music can respond to the space in a meaningful way and I think it does. So the building and the architecture itself starts to govern what goes on and might even colour the fabric of the music itself. These influences will always be more obvious with improvised or experimental music which has room to adapt instantly to its surroundings.

Jack: It seems so. And the audience for sure does. This space can catch people off guard because perhaps they are expecting a warehouse interior and they can go very quiet, there's almost a church-like atmosphere. Their voices drop and that's an amazing thing for music and that's a product of the size and the features and the fact that it's so quiet in here as well. There's nobody else working here when there is music on. About an hour into a set of music, the audience kind of relaxes and you start seeing eyes looking up, drifting around the beams as they listen to the music, it's like visuals in a way.

Miranda: Also, it's kind of a funny little place, it can be an awkward room at times for the audience. There's that pillar there in the way and it's not a custom-

Musician at the Centre for Creative Practices (photograph: CFCP)

made space so you are working in the space that you have. Again, that interrupts the stage versus audience model.

Seán: If this alternative spaces model continues into the future (and we agree that that's likely) perhaps with momentum and continued practice each space may develop its own sound. I really like the idea that a 'Joinery sound' for instance could develop.

Feargal: You can see it the development of some groups in Dublin now. A lot of the experimental things that they now have ended up doing are informed by what they were doing in gallery-type spaces. And it's stuff that they could never have tried out in the traditional venues; you just wouldn't go down on your knees and try out this trumpet stuff for 15 minutes until you got it right in front of an audience! It just wouldn't happen, but in here it's quite natural to do that. It's experimental to the point of work-in-progress, it's not just performance, it's musicians working.

Coda

At the time of writing in July 2011, these spaces and several other alternative, non-profit, artist-run spaces in Dublin continue to present music regularly to local audiences. Current economics and a changing cultural practice point to this becoming a long-term situation. It is fashionable to talk of Ireland's maturing as a nation in the twenty first century, yet I view these developments in that light. Dublin audiences are, today, looking beyond the traditional presentation of music as mediated through an alcohol licence, a promoter, entry policies, profit margins and a circus of other obstacles between the musicians and audience. These artist-run spaces offer a real alternative to this system with many interesting artists working in these spaces today, supported directly by audiences. Fundamentally, though, it is the organisers of these spaces we have to be grateful to for a sometimes thankless job of committing themselves to this work and safeguarding these new spaces for artistic and musical adventure.

Interviewees:

Ian Oliver and Monika Sapielak, Centre for Creative Practices, 15 Pembroke Street Lower, Dublin 2 | www.cfcp.ie

Jack Phelan and Erin Michelle, Hello Operator, 12 Rutland Place, Dublin 1 | www.hellooperator.org

Miranda Driscoll and Feargal Ward, The Joinery, 6 Rosemount Terrace, Arbour Hill, Dublin 7 | www.thejoinery.org

Biographical note

Seán Mac Erlaine is a Dublin-based musician, composer and music producer. He works in a wide variety of settings from free improvisation, contemporary jazz to folk music and experimental theatre performing with a diverse range of musicians and artists reflecting his own versatility and interest in cross-platform work. An accomplished woodwind instrumentalist, Seán plays alto and soprano saxophones as well as clarinet and bass clarinet. He holds a first degree honours Masters of Music (Perf) from DIT and a Diploma in Jazz Performance awarded by the Guildhall School of Music, London. He is currently a PhD candidate at GradCAM, developing a practice-led research around live electronics in solo woodwind performance (www.seanmacerlaine.com).

8

A Fair Deal for Dublin

Dermot Lacey
On Politics

The 'fair city'?

Dublin is often described as the 'fair city' – but is it? Is it a city that treats its people fairly? Is it fairly run? Does it treat all its citizens fairly? Does it protect its culture, heritage and environment fairly and sensibly? Is it a democratic city? Is, as Winston Churchill put it, democracy the worst form of government – except for all the others? Or is democratic consultation and decision making central to the future of Dublin. Does any of this matter?

The answer, of course, is that yes, it does matter – or at least it matters to me. Dublin is my home. It always has been and I hope it always will. It was and will again be one of the finest cities of Europe. It is a great and beautiful city, ideally located between the scenic natural beauty of the Dublin Mountains and the incredibly clean and majestic Dublin Bay. It is a city with a great history and culture; it is a city of literature and with a genuine appreciation for the arts; above all, it is a city and county with a resilient people still enthused by the notion of community. Unlike Margaret Thatcher, Dubliners do believe there is such a thing as society. This is demonstrated every day of every week in the volume of community work, youth and sports activity and community activism actively engaged in by, and for, Dubliners.

It is also, however, a city of unnecessary complexity. It is a deeply undemocratic city, with decisions made at a remove from the people of Dublin and, in far too many cases, at a remove from the democratically elected representatives of those people. It is poorly served by the administrative and governance structures imposed on it by successive national governments. It is scandalously under-funded and under-resourced. It has a confused transport system, unacceptable poverty, inadequate housing and a divided and unequal series of communities. None of this is necessary. We need to imagine a better future for Dublin and we need to create that better future for Dublin.

The tragedy for Dublin and Dubliners is that when times were good and finance available, that we had, in Ireland, one of the least imaginative, backward looking governments in the history of our state. Extraordinarily, it was during the time when Ireland was led by what a disconnected media often referred to as the 'Quintessential Dub' – Bertie Ahern – that Dublin and Dubliners suffered most. It is why we need a new approach to build a new and better Dublin. It is but one of the many reasons why we need a New Deal for Dublin – a Fair Deal for Dublin. It is also a very clear example of why the model suggested by a few commentators of introducing a Minister for Dublin is not the answer. Can we solve Dublin's problems? Yes we can. Can we make it a better place for all? Yes we can. Can we have a democratic and inclusive Dublin? es we can. The pertinent question is how do we achieve at least some of these objectives? How do we make Dublin the inclusive and democratic county that it can be and I want it to be? How do we create our own future for Dublin?

The answer lies in real reform of our local government structures. This does not need to wait, as some would have it, until the country's problems are fixed. Local government reform is not an optional extra – it is, in my view, integral to our country's future. Ireland can be transformed through the reform of local government. We cannot do it any other way. It is not possible to reform our political, economic and public sectors if we do not at the same time reform local government. In the case of Dublin, my preference would be for a directly elected mayor and a new Dublin Regional Assembly. In the course of this essay I hope to outline why that is the case.

A changing county?

While Dublin is a changing city and county, it is a city and county that does not work. The city and county does not work for citizens, for business, for communities, or for Ireland. Despite it being the engine of growth for the economy and the fact that, in a European context, it is the only real city-region in the country, the governance of Dublin has largely been ignored and any real reform avoided since the establishment of the State. The Organisation for Economic Co-operation and Development (OECD) categorises city regions by their population size and the smallest size considered is 1.5 million (OECD *Territorial Reviews: Competitive Cities in the Global Economy*, 2006).

Tinkering with the boundaries in breaking up the old County Councils, reducing the power to seriously drive the region, and a collapse in funding have sadly been the hallmarks of government intervention over the last decade or so. Incompetent interference, followed by inertia, has been the closest thing to positive action from those on 'the inside', those really in power.

The decision by the Minister for the Environment, Community and Local government, Phil Hogan TD, to reverse his previously announced decision to publish the White Paper on Local Government, prepared by the previous minister and government, is therefore a real step backwards. However, if it speeds up publication of his own proposals he might yet redeem the indefensible record of this department – a department which one well known commentator has described as the one Department of State that is actively hostile to the three nouns in its (then) title, Environment, Heritage and Local Government. These proposals must provide for a better future for Dublin because a better future for Ireland must in reality be predicated on Dublin sustaining real economic growth and achieiving administrative and governmental cohesiveness.

Publication of the White Paper or a policy statement is, of course, the easy part: delivery of reform is another matter. Any serious changes will meet undoubted political, departmental and institutional opposition to real reform. For far too long power and authority in Ireland has rested with unaccountable mandarins in government departments and their agents, whether via quasi-independent agencies or through the city and county managers.

Real change is, however, necessary. The 2011 general election proved that Irish people are open to new ideas and new ways of doing business and exercising governance. With courage and vision, and above all a serious commitment to reform from the top, we can have a meaningful, inclusive, democratic and relevant local government system. We can make Dublin work and in turn make our country work.

Since the foundation of the State, local government has been subject to a process that can best be equated to constructive dismissal.
– Ciaran Lynch TD, Dáil debate, November 2010.

Reforming the city – rebuilding the county

Regrettably, what is equally true is that despite all the recent talk of reform,
changes to our local government structure hardly featured at all in public debate. Reform of governance at a local level was discussed not at all during
the 2011 general election. The truth is, however, stark: in my view it is simply
impossible to reform our national political and public sectors if we do not start
on the ground, in our communities and in the chambers of our city and county
councils and the regional authorities.

Before any decisions are taken, or any reforms contemplated, we need
agreement on what is meant by 'local government' itself. Quite simply, we need
a collective 'buy in' on local government. For me, local government is about the
delivery of comprehensive public services in a manner required, demanded and
agreed to by the local community. It must be about the provision of services, in
an accountable and democratic manner, to the people in receipt of, or entitled
to, those services. Without these attributes it is neither 'local' nor 'government'.
Sadly, here in Ireland that is the present reality.

A future for the county?

Bemoaning the plight of local government is also easy. There are library shelves
bursting with reports and analyses. I would like to be more positive and constructive. There are others, more capable than I, who can comment on the
national situation. I hope they do. I want to concentrate on Dublin. It is a city
in which I had the privilege to serve as Lord Mayor and a county where I had
the privilege to serve as Cathaoirleach of the regional authority.

In the context of this essay, as well as defining local government itself, we
need also to define where and what we mean by Dublin. Is it the city? Is it
the county? Is it the Dublin region? Or, as some would have it, is it the larger
metropolitan area? While there are many reasons to define a new governance
area as being the greater Dublin area or, as it has been described, the 'drive-
to-work' Dublin area, my view is that here in Ireland, rightly or wrongly, local
identity is important, loyalty is important and a clear definition of boundary,

in a governmental context, is important. In all respects, therefore, I believe we should focus in on the traditional county of Dublin.

It is this county of Dublin that needs our focus and attention. It is this area that has been and will be again the engine of our economy. Rebuilding and growing that Dublin will help once again to grow our economy and strengthen our society. It will help Ireland grow and develop. Part of our role as advocates for Dublin is to dispense with the old and very outdated argument of 'Dublin versus the rest'. The reality is that what is good for Dublin is invariably good for Ireland. Our future as a people is intertwined. Dublin is our collective capital. For Ireland's sake, Dublin needs to run Dublin. That is the very essence of this argument. The present situation, in which disinterested quangos (largely unaccountable state bodies and often disconnected governmental departments) interfere in the affairs of the county without any appreciable knowledge or sympathy, cannot be allowed to continue. Power and authority currently rests with the unelected and the unaccountable, whilst the elected city and county councillors see powers removed on a near daily basis. Dublin deserves better. Ireland needs better.

The existing situation in which more than 40 bodies have responsibility for traffic is the most obvious example of this. At least ten separate bodies are responsible for Dublin Bay and most absurdly national government appoints the St. Patrick's Day Festival Committee, which largely, though not exclusively, affects Dublin. There are far more examples than this. Surely this cannot continue into the future.

> The introduction of direct democracy with direct accountability to the people should offer us a chance to develop a credible economic recovery plan for Dublin and, consequently, the entire country. A Mayor who is directly accountable to the people could and should prove to be the driving force that the city and the country badly need. – Lucinda Creighton TD, Dáil debate, November 2010.

Dublin needs a political voice

Perhaps, more than anything else, Dublin needs someone who understands how things work, or more accurately, how things do not work, and who will stand up for the city and county. To create that better future that we seek Dublin needs a spokesperson for the whole community. It needs someone, who can be a political advocate armed with the mandate of direct election. That is why I believe that central to any meaningful reform must be a directly elected and longer-term mayor. The mayor needs to be a champion for Dublin, someone who will market and promote the region internationally and who will stand up for it nationally.

The proposal to have an election for a mayor of Dublin would give us an opportunity to create that voice. The election campaign itself would provide an opportunity for a collective debate on the future of Dublin. The visibility and accountability of such an office holder would considerably help inform the public on the choices involved on issues of concern. That is why, with all its imperfections and limited powers, I welcomed the publication by the last government of the Local Government (Mayor and Regional Authority of Dublin) Bill draft legislation in 2010. All political institutions grow and evolve over time, and I believe the implementation of that Bill would have proved no exception.

That legislation clarified some issues. It specified the county as the area involved and provided a new structure for the regional authority. However, the proposal that the mayor would chair the authority, to whom he or she would be accountable, was, I believe, a mistake.

Similarly, the proposal to establish a Regional Development Board was unclear, as was its composition and democratic mandate. Unless the public service agencies are accountable to this body, and not equal participating parties as at present, it will not work. The creation of the proposed Dublin Transport Council was inadequate, but a significant step in the right direction. Yes, there were deep flaws and absences from the legislation. There was a real lack of integration of services and roles. There was uncertainty about the relationship with the department and the minister. It was, however, an important start – unfortunately one not taken. The truth is that it would appear that such an approach is now off the agenda for a long time, but I believe there is still a need for the debate and for the campaign to continue. It remains an aspiration worth pursuing.

I have said before that the proposed salary was disgracefully and unnecessarily high. It was a distraction from what should be a debate about the role of a mayor. This figure has already been reduced and is perhaps the first and only victory of the campaign to create the post. No doubt over the years this might be adjusted downwards even further and that is not something I would oppose. There is no need for a €200,000+ salary for the mayor of Dublin, just as in all probability there is no need for it for government ministers. The essential financial element is that the mayor would have the power and resources to do the job, and the commitment to do it effectively. The absence of an independent source of funding was a major flaw in the previous proposals and must be addressed whenever a future government is serious about reform.

Many believe that we need more than the simple introduction of a directly elected mayor, and they are right. A new mayor can and must drive further reform and a real debate about the future of Dublin.

Two of the arguments used against the introduction of a directly elected mayor are cost and the issue of 'celebrity' candidates. In my view, both are bogus. Properly structured, a newly elected mayor, working with the already existing, though enhanced, Dublin Regional Authority, will see the need for many of the existing agencies reduced and/or incorporated into the mayoral structure with significant savings. On the 'celebrity' candidate issue, the answer is simple: we live in a democracy, so let the people decide. I have great faith that, subject to a fair and balanced media presentation, the electorate will decide intelligently. While not the subject of this essay, it is this issue of media coverage of a campaign – the absence of a fair and informed media on local government matters – that would concern me most. This is particularly true of the national broadcasting service – RTÉ – whose understanding and knowledge of local government in my view is virtually non-existent and for whom access to the airwaves is a rare privilege accorded only to a chosen few. Clear guidelines for their conduct of a campaign and debate on the issues would be crucial if genuine progress is to be made.

Facing down the Custom House

It is clear to anyone interested that our current system of local government requires renewal and reform. Clear too is the fact that the various local councils are directed, unofficially but in reality, by city and county managers, answerable to the Department of the Environment, Community and Local Government and the permanent officials therein. It is striking that the term of office for a city and county manager is seven years and that under our current system the term for a mayor is usually one year. Longevity itself is power.

Understanding that relationship is the key to understanding our present problems, and breaking that relationship is the key to resolving them for the future. Again, the proposals in the Labour/Fine Gael Programme for Government to abolish the role of county managers and replace them with 'Chief Executive Officers' is a step in the right direction. None of this should be taken as a personal reflection on the three very fine public servants, Frank Feely, John Fitzgerald and John Tierney, with whom I have worked during their terms as Dublin City Manager. They all served Dublin well. It is the structural and relationship problem that need to be resolved.

We would now, of course, be experiencing the third term of a directly elected Lord Mayor of Dublin had the contents of the Local Government Act of 2001 been implemented. Alternatively, we could have just commenced the first year of the first directly elected mayor of Dublin, if the repeated promises of the Green Party had reached fruition. Unfortunately, the people of Dublin were denied that opportunity as once again 'the establishment' won out. There is now considerable uncertainty that the proposal will be resurrected at all. At this stage, it is not clear what reforms are envisaged by government beyond the implementation of the EU/ECB/IMF economic 'bailout' package in so far as it impacts on local government.

I believe that Dublin desperately needs a longer-term mayor who would serve for the full local government term, and a mayor directly elected by the people who would have the authority and mandate needed to serve for such a term. We also need substantial reform of the structure of the four local authorities in the Dublin city and county areas – plus Balbriggan Town Council. Such a mayor working with the members of the Council and with sufficient powers and resources is needed now more than ever to rescue this city and county from the clutching, incompetent and disinterested control of central government and administration.

Shamefully, the sections of the 2001 Local Government Act that would have enabled this, courageously introduced by Minister Noel Dempsey, were reversed by his successor, Minister Martin Cullen. Even more shamefully, the Green Party Minister, John Gormley, was thwarted in his efforts to introduce the most recent proposals for a directly elected mayor and regional authority.

A new model for an old city and county

There are many ways in which real reform could be achieved. I want to propose a simple model that I believe would be in the best interests of the future of Dublin city and county. While there may be debate about the appropriateness of retaining the existing four Dublin local authorities, I believe that it is better, for the present, that they remain. This would also allow that for a period of five years in which they would continue to elect their Chairpersons/(Lord) Mayors in line with current practice.

I propose that the number, jurisdiction and roles of the four existing Local Authorities (plus Balbriggan Town Council) be reviewed after a period of five years, or one term of office, of a proposed Dublin Regional Assembly. This period should be used to assess the possibility of eventually introducing a series of genuinely local District Councils serving populations of approximately 100,000 people each in the greater Dublin area. It would also allow for a gradual merging of the roles of Lord Mayor and mayor. Whilst for many this is an obvious step, I believe that there are distinct roles and we should assess the respective merits of retaining them as separate roles or combining them into one.

Essentially these different roles stem from the unique requirement of the Lord Mayor of Dublin to regularly act as the official host for guests to Dublin and Ireland, and often as a sort of unofficial ambassador for the whole country. There is also the role as effectively a civic cheerleader and the ceremonial office holder for appropriate civic occasions. The new role envisaged for a mayor for Dublin will in my view be more executive and more political. I remain open to persuasion as to which is the best way forward.

Contrary to common perception, Ireland has a very low ratio of elected councillors per head of population. The following table gives some idea of the European average. It is worth noting that the UK figures do not take into account the existence of the Scottish Parliament and the Welsh and Northern Ireland Assemblies. The Northern Ireland Assembly has 108 members, the Scottish Parliament 129 members and the Welsh Assembly 60 members. In Dublin, the figure is a staggering figure of 12,400 people to each councillor.

Such district councils as I propose would, over time, replace the existing, South Dublin, Fingal and Dun Laoghaire-Rathdown County Councils and Dublin City Council. In order to enhance a sense of local identity and ownership, these councils should be based on real communities of location and interest. Areas such as Tallaght, Lucan, Swords, Dun Laoghaire and Ballyfermot are obvious possibilities for this. With the increasingly global nature of our world, real social cohesion in the future can be best enhanced through the promotion of the local and community awareness.

Country	Population (m)	No. of Councils	Average Pop. per Council	Pop. per Councillor
France	59.6	36,700	1,600	118
Austria	8.2	2,350	3,500	209
Sweden	8.8	310	28,400	256
Germany	8.3	15,300	5,400	350
Finland	5.2	452	11,500	410
Italy	57.7	8,100	7,100	608
Spain	40.0	8,100	4,900	610
Belgium	10.3	589	17,500	811
Greece	10.6	1,033	10,300	1,075
Denmark	5.4	275	19,600	1,115
Portugal	10.1	308	32,800	1,131
Netherlands	16.0	548	29,000	1,555
Ireland	4.0	114	35,000	2,500
UK	59.6	468	127,350	2,603

Source: Hughes, Clancy, Harris and Beetham (2007), *Power to the People: Assessing Democracy in Ireland*, Dublin: New Island.

Pending completion of the overall reform project, there is no reason why such pilot town or district councils could not be established at an early stage. Composition of these councils should also be used to create greater equality in terms of councillors and population with the rest of the country, and a consequential equalisation of Seanad voting rights if the Seanad is to retain its present form.

I am also suggesting that in order to provide a local/national link that the directly elected mayor would be an ex-officio member of Seanad Éireann and that a similar provision be made should directly elected mayors be introduced for the other larger cities. This should be done without increasing the overall membership of Seanad Éireann and could be done in tandem with other proposed reforms of the Seanad.

A Dublin Regional Assembly

Dublin also needs an over-arching strategic regional approach. In that context I suggest that a new Dublin Regional Assembly be established. Such an assembly would be comprised, as with the existing Dublin Regional Authority, of 30 members. This would entail six constituencies electing five members each.

In order to ensure best internal regional balance there would be two north-side constituencies, two south-side constituencies and two to the west of the county. This would enable a sufficiently broad-based (political and regional) membership to ensure a robust and inclusive assembly. The assembly would have one committee for each of the policy areas listed in the next section.

An alternative model would be to have three such constituencies, north, south and west, with five members each leading to the election of what would effectively be a fifteen member executive for the county. Each policy area would be overseen by three members of the assembly who would have executive responsibility for the area involved. In this scenario, the overall scrutiny and monitoring role would be provided by members drawn from the four Dublin local authorities on a basis similar to the present Dublin Regional Authority. The Leader of the assembly would be the directly elected mayor of Dublin.

Powers of the Assembly

I am suggesting that the powers and responsibilities of this suggested assembly would be as follows:

1) Land Use Planning and Strategic Development. This would deal with devising strategic planning guidelines and monitoring and planning development across the region. Responsibility would also include implementation of national spatial strategies and economic development.

2) Traffic and Transport Co-ordination. The assembly would be the Dublin Transport Authority and would provide for an accountable and integrated approach to traffic and transport, including responsibility for all public transport and taxi provision and regulation in the Dublin region.

3) Social and Affordable Housing. The assembly would replace the existing Affordable Housing Partnership in the Dublin area and co-ordinate housing provision and allocation across the Dublin region. It would also have responsibility for developing new initiatives for housing provision and responding to the issue of homelessness.

4) Dublin Bay, Waterways and Mountains. These great assets of the region are at present largely under-appreciated. The Dublin Mountains Partnership

initiated by Dun Laoghaire-Rathdown and South Dublin County Councils has shown the possibility that does exist with imagination in this area.

5) The Assembly would also have a coordinating and/or monitoring role in relation to county-wide services provided by agencies such as the HSE, VEC/ Local Education Boards, Enterprise Ireland, tourism development, policing and relations with other regional authorities and relevant bodies. One of the first tasks in this area would be to develop co-terminous boundaries for all public service providers in the Dublin region. It would also have specific responsibility for the proposed Regional Development Board.

Some of the above could be done in conjunction and co-operation with the existing local authorities.

I am also suggesting that the Dublin Regional Assembly would provide a forum to which the Dublin members of the European Parliament could report back and consult on issues of relevance to their work. This would significantly enhance engagement with the European institutions and improve the opportunity for Dubliners to engage with and benefit from European Union initiatives.

In addition to the elected assembly, I would like to see a Dublin Civic Forum established, comprising representatives of civic society across the county. The forum members would receive no payment and would convene as appropriate to advise the assembly on matters of relevance.

I have previously suggested that the Dublin Regional Assembly should be based in the old Parliament Building on College Green with the remainder of the building housing an Institute for Dublin Affairs and a much-needed Dublin museum. The institute would be a collaborative model drawing on the expertise of the third-level institutes in Dublin and would act as a policy feeder to the assembly. It would build on the experience of the creative alliance established by the Dublin City Manager that already draws together in loose form many of the relevant agencies and bodies. The old Parliament building would also be the location for meetings of the Civic Forum. This could all be done in conjunction with proposals by the Minister for Arts and Heritage to develop the building as a National Cultural Centre and the creation of a major public plaza to the front of the buildings. Transferring ownership of the former Parliament Building might provide some recompense for the €8.5

billion pumped into Bank of Ireland in recent times, and relocating the bank headquarters to the docklands might help the rejuvenation of that area.

There is also much scope for the development of new forms of democratic participation such as citizens' juries and participative budgeting. These could be facilitated through the Dublin Regional Assembly office and could enable citizens to engage with public service providers in a meaningful way.

Reform again?

There is a widespread consensus amongst politicians, commentators, academics and the public that we need to reform local government. This is articulated regularly in a general rather than specific sense and is thrown into the wider debate about political reform. However that is where the consensus ends. The promise offered by the optimism of the Better Local Government project initiated by Brendan Howlin TD, and the early enthusiasm of Noel Dempsey TD, were followed by inaction, inertia and, on occasions, outright hostility to democratic local government by the very government department that should have been its champion, reformer and defender.

Of course, we need real reform, and of course we need councillors to take more responsibility. As Lord Mayor of Dublin, in difficult circumstances, I did accept such responsibility in relation to the city budget. Since then the majority in favour of the budget has increased with each passing year.

A directly elected mayor should only be one small – though important – part of a total reform of the failing system of local government. Powers which have been stripped from elected representatives and handed over lock, stock and barrel to city and county managers, effectively if not officially, answerable to the minister of the day, need to be restored to city and county councillors across the country. If we are truly to build a better future for Dublin and for Ireland, local government must be the heart that drives that forward.

Paying the price

The issue of the financing of local government also needs extensive review. Quite simply, there is no real governance role without independent finance raising responsibilities. There must be a clear link between local spending and local revenue and the accountability of the councillor. The successful operation of the BIDS (Business Improvement District Scheme) scheme in Dublin city centre shows that there is a willingness to work such initiatives if there is sufficient benefit and adequate explanation and consultation. Local government also requires more opportunities to introduce appropriate local taxation, subject of course to the law and the right of the people to comment on same through local election campaigns and possibly local referenda.

At present, Dublin City Council is losing out on millions of euro every year (€28 million for 2010 alone) from commercial rates which the government has abdicated its responsibility to pay. While applicable across the entire country, this has hit Dublin more than anywhere else and is a further example of the cost involved in being the capital city. Since the expedient abolition of domestic rates in 1977, every local authority has lost significant income. The promise to allocate a sum equal to the amount that would have been raised has been consistently broken. For the year 2009 alone, the shortfall was approximately €130 million. The financial burden faced by local authorities was intensified by the costs of the benchmarking agreement. Again, local government was denied any opportunity to participate in negotiating. The concept and practice of 'social partnership', it would appear, included everyone except the democratically elected arm of local government. Once again, as in so many instances, it was a case of national government decides, local government pays. A proposal some years ago by members of Dublin City Council to introduce a €1 per night hotel/bed tax for all visitors would have, on average, delivered approximately €26 million additional resources to the city. Despite the fact that, at the time, some hotels were charging rates of up to €500 per night, the proposal met with outright hostility from the trade and, as ever, a compliant, not to say hostile, department and government refused to introduce the necessary legislation. This money could have been invested directly into providing better experiences and facilities for all, visitors and tourists alike, and would, over a four-year period have delivered approximately €150 million to make Dublin a better place at relatively little cost or inconvenience.

A reduction in the number of agencies and quangos, with their roles and responsibilities transferred to local councils would enable swifter and more 'on the ground' decision making. It would ensure a better integration and delivery of services and would also save money. Consequently, it would enable the transfer of a fairer share of the national resources to Dublin and a more efficient expenditure of same.

National forum on the financing of local government

I have previously proposed that a national forum on the financing of local government be established as a matter of urgency. The forum would draw its membership from the main political parties, the three councillor representative bodies and the social partners. It would be given six months to a year, to agree an approach that would provide sufficient funding, on a nationally agreed basis, and one that would allow some degree in local flexibility as to appropriate local fundraising.

And finally

Introducing the direct election of longer-term mayors is not the panacea for all our problems, but it would be a major starting point. Quite simply, the people whom we are meant to serve deserve better. The current mess suits no one except the mandarins in the Custom House and their temporary ministerial masters. This cannot be allowed to prevail. We need to dream of a better future and to turn those dreams into realities. We need to create a Dublin that is all the things we want it to be. But let us do more than just imagine – let us truly create it. With a new form of governance we have an opportunity to put behind us the mistakes and the errors of the past and to learn from them. As a society we need not be bound by old agreements, old alliances or old commitments. Indeed, we must not be bound by them. We have the opportunity and duty to fight back and to stand up for real local decision making and to build a truly inclusive, progressive and sustainable city and county. We can and must build a better future for Dublin and Dubliners. In short, we have an opportunity to stand up for Dublin. In doing so, we are also standing up for Ireland. If we don't, no one else will.

Biographical note

Dermot Lacey has been a Labour member of Dublin City Council since 1993, currently representing the Pembroke–Rathmines area. He is presently Chairperson of the Housing, Social and Community Affairs Strategic Policy Committee and a member of the Corporate Policy Group. He is a former Lord Mayor of Dublin and Cathaoirleach of the Dublin Regional Authority. He is also a member of the City of Dublin VEC, the Southern and Eastern Regional Assembly and a former member of the Dublin Docklands Development Council. Dermot is a life-long member of the scout movement whose ethos is reflected in his political and community activism.

9

Who Will Remember Us?: Memorialising the Multicultural City

Katrina Goldstone
On Ethnic Legacy

First thoughts

> But will there be anyone to remember us in another thousand years? . . . Still surely it's not possible that not one single molecule will be found for us, like a yellowing manuscript at the bottom of a forgotten drawer whose very cataloguing guarantees its eternity even if not a single reader ever discovers it? But will the catalogue itself survive? Or will some totally different cipher fuse and scramble everything that has gone, so that our image can never again be intertwined as we imagine it to ourselves? – A.B Yehoshua, *A Journey to the End of the Millennium*

It may seem strange, in a volume on future visions of Dublin, to focus on the past. But sometimes we need to go back before we can move forward, to look at more nuanced versions of 'the Past' than nationalist shibboleths will allow for, because the version of the past that gains currency now shapes the societal developments of the future. Our today is tomorrow's past. So I want to project myself forward, into a future I might not live to see, whilst looking at how we have reconfigured the past today, to look at who we've remembered and how we've marked these memories on the cityscape or in institutions, in order to guess who it will be important to commemorate and whose achievements will be marked on the cityscape of Dublin circa 2050. In particular, I want to consider how the rush and fury of the last decade, and one of its key phenomena – the development of Dublin as a capital city that is home to diverse migrants – might be looked back on and commemorated.

I want to put some tentative markers out, to reflect on cultural memory, erasure and selective amnesia. How might these play out and influence the monuments of the future, the commemoration and memorialisation; how will this predicate what will be picked out on the mid-twenty-first century public political landscape? Will the cultural practices of memory be adequate in relation to the rich diversity of multiethnic Dublin, to capture the energy and drive that has spurred many different peoples to make their home here? And to do justice to the way migrants have re-configured Dublin as multicultural city? In what way might the spectral traces of these groups be excavated? How might we memorialise the histories and traces of today's minorities? And might the remembrance of the migrants of today inspire the minorities of tomorrow, be more than a passing nod to a pluralist democratic society with Dublin at its heart?

The future of diverse Dublin?

I want to imagine what the scholars and the heritage merchants might make of these times, to allow myself to reflect on that other possibility – the vision of the bigots and naysayers – that in 2050, the concept of a diverse Dublin, a multiethnic Dublin with different minorities, may seem as strange to future Dubliners as the lost city of Atlantis does to us now. Fifty years hence, will our national monuments and heritage industry celebrate only a limited notion of citizenry which ignores or exoticises minorities, or will our cityscape reflect the nuanced realities of a pluralist past? And I want to reflect on the possibility that one of the longest established minorities in Dublin – Jews – may be greatly diminished. My anxiety is not only that there will be very few Irish Jews left, but that the rich history of the Jewish presence in Ireland – and indeed that of current groups of migrants – will be erased and buried. Or worse, – it will be 'Kitschified' with a capital K.

This type of phenomenon is already occurring all over Europe in relation to lost Jewish communities – particularly in the countries of eastern Europe, and in more recent years in Spain, where traces are being frantically sought in medieval towns for a population persecuted and expelled in the fifteenth century. As pointed out by Diana Pinto in her essay 'Jewish Spaces vs. Jewish Places', the motivations behind these European initiatives are mixed and complex. Some are questionable, carried out in a cack-handed fashion by those nostalgic for a bit of 'ethnic spice' or who want to climb on the 'intercultural dialogue' bandwagon without actually engaging on equal terms with the minorities whose 'culture' they're hijacking; initiatives which are predicated on crude, one-dimensional and stereotypical notions of 'Jewishness', tapping into a cosy faux nostalgia, and barely masking another form of unintentional disdain. So my vision of Dublin in, say, 2050 is one which might embrace the Irish Jew as lost artefact or quaint anthropological curiosity, if care is not taken. On the other hand, a richer and more nuanced version may be celebrated in a state-of-the-art professional Irish Jewish Museum or in thought-provoking, challenging public art. The decisions made now will lay the foundations for one or another mode of memorialisation.

Complex heritages

Already, to a certain extent, Jews have been fetishised and turned into heritage fodder. Every June, the sixteenth, to be precise, the Irish tourism industry turns a gaudy and intense spotlight on a fictional character, a Jew-not-a-Jew, Leopold Bloom. On that day Joyce aficionados and assorted tourists traverse the cityscape in the footsteps of Bloom. There is something peculiarly postmodern in the notion that 'Themepark Ireland' has recruited Bloom – the creation of James Joyce, a former pariah – to the first rank of 'Oirish heritage'. Not only that, but the focus on the fictional Bloom, not halachically Jewish at all, overshadows spectacularly the real histories of Jewish people in Ireland. In the august realm of heritage paddywhackery, Irish Jews have, until relatively recently, been practically erased, and yet on the other hand given a certain kind of faux prominence. Sites of Irish Jewish historical importance in Dublin can go unacknowledged, or are demolished in the city's relentless quest for post-modern hipness. In 2050 is it conceivable that the pendulum may have swung again and the city fathers, looking for another angle to bolster the tourism industry, will scrabble to uncover the site of Stratford and Zion Schools?

Or that a corridor in the Museum for Forgotten Migrants will be devoted to the Jewish community and visitors will stare at a sepia digital screen showing blurry images of the Briscoes, the Solomons, the Abrahamsons, with as much bewilderment as we today look at the fabulous artefacts of Tutankhamun and Nefertiti?

I got a not altogether welcome taste of what this futuristic heritage tour might be like a few years ago. On 27 May 2008, I was asked to be part of the first historic walking tour of 'Jewish Dublin' organised by Dublin City Council. Over 200 people turned up on a rainy weekday evening to hear about the history of Dublin's Jewish community. Whatever about the motivations and expectations of the assembled walkers, over the course of the two hour walk, a number of clichés and stereotypes were trotted out as part of the accompanying lecture to the tour. There was an attempt to downplay the government policy which limited the entry of Jews into Ireland during World War II. Stopping outside the Bretzel bakery, there was a reference to the fact that generations of Dubliners liked to go there. Yet the numbers of Jewish-Irish steadily diminishes, in part because of the difficulty of maintaining a full commitment to a life based on strict religious observance and keeping kosher in a city where there are no longer the kosher butchers and grocers of yore. Dubliners can wallow in a faux-nostalgia for Bretzel's onion bread and for a dwindling community with whom not that many had sustained meaningful contact.[1] In twenty-first century Dublin, branches of the Bagel Factory proliferate whilst actual kosher outlets are limited to a section in Supervalu Rathfarnham. (The Bretzel bakery's bread has also had its kosher status restored in recent years.) Iris Weiss, in her essay 'Jewish Disneyland', was perplexed by the ease with which non-Jews seek to consume or appropriate a manufactured Jewish culture – smoked salmon bagels and klezmer music CDs. In the Irish case, it is in stark contrast to the difficulty for observant Jews to maintain *yiddishkeit* in a Dublin without any proper kosher butchers. Clanbrassil Street and the environs of the South Circular Road, once the heart of a vibrant Jewish district, boasted a plethora of Jewish-owned shops, bakers, butchers, grocers. Today the area is home to a rich diversity of cultures with a scattering of halal butchers and a mosque.

Cohen's shop on Liffey Street, Dublin 1 (photograph courtesy of the Knowles Collection)

The politics of remembrance

> We excavate the history we need, bend the past to colonize the present. – Iain Sinclair 'Mobile Invisibility', in *Rodinsky's Room*

What gets marked out on the cityscape, and what gets forgotten, is part of how a nation constructs itself or chooses to view itself. No monument or political marker in a city is without its agenda. On the one hand we have a veritable proliferation of historicism and ennobling of one version of 'the Past' which has certainly excluded many stories. Yet historical amnesia can also exacerbate the invisibility of minorities in contemporary society. So today, just as it will be in 2050, it is important how the stories of Jewish Dublin are told and by whom. The small Jewish museum off Walworth Road is in the heart of what was once the Jewish district of Dublin. That it exists at all is very much due to the energies of two Jewish men, Asher Benson (the original archivist) and Raphael Siev (the curator), plus the efforts of a devoted group of volunteers. Since the death of Raphael Siev in January 2010, the running of the museum has undergone a change, with an extension in opening hours and an ambitious fundraising campaign in place to expand the museum and secure its future and additional advisory support from the Heritage Council. If the fundraising campaign is successful, there is a very good possibility that the stories that are told in the future will indeed be shaped and shared by Jews themselves and that these narratives will demonstrate the diversity of Irish Jewry rather than sticking to one 'official version', static, monolithic and homogenised. There are the other stories to be told that will include rebels and radicals, women, artists, scholars, intellectuals, tailors and cabinetmakers. A nuanced history of the Irish Jewish community would embrace the secular and Progressive traditions as well as Orthodox Judaism. A story that is less frequently repeated is the history of Jewish artists, intellectuals, progressives and radicals like Leslie Daiken, Harry Kernoff, the Sevitt sisters and Maurice Levitas.

One strand of the story is of Jewish sites of worship that date back to the eighteenth century and earlier and range from the baroque showy splendour of Greenville Hall on South Circular Road to the cramped feverish atmosphere of the tiny prayer rooms or chevrot which were once dotted all around the streets off South Circular Road. In the 1920s they could be found at no. 7 St. Kevin's Parade, and at 52 Lower Camden Street, 46 Lombard St West, Walworth Road and Lennox Street. When I hear about the numerous African places of worship all over Dublin today, some of them just in people's front rooms, I am reminded of those turn of the century Jewish newcomers (mainly from what is modern day Lithuania) with their old time religion, praying intensely, their voices rising in the tiny upstairs rooms of their new Irish home. Jews have been here a long time, some records say back as far as the eleventh century. The pain of some of the nineteenth century migrants was captured starkly in this extract from the Church of Ireland's Jews' Society (a conversionary organisation) Report of 1897:[2]

> The owner of a house into which I went to shelter from the rain, turned out to be a Jewess, she could speak but little English. I spoke in German, she in Yiddish, and we got quite friendly. The tears rolled down her cheeks as she told me how lonely she felt, her brothers, sisters and parents being far away in Russia.

But yet, take a walk round Dublin with a sharp eye and certain facts, and you will see a different city, hear other ghostly voices whispering through the brickwork and the Georgian facades. When I walk around the city and pass the Coombe corner of Francis Street I think of Harold Mushatt and his famed herbal remedies, 'the saviour of the sick' in tenement lore. Passing the Gaiety Theatre, I think of Louis Elliman, presiding over a showbiz empire and the years of entertainment and icons of popular culture enjoyed by generations of Dubliners as a result. The Dublin Jewish Amateur Dramatic Society even trod the boards of the Gaiety in the 1920s. On the Leeson Street corner of St. Stephen's Green there is the Three Graces monument, the gift from the German people to the Irish in gratitude for taking in groups of German children post-war. I think about the Jewish children who didn't get to come here and their fate. At Harrington Street, no. 3 to be precise, I think of all the good folk who might have crossed the threshold when it was home to the Dublin Jewish Literary and Social Club.

The ugly highway of twenty-first century Clanbrassil Street is overlaid on a street which in Irish Jewish history is the equivalent of O'Connell Street, once the bustling and vibrant host to myriad Jewish shops in the 1920s and the source of much nostalgic reminisce. So many community memoirs paint Clanbrassil Street in the golden light of nostalgia, infusing recollections of it in the warm fug of sentimentality. Both A.J. Leventhal and Leslie Daiken wrote about the territorial skirmishes in the 1920s around Synge Street with each gang of boys, Christian vs. Jews, and occasionally Protestants, shouting their sectarian chants. Writer June Levine, as Cormac Ó'Gráda pointed out in his socio-economic history of Irish Jewry, had a less positive perception of what Clanbrassil Street signified. To her it was 'claustrophobic'.

In Ireland, the overwhelming proportion of Jews has always lived in Dublin, *Dubh Linn*. One of the earliest established synagogues appears to have been of Sephardic (Spanish and Portuguese) origins. Both Capel Street and South Circular Road are locations where new waves of migrants have set up homes and businesses. Capel Street in particular, in the nineteenth century, was an early location for Jewish businesses. This 'layering' of migrant and minority histories is not uncommon. Look at London's Brick Lane and Whitechapel, areas which first played host to thousands of east European Jewish immigrants and is now an established Bengali centre; New York's Lower East Side, where again Jewish, Italian and Irish immigrants lived at times in acrimony, now houses later generations of new immigrants from other shores. And the South Circular Road, which once boasted the greatest concentration of Jews in Dublin, now has more Muslims drawn from Bangladesh, Somalia, Pakistan and Malaysia living in the side streets off its long and sinuous bends.

The figure that came to embody early Jewish visibility was the Jewish peddler. Those who talked about the strangeness of seeing many black faces on Irish streets in the first waves of 1990s migration should time travel back to the 1880s and 1890s and imagine the visual impact the Jewish 'weekla man' had tramping the roads of rural Ireland in his long black coat or making his round in the Dublin suburbs. Louis Hyman cites the example of Cork city where in the first wave of migration 'the people flocked to the neighbourhood of Hibernian Buildings, where the Jews had found lodging, and clamoured to be allowed to see what the Jews looked like'.[3]

What do we remember? What do we forget?

Jewish people put the clothes on Dubliners' backs – literally. At the turn of the century a goodly number of Jewish immigrants signing on the aliens' register were tailors, tailors' pressers, and machinists. They also furnished Dubliners' homes as a number were cabinet makers.

The role of Jewish tailors in radical union activity was highlighted through the research of Manus O'Riordan (now retired research officer at SIPTU).[4] A plaque to honour this small forgotten group was unveiled at 52 Lower Camden Street in 2005, highlighting a hidden history of Jewish radicals and trade unionists. In the climate of selective recall it is forgotten that Jews all over the world helped with donations to the Famine. We forget – at least until relatively recently – that the Irish state was reluctant to let Jewish refugees in to Ireland in World War II. We remembered over and over that there was a pogrom in Limerick but we forget that two Jewish men were shot down in 1923, asked if they were Hebrews and told to run for it; a small stained glass window in the Dolphin's Barn Cemetery the memorial to this event. We forget that in eighteenth century Dublin, then the second city of the Empire, a section of the population were African; that there were other waves of migration that have left indelible yet subtle traces on both Dublin life and on the cityscape: the Huguenots – whose descendents are still marked out by their distinctive French names like La Touche, and Jeremy D'Olier who provided the moniker for D'Olier Street – and of course the Italians who amongst many contributions to society, changed the Irish diet forever.

Monuments to the future

Will we also look back at the Great Migration of the 1990s–2000s, which brought Poles, Nigerians, Somalis, Bengalis to our shores? Will that incoming of people be bathed in the light of faux nostalgia? Will there be heritage tours for Poles and Nigerians – particularly perhaps for 'Irish-born children' whose parents have been unceremoniously booted out of this country? Will tour guides tell them 'this is where your parents were held before deportation'? And 'here is the site of the direct provision hostel where your parents had to live for years'? I can't see Fáilte Ireland quite rising to the complexity of that one. In 2050 what monument will there be to the contribution of foreign migrants to our now shattered economy? What trace will there be in sites of care homes and hospital corridors – if we still have any – of the Filipina women looking after both the young and the old? What marker of gratitude will be erected to those brown skinned child-minders, the ersatz mothers who have given an entire generation of young Irish people an intimate experience of love, affection and caring? Surely that will inspire a slew of nostalgia novels – Irish mini-versions of the Deep South or South African memoir genre, where pampered white females remember and reminisce about their black Nannies. That extraordinary contribution to an affective culture is invisible even today – what chance is there that it will be remembered and celebrated in 2050? Let's look at some of the statistics that may be forgotten by 2050: 'Between 1999 and 2005, 3,000 Filipino nurses took up assignments in Irish hospitals, and several thousand others were recruited to work in the caring and service sectors.' That reference was mentioned in the Migrant Networks exhibition held in 2010, which documented the achievements of eighteen individuals and organisations in many diverse areas of civic life – rights advocacy, gender issues, culture, the media, and religion.

At the launch Dr. Ronit Lentin of the Migrant Networks Project, School of Social Science and Philosophy, Trinity College Dublin said:

> ... this exhibition is our way of showcasing and saying thank you to some of the migrant leaders we have worked with over the past eighteen months for the contribution they and their networks are making

to Ireland's cultural, social and political lives. These leaders are showing Ireland how, often in difficult situations, with little funding and
support, migrants are advocating for their communities in the areas of
religion, culture, gender and media, and thus not only enriching the
lives of their communities, but also transforming Irish society.'

Will any of the personalities featured in the Migrant Networks exhibition
be acknowledged in the cityscape in fifty years' time?

We can only hazard a faltering guess at how future historians and heri-
tage-peddlers will interpret this catastrophic era. But migrants were key to
building the 'Celtic Tiger' economy and they are now suffering disproportion-
ately in its downfall. But will they be written out altogether of the many, many
assessments there will be of this seismic period of Irish history? There are
many immigrant families who are a part of Ireland now and who intend to stay
here, and have their children and grandchildren grow up here. The preliminary
statistics from Census 2011 indicate that the exodus of migrants in media lore
has not taken place so dramatically. The complexities of the picture will not
emerge fully until the full Census publication in 2012.

Will history repeat itself?

In terms of fears of the demise of the Jewish community, we have been here
before of course, indeed several times over. The Jewish population in Ireland
increased markedly between 1871 and 1911 going from 285 (north and south)
in 1871, to 5,148 in 1911 (again, north and south). By the late nineteenth century, the Jewish population in Ireland had increased by 203 per cent, augmented
by those fleeing real or potential persecution as well as by Jews simply seeking
better economic circumstances. This was just a fraction of the tide of Jewish
humanity that washed up on many foreign shores in the great migration of
the 1880s–1900s, a mass movement of people that happened to bring my own
grandparents to the cold gray city of Manchester. In the decade of 1881–1891,
Jews constituted 14 per cent of that city's population.

The Jewish refugee crisis of the 1930s was a prelude to genocide. Those
Jews that could escape were scattered to the four corners of the earth. But the
Irish Jewish community was not augmented substantially, indeed scarcely at all,
because of a restrictive Irish government policy towards Jewish refugees. The
likelihood of a worldwide twenty-first century Jewish exodus, which might in

turn mean an increase in the small Jewish community in Ireland, can only be conceived if one can conjure up a vista of modern-day pogroms and expulsions. This is a vision no-one but the extremists of the far right want to entertain.

Extract from the 1911 Census (National Archives)

Forgetting to remember?

In Ireland commemoration and tropes of memory in relation to the national story, the freedom struggles and independence, are deeply rooted in Irish cultural practices of the Irish nation. Commemoration and the alternative modes of representing cultural memory, as highlighted by nigh on twenty years of debate on memory across several disciplines, is not just a 'call to remembrance'. There are tensions between official and vernacular memory and new tropes of commemoration, as represented by the work of artists such as Jochen Gerz and Shimon Attie. Cultural memory is disputed, shaped and forged in a tumultuous crucible. Michael Kammen's thesis that 'societies in fact reconstruct their pasts rather than faithfully record them, and that they do so with the needs of contemporary culture clearly in mind – manipulating the past in order to mould the present' has interesting resonances for the business of reconstructing a multi-ethnic past for Ireland, one that will be relevant to a genuinely democratic nation in forty years' time with whatever proportion there will be of its populace from Elsewhere.[5] Who is doing the remembering, and what are key questions in the politics of remembrance? If one follows Kammen's argument, might not the physical marking on Dublin's cityscape of the contribution of the Jewish community, Ireland's longest established racialised minority, act as a small bulwark against antagonism to today's migrants, an antagonism which diminishes, denies and erases their key role in building the Celtic Tiger society?

On an optimistic note, fifty years ago the notion that there would have been a museum devoted to the Irish Jewish experience was probably unthinkable. A museum or repository for Jewish archives was one of the cherished dreams of Asher Benson, a long time chronicler of the Irish Jewish community. It was fulfilled before Asher's death and carried on by the energy of Raphael Siev, its curator. Today a campaign to improve and expand the museum has an ambitious remit. As long as it results in a professionalised museum experience that avoids the trap of cosy nostalgia and kitsch, it will be a worthwhile endeavour. We may look forward to a mid-twenty-first century experience of time travelling back into the past and virtual tours of the area of Clanbrassil Street that mimic exactly the experience of the street in the 1920s when it was a bustling hub for Jewish shops and a centre for the swopping of communal gossip.

As artist Shimon Attie has put it, his work on memory 'seeks to give visual form to the personal and collective histories that are latent – but not visible – within our cities' architecture'. I hope the artists of the future will be inspired by the diverse histories of all the different groups of people who have come here from other places – the Italians, Hungarians, Chileans, Brazilians, Chinese, Asians, Nigerians, Cameroonians, Somalis, Lithuanians, Latvians, Polish and Rumanians – just some of the folk who, in the steps of the Huguenots of the seventeenth century and Jews of the nineteenth century made Dublin their home. We have their legacy already in new food shops, new places of religious worship, dynamism and vitality.

This reflection on how we re-configure 'the past' to suit our needs is also to provoke thought on the possibilities of a future Dublin, reflecting the complexity of 'the now' for future generations, espousing authentic memorialising of a multicultural city, allowing the whispers and traces of the many as opposed to the few. This decade has been one of seismic change. May our descendents see themselves reflected back, not erased or barely visible through the crooked glass of a distorting mirror.

My hope is that in fifty years' time there will be artists to take up the challenge of memorialising the history and presence of diverse groups in Dublin. Like Shimon Attie and the many other artists who work on cultural memory, may they reflect on the ways art can reconfigure what Karen Till calls 'orthodox memorial narratives'. Might the Dublin of 2050 show a cityscape of imagination and daring, where 'heritage' and 'memory' are playfully deconstructed, and artistic interventions construct an altogether more lively and democratic memorialisation; availing of a rich plethora of mechanisms to remember all of us.

An 'other' cartography? Just a few plaques for a diverse Dublin in 2050

There already is a plaque at 52 Lower Camden Street to both the Jewish Tailors Union and an earlier synagogue.

- *The former Tara Street Baths* – where in 1880s Jewish women were allowed to use the baths as Mikvah[6] during a water shortage in the city.

- *The Gaiety Theatre, South King Street* – Louis Elliman owned the Savoy Group and the Gaiety; under Elliman's management, the annual 'Pantos' became a regular feature at the Gaiety and hundreds of Dubliners flocked to them.

- *Mushatt's Chemist, No. 3 Francis Street* – hundreds of working class Dubliners might have died had it not been for Harold Mushatt's renowned homemade remedies. In particular for the poor, who could not afford medical attention, his expertise was indispensable.

- *Trinity College* - graced by the presence of many distinguished Jewish scholars including Professor J. Weingreen whose *A Practical Grammar for Hebrew*[7] has been a seminal text for nearly fifty years; and A.J. 'Con' Leventhal, friend of Sam Beckett and great promoter of the work of James Joyce.

- *[Mendel] Stein's Opticians, Grantham Street* – generations of Dubliners got their glasses from Stein's; but Mendel was also a fitness fanatic and trained many boys in boxing and 'physical jerks'.

- *No. 3 Harrington Street* – used to be the Dublin Jewish Literary and Social Club in the 1920s.

I would also suggest a monument is erected to Filipina nurses, carers and child-minders (location optional) and also a monument to the Unknown Foreign Kitchen Worker.

Further reading and references

Hyman, L. (1972) *The Jews of Ireland from Earliest Times to the Year 1910,* Shannon: Irish University Press.

Keogh, D. (2008) *Jews in Twentieth Century Ireland: Refugees, Anti-semitism and the Holocaust,* Dublin: Gill and McMillan.

Ó Gráda, C. (2006) *Jewish Ireland in the Age of Joyce A Socio Economic History,* Princeton: Princeton University Press.

O'Riordan, M. (2008) 'Citizens of the Republic' in *Dublin Review of Books* (Dublin)

Pinto, D. (n.d.) Jewish Spaces versus Jewish Places? Jewish and Non-Jewish Interaction Today, available at: http://humweb.ucsc.edu/literature/course_materials_literature/documents/PintoJewishSpacesVersusJewishPlaces.pdf.

Till, K. (2011) Mapping Spectral Traces, available at: http://www.isce.vt.edu/files/MappingSpectralTracesCatalogFull.pdf.

Weiss, I. (2002) 'Jewish Disneyland – the Appropriation and Dispossession of Jewishness', in Golem no 3 6, available at: http://www.hagalil.com/golem/diaspora/inhalt.htm.

On the black population in Ireland:

Hart, W.A. (2002) 'Africans in Eighteenth-Century Ireland', *Irish Historical Studies,* May.

Rolston, B. and Shannon, M. (2002) *Encounters: How Racism Came to Ireland* Belfast: Beyond the Pale.

Migrants hit hard by recession:

http://www.irishtimes.com/newspaper/ireland/2011/0504/1224296002802.html

MRCI Report (2010) Hidden Messages Overt Agendas, available at: http://www.mrci.ie/media/128716146816_HIDDEN_MESSAGES_OVERT_AGENDAS.pdf

LEADERS Migrant Networks' Leaders. A photographic exhibition showcasing the contribution made by leaders of migrant networks in the fields of advocacy, religion, culture, media, and gender, organised as part of the ongoing Trinity Immigration Initiative Migrant Networks Project http://www.tcd.ie/immigration/networks/index.php.

Endnotes

[1] For other reasons for Jewish emigration from Ireland see Ronit Lentin (2000) *Ireland's Other Diaspora: Jewish-Irish within/Irish-Jewish without*, Golem 3, http://www.hagalil.com/golem/diaspora/irland-e.htm.

[2] 'Extracts from *Our Missionaries' Journals*, Church of Ireland Jews' Society Committee Report year ending 1897.

[3] Hyman, L. (1972) *The Jews of Ireland from Earliest Times to the Year 1919* Shannon: Irish University Press.

[4] Services, Industrial, Professional and Technical Union.

[5] Kammen, M. (1991) *Mystic Chords of Memory: The Transformation of Tradition in American Culture* (London: Random House). For a summary of debates on memory see Kirk Savage, *History, Memory, and Monuments: An Overview of the Scholarly Literature on Commemoration*, an online essay commissioned by the Organization of American Historians and the National Park Service, at http://www.nps.gov/history/history/resedu/savage.htm.

[6] A bath used for ritual immersion in Judaism.

[7] First published in 1939, it is still available from Oxford University Press.

Biographical note

Katrina Goldstone is Communications Officer at Create, the national agency for collaborative arts. She has also been a regular contributor to RTÉ programmes and Irish print media, writing on and discussing arts and culture, the Holocaust, Jewish literature, Jewish history and the Jewish community in Ireland. She did the research and co-wrote the script for the RTÉ documentary No More Blooms: Ireland's Attitudes to Jewish Refugees *(Louis Lentin, 1997). Her essays appear in* Cultivating Pluralism *(Oak Tree Press, 2000);* Racism and Anti-racism in Ireland *(Beyond the Pale Publications, 2002); and* Irish Studies *('Twilight Zones', an interview with poet Gerald Dawe on the Holocaust in literature, May 2005). Online: 'Now You See Us Now You Don't: Jews, Dublin and Historical Amnesia', in* Translocations, *Winter 2008, Volume 4, Issue 1, pp. 102-109. Her conference contributions include papers at 'The Expanding Nation: Towards a Multi Ethnic Ireland' (Dublin, 1999) and 'Emerging Irish Identities' (Dublin 2000). She contributed as a guest lecturer to the Holocaust Education Trust Summer School for Teachers (2009-10). She was a founding member of the Irish Association of Minority Ethnic Women and served on the board of the Irish Refugee Council and advisory board of AkidWa.*

10

From Dependent City to Sustainable City: Weaning Dublin Off Fossil Fuels

Patrick Daly
On Energy

Crises afoot? Global crises

The last century has seen massive growth in the world's population, which is estimated to soon reach the seven billion threshold, a seven-fold increase from 1804 when it reached its first billion. Most of this growth has occurred in the last century alone, with a billion being added in just over the last decade, and though the rate of increase is decelerating, the world's population is projected to reach over nine billion by 2050.[1]

This growth has been coupled with rapid increase and disparity in living standards including an inequitable consumption of resources such as energy; for example, an estimated 1.6 billion people, mainly in developing countries, have no access to electricity.[2] The richest countries, taking the OECD[3] nations as representative, having approximately one-quarter of the world's population are estimated to consume over 50 per cent of the world's energy, and emit over 50 per cent of the world's carbon emissions.[4] Taking historic emissions into account, it is claimed that wealthier countries collectively account for some 7 out of every 10 tonnes of CO_2 that have been emitted since the start of the industrial era.[5]

Such massive population growth has also coincided with an increasing shift from rural to urban living, and cities are now set to be the principle locus of future population growth. Some 50 per cent of the world's population are now living in cities and in Europe urbanisation is even more pronounced with 72 per cent of the population being urbanised.[6]

This population and consumption explosion has been founded on the scientific, engineering and technological advances of the industrial and modern eras, which themselves have been powered by an energy revolution based mainly on the use of fossil fuels such as coal, oil and gas. There is a growing consensus among the international scientific community and increasing evidence of critical environmental impacts arising from the fossil fuel era, notably rising temperatures resulting from increased levels of greenhouse gases (GHG) such as carbon dioxide into the atmosphere.[7]

Concern is growing not only in relation to the extent of resource consumption, particularly of fossil fuels, but also the availability of key resource reserves, especially energy resources such as oil, which many experts claim has already hit its 'peak' with diminishing reserves and demand levels outstripping new finds, thus impacting on price.[8] Given the dependency of our modern cities on limited fossil fuel energy, there are clear concerns about the 'security' of such energy supplies and the potential economic and social impacts of limitations or restrictions in availability of such key resources.

The combined risks of global warming and energy security, with their economic, social, health and environmental impacts, are perhaps the most significant drivers behind international calls for action on reduction of carbon emissions and also in shaping energy and environmental policy direction in the EU and, in turn, Ireland. The United Nations Intergovernmental Panel on Climate Change (IPCC) has called for a 50 per cent reduction in all greenhouse gas emissions by 2050 and for developed countries to reduce their CO_2 emissions by 80 per cent by 2050 in order to just stabilise average global temperatures. Achieving this would require a radical shift in the way we live and function in our cities, including substantial changes in the energy sector and key infrastructure.[9]

The Kyoto Protocol is the international agreement in which Ireland, as part of an overall EU accord, committed to limit its growth in annual greenhouse gas emissions to 13 per cent above 1990 levels in the period 2008 to 2012 (equating to a limit of 62.84 Mt CO_2 eq.), with a collective EU-15 target of an 8 per cent cut for the same period.[10] Ireland's limit was first breached in 1998 and in all years up to 2009 when, due principally to the economic downturn, it declined to 62.32 Mt CO_2 eq.[11] However, in 2008 the EU also agreed a Climate Energy Package with a target to reduce GHG emissions across the EU by 20 per cent below 1990 levels by the year 2020.[12] Irish environmental policy and legislation is principally determined by Europe – indeed, many would argue that we would have little energy or environmental initiative here in Ireland if it were not for directives from Europe – and the most recent Government White Paper on Energy, *Delivering a Sustainable Energy Future for Ireland* (2007), sets out an Energy Policy Framework for 2007-2020 tackling the key concerns of security, sustainability and competitiveness of energy supply. The paper cites specific challenges for the Irish context being its (then) 'economic growth', a 'small energy market', a 'peripheral' location on the western edge of Europe and its 'limited indigenous fuel resources', the latter of which clearly refers to fossil fuel resources and not the abundant potential renewable energy resources we have of solar, wind, tidal, hydro and bioenergy including biomass.[13]

Living in the fossil fuel age

Ireland is a hugely import-dependent state with some 89 per cent of our energy coming from imports, mainly fossil fuel-based, and with some 90 per cent of our energy use in the form of fossil fuels we are clearly still in the fossil fuel age.[14] So it's not surprising that Dublin, its capital, with a county population of 1.27 million[15] people and the city at approximately half a million inhabitants, is predominantly a fossil fuel 'guzzler' of a city, living mainly on a diet of oil, coal and gas. Economically, this import dependency presents a major financial haemorrhage for Ireland with a reported €6 billion or so leaving the economy annually on fuel imports.[16]

With total primary energy consumption in Ireland in 2009 estimated at 14.9 million tonnes of oil equivalent,[17] or 173.3 terawatt-hours (TWh), this would equate, on a pro-rata population basis, to 45.7 terawatt-hours for Dublin county and 19.5 terawatt-hours for Dublin city. This compares to an estimate carried out by Dublin City Council of 22 terawatt-hours of primary energy per annum, at 5 million tonnes of carbon dioxide (CO_2) per annum, equating to an energy-related carbon emission of just under 10 tonnes CO_2 per person per annum for Dublin City.[18]

With energy prices envisaged to rise (due to increasing demand and diminishing resources), Dubliners are likely to experience higher energy price impacts on production, business operations and consumer spending with a potential loss of competitiveness in the global market, which is quite negative given that the city is increasingly focused on internationally traded services.[19] Rising fuel costs in energy inefficient housing also increases risks associated with 'fuel poverty' (an inability to afford adequate warmth), with potential rises in co-related 'excess winter deaths', currently estimated at some 1,500–2,000 deaths per annum in Ireland.[20] Given the prevalence of pre-building regulation housing (1991) in the capital, this is a serious concern.

Environmentally there are critical global impacts of rising temperatures and sea levels in terms of agriculture and food, water shortages, and increased extreme weather events such as flooding which in turn will have enormous human impacts in certain regions.[21] Ireland will not be immune from such impacts and Dublin is likely to experience an increase in 'urban heat island effect' (a phenomena that gives rise to increased city temperatures compared to average, due to the extent of urbanisation – hard surfacing and absence of vegetation etc.), which will have health effects from for example increased heat-stress, as well as energy impacts from air conditioning and ventilation demands. Water shortages are likely to increase during the summer months combined with increased flood risks in winter.[22, 23]

Dublin's energy profile

While popular thinking may tend to see industry as the principle carbon polluter, the collective energy consumption from the thousands of individual houses and apartments amounts to a significant energy consuming sector. In fact housing is the biggest consumer and polluter compared to the other sectors in Dublin city at an estimated 35 per cent of the city's primary energy consumption with transport at 23 per cent, services 22 per cent and manufacturing 20 per cent. In energy and carbon terms, this equates to 7.8 TWh (1,570 ktonnes of CO_2) per annum or 32 per cent of the city's energy-related CO_2 emissions. Critically, 80 per cent of the residential sector's energy use derives predominantly from a pre-building regulations housing stock, a legacy of previous decades of political inaction and short-sightedness, and would only achieve an 'E' rating on the Building Energy Rating (BER) scale, the second lowest band! Gas is the principle energy source for Dublin city residents, at 56 per cent, followed by oil at 30 per cent and electricity at 14 per cent.[24, 25]

Getting about in Dublin has changed radically in recent years with transport now accounting for nearly a quarter of Dublin city's primary energy and carbon emissions. Notwithstanding the various welcome and important public transport measures such as the LUAS, bus lanes and bus corridors, there has been an explosion in numbers of road vehicles in Dublin, growing more than 100 per cent from 1990 to 2006, and estimated to consume 5 TWh of primary energy and emitting 1,240 kilo-tonnes of CO_2 annually (Dublin city and county). Dublin is a city clearly dominated by the private car with the 470,952 private cars registered in Dublin city and county (based on 2006 data) estimated to use 64 per cent of the transport sector's primary energy consumption. Cars are also the main commuter option with 55 per cent of passenger journeys undertaken in private cars and taxis (compared to public transport), yet using 93 per cent of the combined private-public transport energy demand.[26] Vice versa, public transport accounts for only 22 per cent of passenger journeys yet consumes only 7 per cent of the combined energy demand. The poor ould bicycle was, in the main, abandoned by Dubliners, who perhaps for a variety of reasons (weather, safety, security, etc.) have taken to their cars (in ever newer models and with bigger engine sizes) in large numbers. Recently, however, the bicycle is making a comeback for commuters and the dublinbike rental scheme has been a huge success with, for example, a recent peak rental of over 6,000 uses on one day in July of 2011 alone.[27] But Dublin has some serious infrastructural development to undertake in order to facilitate the levels of bike usage seen in some other European cities. In pedestrian terms, the compactness of the city centre perhaps aids the experience of Dublin as being a positive pedestrian city with most city centre facilities being within reasonable walking distance, something that I have always loved about Dublin and giving it what I would call a 'town feel'.

The commercial sector in Dublin city employs over 260,000 people and needs secure and cost-competitive energy to function effectively. Dublin's commercial sector is predominantly services-based with manufacturing accounting for 6 per cent of employment with the majority of enterprises being in the small and medium-sized category; this shift from manufacturing to services is predicted to continue. Combined, the services and manufacturing sector make up 42 per cent of the energy use of Dublin with a predominantly electrical energy base.[28]

Benchmarking

In international and EU comparisons, Ireland rates poorly in terms of its energy import dependency, ranking with the five most 'import-dependant' states in the EU – not a very secure place to be, especially given our current economic context.[29]

In terms of carbon emissions, following our economic downturn, Ireland's total GHG emissions fell to 62.32 million tonnes of CO_2 equivalent (a per capita emission of circa 14 tonnes), with energy-related emissions of 67 per cent, equating to 41.7 million tonnes or 9.2 tonnes per capita.[30] The Dublin City Sustainable Energy Action Plan (SEAP) estimates energy-related CO_2 emissions for the city at just 9.87 tonnes per capita annually.[31] Total GHG emissions in CO_2 equivalence would include more than energy-related emissions and as such would be higher, which, given the absence of agriculture in the city, I would suggest could be in the in the 10-11 tonne per capita range, and for the county in the 11-13 per capita tonne range.

Comparing this indicative total GHG emissions range for the city to data on GHG emissions for other cities gives an indication of where Dublin ranks on a world scale: Kolkata in India is an example of one of the lowest emission cities in the world at 1.1 tonnes CO_2 equivalent per capita; Tokyo is also low at 4.9 tonnes; some exemplar European cities are Stockholm in Sweden with 3.6 tonnes and Barcelona with 4.2 tonnes. Dublin compares more to major capitals such as London (9.6) and New York (10.5).[32]

On a broader basis there are a number of environmental indices or rankings for cities, and the Siemens Green City Index, undertaken by the Economist Intelligence Unit (EIU), is one example of a comprehensive index based on 30 major European cities from 30 European countries and including a range of environmental criteria, with energy being one of its eight categories: CO_2 Emissions, Energy, Buildings, Transportation, Water, Air, Waste/Land Use, and Environmental Governance. The index ranks Dublin in the lower division at 21st, next to Athens, and being outdone by many of the major Eastern European cities. The Scandinavians take the top honours (Copenhagen is rated the greenest major city next to Stockholm and is followed by Oslo), with energy-efficient buildings, extensive public transport, and renewable energy production being key factors in their success. Importantly, the ranking allows comparison of specific categories and indicators between cities and includes key facts and statistics, no doubt to inspire and raise the bar. For example, 68 per cent of Stockholm residents cycle to work (in stark contrast to Dublin's car-dependent and stressful commuter experience), and a further 25 per cent of commuters use the public transport system, which includes ethanol-powered buses and intelligent traffic guidance systems that ensure smooth traffic flows![33]

There are also numerous examples of cities across Europe with excellent energy, waste and water initiatives. The European Green Capital Award has nominated the following four cities as Green Cities with strong achievements to date and some visionary targets: Stockholm with a population of 800,000 citizens (nominated as European Green Capital for 2010), boasts a comprehensive and integrated approach to sustainability, with many excellent initiatives. For example, all trains and inner cities buses run on renewable fuels and the city has a vision to become independent of fossil fuels by 2050. Hamburg, with a population of 1.8 million, is Germany's second largest city and was nominated for 2011, and has achieved a 15 per cent reduction in CO_2 emissions per person from 1990 levels with plans to reduce is CO_2 by 40 per cent by 2020 and 80 per cent by 2050. Vitoria-Gasteiz, capital of the Álava province in the Basque Country, will hold the title in 2012 with exemplar green belt standards and a major water efficiency initiative underway. And Nantes, France's sixth largest city with a population of 600,000 will hold the title in 2013 with an exemplar transport initiative in progress, including the re-introduction of electric trams, quality bus services, bicycle routes and pedestrianisation. To date, Nantes's climate action plan has reduced CO_2 by 4.77 tonnes per capita.[34]

Freiburg eco-city

Perhaps the most known exemplar city in Europe is Freiburg in Germany. With a population nearing a quarter of a million, it not only boasts an array of sustainable energy initiatives but also has a strong green economic sector, including significant job creation, particularly through its green industry and tourism sectors, with an estimated 12,000 people employed in the environmental and solar industries alone.

A green movement first emerged in Freiburg some 30 years ago in a campaign against a proposed nuclear power station, and in the wake of Chernobyl it was one of the first cities in Germany to establish an Environmental Protection Office. In 1992 it was chosen as Germany's 'Environmental Capital', and since then has been honoured with various awards for its many initiatives, including the European Public Transport Award, the German Solar Prize, the Federal Capital for Climate Protection, and the European City of the Year in 2010.

Freiburg first established a Climate Protection Policy in 1966 with a target to cut emissions by 25 per cent by 2010, and their current target is to achieve climate neutrality by 2050. The city hosts award-winning architectural and renewable energy projects including a solar village, zero energy housing and even a football stadium that has a solar energy plant on its roof. There are significant waste and recycling facilities with incineration reserved for non-recyclable waste only. The residents also have a four-part separation of domestic waste – grey, yellow, brown and green. The city has capitalised on its green credentials and has an expanding eco-tourism sector supported in part by strategic city initiatives, including for example hosting national and international conferences, and a twinning programme to support green collaborations, including commercial ventures, with other cities; currently nine cities are twinned to Freiburg. Transport policy and planning is built around a traffic reduction strategy with pedestrian, bicycle and public transport given full priority and integrated across the city into all local planning. No new housing development could happen in Freiburg without it being on the integrated public transport hub.

Economically the city has benefited greatly from its green journey and hosts a number of private and state research centres studying renewables such as the Fraunhofer Institute for Solar Energy Systems (ISE), Europe's largest solar research institute, and hundreds of spin-off enterprises. Some of the green businesses include green architects, a zero emissions hotel, organic foods, as well as raft of manufacturing firms with products supporting the sustainable energy sector. The city has even provided specific and specialised third-level programmes in the green sector including green economics.

Freiburg has a heritage that is deeply respectful of nature. With high levels of environmental awareness amongst its citizens, these achievements have been realised due to significant political initiative and leadership which have been translated into integrated environmental policy, involving multi-stakeholder engagement and commitment, including private citizens, companies, utilities, universities, media, etc. The city's sustainable urban planning is advanced and includes an integrated approach with sustainable energy optimisation required in all development planning. This includes building alignment and siting for solar access, and a mandatory requirement for energy proposals to be included at planning stage with a contractual obligation to proceed with the most compatible energy supply option at a same or low additional cost. The city has also developed an energy master plan and specific tools for assessing energy demands to inform the planning process from a sustainable energy perspective. The city's overarching planning strategy, 'Land Use Plan 2020', was developed in 2003 from significant citizen involvement and input including the drafting of 'visionary goals' with 19 working groups to advise on specific development areas.[35]

First steps

Despite some significant differences, perhaps the most striking of which is the very nature of local government itself (with continental and Scandinavian municipalities exercising a radically more holistic 'development' function and scope than the mere development control/zoning and basic 'service provider' role of the Irish equivalent), Dublin has much to learn from cities like Freiburg. While we may have certainly started the journey much later then Freiburg, and made many mistakes in the interim, such as allowing rapid urban sprawl and facilitating car-dependent low-density development, Dublin has its own set of unique assets and resources, including an increasing environmental awareness and engagement amongst its citizens, and can – indeed must – move forward.

There are glimmers of change on the horizon for many cities across the world, evidenced by the growing number of organisations and movements promoting change and transition toward more sustainable cities, including the UN, the EU and various types of non-governmental organisations operating at local, regional, national and international levels.

For example, *Sveriges Ekokommuner* (National Association of Swedish Eco-municipalities) is a voluntary movement of 80 local and town Swedish authorities which have committed to agreed environmental targets and to monitor and report on these, with a similar movement developing in Canada. A Canadian-based movement is the 'Sustainable Cities International Network', a network of cities, towns and regions sharing their experiences, expertise and tools to undertake urban sustainability plans and projects; and based in the UK is the 'Transition Towns' movement, which had its beginnings in Kinsale, County Cork with some 47 groups now active in Ireland seeking to promote sustainable living including developing local action plans.

One example of a European movement that is now impacting directly on energy policy in Dublin is the European Commission 'Covenant of Mayors', a voluntary network of over 2,000 regional and town authorities committed to going beyond the objectives of EU energy policy (climate and energy package targets), with Dublin City Council being the first Irish authority to sign up in March 2009, following the preparation of its first Climate Change Strategy for Dublin city. As part of its commitment to the covenant, Dublin City Council had to develop a 'Sustainable Energy Action Plan' (SEAP) for the city, including a baseline (2006) energy inventory of consumption of energy in the city for residential, transport and commercial sectors (which has been drawn on in this chapter), and propose a strategy for significant energy and carbon reductions in the city.[36]

The Dublin City Council 'Sustainable Energy Action Plan' has committed to exceed the EU target of a 20 per cent reduction in emissions by 2020, and in relation to its own assets, to achieve a 33 per cent reduction, both of which support the targets in the National Energy Efficiency Action Plan for Ireland 2007-2020. In addition, it states a long-term vision to be an 'Energy Smart' city by 2030 achieving a 50 per cent carbon emissions reduction. Its overall objectives are to reduce energy costs for citizens, council and business, to reduce energy use, energy import dependency and CO_2 emissions, to improve the competitiveness and attractiveness of Dublin as a business location, to increase the share of renewables and to improve the environment.

The plan includes a range of eighteen concrete proposals, each of which has been assessed in energy/carbon abatement and costs terms with an investment of around €0.5 billion per year to a total investment of €6 billion, which, taking energy savings and carbon costs into account, would equate to a total net cost of €2.4 billion.

For the residential sector the proposals include the refurbishment of housing stock, notably the pre-building regulations stock, with measures such as low-energy lighting, attic insulation, wall insulation, boiler upgrades, window replacement and renewable energy; the development of a district heating scheme for the city utilising waste heat; improved efficiency of new homes from improved national building regulations; and changes in user behaviour. Proposals in the commercial sector include refurbishment of buildings, including upgrading of lighting, heating and ventilation systems and improved user operation; proposals for the transport sector including measures for alternative work and school travel plans, a cycle initiative and eco-cars and low-consumption driving.

The plan is a very welcome initiative and presents important baseline information on the energy and carbon profile of the city with energy and cost comparisons of a diverse range of actions, some of which are national programmes, some requiring commitment from various stakeholders in the city and others within the Council's own remit. Dublin city now at least has a target to achieve (over 40 years after Freiburg!), but its 2050 target falls short of the UN call for an 80 per cent reduction. Still, given our current high levels of fossil fuel energy consumption and carbon emissions, the target would represent a major shift in our current trends and will require a substantial commitment from all sectors including government and Dublin City Council. Whether the plan includes the level of multi-stakeholder engagement required to achieve such targets and the financial commitment and resources can be availed of remains to be seen. However perhaps the most serious limitation of the plan is its scope, in that its focus is on Dublin city only and as yet there is no equivalent plan for the other Dublin authorities.

Greater Dublin

Dublin city is part of a greater entity that is Dublin and its surrounding region. Dublin is fundamentally connected and inter-related to that region in many ways, especially for key resources such as water and food, and the very resources that may assist Dublin and the whole region in its transition to a sustainable future. Importantly, this greater Dublin region is predicted to grow significantly over coming decades thus creating more resource demands for water and energy, including significant further growth in transport energy.

Currently estimated to have a population of approximately 1.8 million, the National Spatial Strategy indicates that the greater Dublin area could reach a population of some two million by 2020. A future planning model of the region indicates further outward expansion of the city with Dublin likely to develop from a mono-centric to poly-centric model with key relationships to neighbouring conurbations, especially to towns on the northern axis where growth is predicted to be strongest.[37]

The solution for a sustainable Dublin lies in part in an overall solution for the greater Dublin area, with integrated strategic master planning combating low density and car-centric development. This greater Dublin region is also where additional and alternative renewable energy resources can be utilised compared to more limited renewable energy options within Dublin city itself, and these have the potential to be developed on a larger scale.

Our energy resources

Dublin and its region have enormous renewable energy resources to be exploited. Despite our high levels of rainfall, average solar radiation on average equates to 900-950 kWh per square meter per annum on a vertical surface, increasing to 11,000-12,000 kWh per square meter per annum on a southerly inclined orientation. This energy can be harvested directly through passive solar access to heat buildings, or via renewable energy systems such as solar thermal for hot water or photovoltaic for production of electricity. There are many examples across Europe of cities implementing measures to capitalise on this abundant energy source, such as the Barcelona Solar Ordinance. Given that much of the energy demand in Dublin is thermal energy for heating buildings and hot water, this is certainly one energy source that needs to be central to any sustainable energy strategy for Dublin.

Harvesting wind energy in a city has some limitations in terms of scale, height, wind disturbance etc., however there are many types of solutions from building integrated systems to medium-scale turbines that could be applied in many local areas of Dublin, and if we are to see the type of transition we need, every available opportunity for such localised energy production will have to be seized. On a larger scale the wider region could be the focal point of some significant scale wind energy developments (including coastal and mountain), which although they may not have the type of wind speeds available on the west coast, they have the advantage of a more developed electrical distribution system with much greater capacity than in the west and the benefit of reduced transmission losses given its proximity to demand.

The greater Dublin area could also be utilised as a bioenergy production and supply belt for the region and city, producing a diverse range of alternative energies such as biomass (a competitive alternative to oil), biogas (with potential to be upgraded for use in gas distribution network), and biofuels to provide an alternative and local fuel/component for the city's and region's transport demands. Indeed, much of the waste that Dublin produces could be used to create biogas instead of being dumped to landfill and rotting with all its associated pollution impacts.

Given our proximity to Wicklow, hydro is an important renewable energy resource that we have exploited in the past and we need to examine this resource again, with clear potential as a significant energy source for the city, and importantly one that can be used as an energy store, perhaps utilising night time excess wind energy.

Waste resources also offer energy generation alternatives including biogas generation, with the potential for urban and suburban systems, and with incineration being utilised only for non-renewable and non-recyclable wastes. Food is also a key part of a sustainable energy strategy with current food production – especially food imports – meaning that many of our foods are hugely energy intensive and this again needs to be reduced. Again, the regions surrounding Dublin should be strategically supported to become Dublin's 'bread basket' with an increasing emphasis on localised food production over imported foods.

Dublin – a model city?

Cities are the world's principle energy consumers and carbon emitters, and with an increasing proportion of the global population base they represent a significant opportunity for energy and GHG reduction. Dublin, with its population of just over a million, nearly a quarter of Ireland's population, presents a major opportunity for significant reduction in carbon emissions and should be leading the way nationally.

And why can Dublin not be among Europe's leading examples of a sustainable city, based firmly in the age of sustainability and out of the fossil fuel age and the dependence on energy imports, a dependency which perhaps started as long ago as the Georgian period? Could we not see Dublin becoming a Zero Emission City?; a city weaned off its imported fossil fuel diet and being substantially self-sufficient in energy terms, with a significant renewable energy sector supporting it? Why could we not achieve a city where the sustainable energy sector is a significant part of the region's economy, supporting thousands of jobs and retaining billions in the economy?

While the challenges to achieving this are enormous they are not insurmountable. Others are pioneering the way, and Dublin can draw from these examples and reshape their solutions and strategies in finding its own path to a sustainable future. In the most simple of terms, we effectively need to apply some key basic principles across all aspects of life in Dublin, which are to radically reduce our energy demand and supplant our imports with energy generated from our own low carbon and renewable resources. This basic quest for resource efficiency/demand reduction and a transition to indigenous sustainable energy sources needs to be owned and applied by all sectors of society, from individuals to households to neighbourhoods, communities, businesses, organisations, and public bodies if we are to see the momentum needed to create such change. History has shown that humans have the potential to respond and initiate major change in society. From the abolition of slavery to the suffragette movement, from the civil rights movement to the current Arab spring, we have shown the ability to transform society. Perhaps we can do so again?

Making the transition

At the national level this energy efficiency/demand reduction/indigenous renewable energy strategy would require a level of vision and political leadership that would implement whatever appropriate changes were necessary in order to achieve such a goal. Government needs to provide a positive and supporting national framework for cities, towns, local communities, businesses and individuals to be facilitated in this transition, as opposed to being curtailed, restricted and inhibited.

Perhaps one of the most urgent aspects of reform required from national government, which could have enormous benefits in terms of sustainability, including energy, is the reform of local government, with a pressing need to have a form of local authority that is much more than that of 'planning control' and 'services provider' but based more on the European model, which takes a more holistic role, remit and responsibility for the overall and integrated development of local areas, towns, counties and regions, including its economic development, its environmental development, and its social development. Currently local authorities in Ireland are in the main providing a development control function, with little strategic master planning, and some of the basic local services to their catchment, with other key services provided by a fragmented, diverse and complex range of bodies and organisations resulting in a lack of integration. This lack of overall holistic and proactive local development responsibility and leadership, combined with fragmented authorities and lack of co-ordination, impacts significantly on sustainable issues, including local energy policy, and is inhibiting for such a small country.

A second key area that national government could support is in creating a fiscal context that supports and promotes sustainability including sustainable energy. And this does not necessarily have to result in cost to the taxpayers, but could assist in retention of finance in local economies, business development and job creation.

One fiscal model I would propose is for national government to create a structure that would encourage the billions of euro that Irish people have in savings, investments and pensions to be invested in strategic sectors for the benefit of Ireland as a whole. For example, according to the Irish Association of Pensions Funds, the value of Irish-owned pensions is in the region of €72 billion, an enormous amount of wealth and capital, but only a small portion of this wealth is actually invested in Ireland with most of it in the global economy. For example, only 5 per cent is invested in Irish equities. If a supportive structure was put in place to encourage the allocation of even 10 per cent of such assets into strategic sectors and investment in the Irish economy – such as the sustainable energy sector – it would release some €7 billion of investment into a much smaller economic pond with a greater effect for Ireland. The Irish Pension Reserve Fund could also be used in this way.[38]

There is also a clear need for a Greater Dublin Authority to strategically direct and support the region's development in a sustainable way with integrated planning of sustainable energy solutions. At the local authority level, Dublin authorities should tackle the sustainable resources issue on a more co-ordinated basis, with perhaps the four authorities being directed by a regional authority in this regard. Any sustainable plan for Dublin needs to be for Dublin and its surrounding region as this relationship is critical for a sustainable energy future and sustainable exploitation of the region's renewable energy resources.

Integrated sustainability planning will be required with energy modelling informing proactive master planning at all levels. Planning in Ireland is dominated by the concept of control and zoning rather than active and intentional master planning, whereas more strategic direction or planning intervention is required to ensure we have optimal sustainable development and renewal.

Under Ireland's National Energy Efficiency Action Plan (NEAP) public bodies and agencies are now mandated to lead the way in terms of sustainable energy and rightly so. Such bodies should be developing clear strategies, and ensure appropriate support and direction to those they serve in assisting them toward a sustainable energy future.

The commercial sector has much to gain if we transform to a sustainable energy future and perhaps significant pain if we do not. There is the clear risk of rising fossil fuel energy prices and shortages impacting on competitiveness; and there are also commercial and business opportunities to be capitalised on in the transition to a green economy, whether it is the supply of components to a green energy company or eco-tourism – change provides opportunity. All business should be developing their own sustainable energy action plans with clear assessments of their current usage and setting out short, medium and long-terms plans to reduce energy use and transition to renewables, which should provide both commercial and social benefit. However it is critical that policymakers and the public and state services support this sector in every way, especially with fiscal measures to ease financial burden.

The need to change to a sustainable future also presents neighbourhoods and communities with both challenges and opportunities, and a possible focal issue around which to re-centre and engage as communities. Communities could, I believe, develop their own energy companies, and seek to implement local sustainable energy measures, be it the insulation of houses or developing a local energy centre. Communities could build and own their own energy projects such as hydro, wind, or biogas and even develop relationships with resource providers in the region, such as farmers, for biomass. Why could we not even see a community-owned farm that provided that community with food, biomass or biofuel, or a community-owned wind farm? The co-operative model would be an excellent platform to undertake such projects and local schools, churches, community centres and clubs such as the GAA, could provide excellent focal points or locations. Indeed all these 'third sector' organisations have a crucial role to play in being catalysts for change in their communities and in helping to create the shift necessary for the major culture change that is required if Dublin is to become a sustainable city/region. Communities should actually consider developing their own sustainable action plans, with multi-stakeholder involvement, and seek to have local authorities' and public body's engagement and support in these.

And every single household will need to play its part, remembering that each of us live in homes that consume energy, often in excessive quantities. We generally get around in fossil fuel modes of transport, work in energy-intensive buildings and study in energy-intensive educational institutions. In each of these contexts we can be promoters of change. And there is a lot we can do. Perhaps developing our own household action plans with some short, medium and long-terms goals would be a useful exercise. Our homes need to be radically upgraded, which could be done in stages perhaps over a 10-15 year period, with a specific energy target in mind. Perhaps we should be thinking of tackling this on a street or community basis and not just our individual homes. This could allow synergies to be developed via shared resources and even shared and improved purchase power. We need to implement alternative energies in our own homes and indeed in our neighbourhoods. We can seek alternative public transport or use alternative fuels. We can recycle and even grow some of our own foods.

We can do more than exercise the power of consumer choice itself – we can seek to pioneer and implement changes in our, homes, neighbourhoods, communities, schools, workplaces and even in our institutions of governance and service. At the end of the day, it boils down to us. We are after all nothing more than a very, very big village or perhaps a city of villages, and Dubliners will need to fashion the type of village they want for the future. The future is ours and it will need a major shift in paradigm if we are to see the level of cultural change to seriously engage in the issue of a sustainable future for our children and theirs. In many ways, the future of Dublin is in our hands.

Endnotes

[1] U.S. Census Bureau, *International Brief on Global Population*, 2004.

[2] International Energy Agency, *World Energy Outlook*, 2002.

[3] Organisation for Economic Co-operation and Development.

[4] U.S. Department of *Energy, Energy Use and Carbon Emissions: Non-OECD Countries*, 1992.

[5] United Nations Development Programme, *Human Development Report 2007/2008*.

[6] UN Department of Economic and Social Affairs, *World Urbanization Prospects*, 2007.

[7] Intergovernmental Panel on Climate Change, *The Physical Science Basis*, 2007.

[8] ASPO (Association for the Study of Peak Oil & Gas), *Understanding Peak Oil*, 2008.

[9] Dublin City, *Sustainable Energy Action Plan*, 2010.

[10] United Nations, *Kyoto Protocol to the UN Framework Convention on Climate Change*, 1998.

[11] Sustainable Energy Authority of Ireland, *Energy in Ireland, 1990–2009*.

[12] Commission of the European Communities, *Europe's Climate Change Opportunity*, 2008.

[13] Government White Paper, *Delivering a Sustainable Energy Future for Ireland*, 2007.

[14] Sustainable Energy Authority of Ireland, *Energy in Ireland, 1990–2009*.

[15] Central Statistics Office, 2011.

[16] *Sunday Times*, 16 November 2008.

[17] Sustainable Energy Authority of Ireland, *Energy in Ireland, 1990–2009*.

[18] Dublin City, *Sustainable Energy Action Plan, Baseline Emission Inventory*, 2006.

[19] The Economic and Social Research Institute, *Medium-Term Review, 2008-2015*.

[20] *Journal of Epidemiology & Community Health*, 'Housing standards and excess winter mortality', 2000.

[21] Intergovernmental Panel on Climate Change, *Impacts, Adaptation and Vulnerability*, 2007.

[22] IIEA, *The Climate Change Challenge: Strategic Issues, Options and Implications for Ireland*, 2008.

[23] Community Climate Change Consortium for Ireland, *Ireland in a Warmer World*, 2008.

[24] Dublin City, *Sustainable Energy Action Plan*, Version 2, 2010.

[25] Construct Ireland, *Ireland's Housing Stock Legacy*, 2007.

[26] Dublin City, *Sustainable Energy Action Plan, Baseline Emission Inventory*, 2006.

[27] www.dublinbikes.ie.

[28] Dublin City, *Sustainable Energy Action Plan, Baseline Emission Inventory*, 2006.

[29] Euro Stat, European Commission, *Energy in the EU 25*, 2005.

[30] Sustainable Energy Authority of Ireland, *Energy in Ireland 1990–2009*.

[31] Dublin City, *Sustainable Energy Action Plan, Baseline Emission Inventory*, 2006.

[32] International Institute for Environment and Development, *Cities and GHG Emissions*, 2011.

[33] Economist Intelligence Unit, *Siemens Green City Index*, 2009.

[34] European Commission, European Green Capital Award.

[35] Green City Freiburg – *Approaches to Sustainability*, 2010.

[36] Dublin City, *Sustainable Energy Action Plan*, Version 2, 2010.

[37] EC, European Environment Agency, *Urban Sprawl in Europe – The Ignored Challenge*, 2006.

[38] Irish Association of Pension Funds, *Pension Investment Survey*, 2009.

Bibliography

Brennan, P. and Curtin, J. (eds.) (2008) *The Climate Change Challenge: Strategic Issues, Options and Implications for Ireland*. Dublin: IIEA.

Breyer, F., Richter, M., Kern, N., Lang, F., Halter, M., Horstkötter, N., Zinthäfner, P. and Ahuis, M. (eds.) (2010) *Green City Freiburg – Approaches to Sustainability*, Freiburg Wirtschaft Touristik und Messe GmbH & Co. KG.

Campbell, Colin J. (2008) About Peak Oil: Understanding Peak Oil. [Internet] ASPO. Available from: http://www.peakoil.net.

Central Statistics Office (2006) Census [Internet] www.cso.ie.

Clinch J.P. and Healy J.D. (2000) 'Housing standards and excess winter mortality', *Journal of Epidemiology and Community Health*; 54: 719–720.

Community Climate Change Consortium for Ireland (C4I). (2008) *Ireland in a Warmer World: Scientific Predictions of the Irish Climate in the 21st Century.*

Commission of the European Communities (2008) *20 20 by 2020 Europe's climate change opportunity*, Communication from the Commission to the European Parliament, The Council, The European Economic and Social Committee and the Committee of the Regions, Brussels.

Daly, P. (2007) *Laughing Stock – Ireland's Housing Stock Legacy*, Construct Ireland, Temple Media, County Dublin.

Department of Communications, Marine and Natural Resources (2007) *Delivering a Sustainable Energy Future for Ireland: Energy Policy Framework for 2007–2020*, Government White Paper, Dept of Communications, Marine and Natural Resources, Ireland, Dublin.

Dublin City Council (2008) *Baseline Emission Inventory for Dublin City Sustainable Energy Action Plan 2010-2020.*

Dublin City Council (2010) *Sustainable Energy Action Plan 2010–2020* Version 2.

Economist Intelligence Unit (x) Siemens Green City Index [Internet] www.siemans.com/innovation.

European Commission, Euro Stat (2006) *Energy in the EU: First Estimates 2005.*

European Commission, (2006) *Urban Sprawl in Europe - The Ignored Challenge*, European Environment Agency Report No 10/2006.

Fitzgerald, J. (2008) *Medium-Term Review 2008-2015*, Dublin: The Economic and Social Research Institute.

Hoornweg D. et al. (2011) *Cities and Greenhouse Gas Emissions: Moving Forward*, International Institute for Environment and Development (IIED) Vol XX(X): 1–21. DOI: 10.1177/0956247810392270 Sage Publications.

Irish Association of Pension Funds (2009) Pension Investment Survey.

Intergovernmental Panel on Climate Change (2007) *The Physical Science Basis, Contribution of Working Group I to the Fourth Assessment Report of the Intergovernmental Panel on Climate Change*, Cambridge: Cambridge University Press.

Intergovernmental Panel on Climate Change (2007) *Impacts, Adaptation and Vulnerability Contribution of Working Group II to the Fourth Assessment Report of the Intergovernmental Panel on Climate Change*, Cambridge: Cambridge University Press.

International Energy Agency (2002) *World Energy Outlook*, Ch. 13 Energy and Poverty.

Stern, N. (2008). *Key Elements of a Global Deal on Climate Change*, London: LSE.

Sustainable Energy Authority of Ireland (2010), *Energy in Ireland, 1990–2009* Dublin.

United Nations (1998) *Kyoto Protocol to the UN Framework Convention on Climate Change.*

United Nations (2008) *World Urbanization Prospects: The 2007 Revision*, Department of Economic and Social Affairs Population Division, New York.

United Nations Development Programme (2008). *Fighting Climate Change: Human Solidarity in a Divided World in Human Development Report 2007/2008*. New York: Palgrave Macmillan.

U.S. Census Bureau (2004) *Global Population at a Glance 2002 and Beyond, International Brief*, U.S. Department of Commerce Economics and Statistics Administration.

U.S. Department of Energy (1992) *Energy Use and Carbon Emissions: Non-OECD Countries*, Energy Information Administration Office of Energy Markets and End Use, Washington, DC

Biographical note

Patrick Daly was born in Dublin and grew up in Ballyfermot. He studied Architectural Technology in the Dublin Institute of Technology before emigrating to the UK (in the 1980s recession), where he worked as a technologist and later retrained as a teacher of Design and Technology (during the UK recession). Returning to Dublin in the mid-1990s he worked in a number of architectural practices and studied Project Management in Trinity. Patrick later founded his own small technical practice while undertaking a Masters in Architecture in Advanced Energy and Environmental Studies. Patrick has lectured part-time in the School of Architecture in the DIT in the areas of technology, energy and environmental design. In 2005 he established his own energy and environmental consultancy (BESRaC), providing research, consultancy and training to a range of clients including public and private sector bodies. He is currently consulting on the Dundalk 2020 project with SEAI, has recently completed an EPA-funded study into the potential of hemp and lime as a construction material in Ireland, and is working on a European energy project promoting bioenergy in the Midlands. Patrick now lives in Mullingar where he has designed and built Ireland's first net energy positive house. See www.patrickdaly. net www.besrac.net.

151

11

The Bridge Gathers the Earth as Landscape around the Stream[1]

Noel J. Brady
on Crossings

Axis Mundi

In ancient Egypt the Nile served as an Axis Mundi around which the Egyptian world view was constructed. It served to re-affirm their cultural supremacy coincidental as it was to the axis of the earth, revolving around the Polar star. Around this axis they assembled a culture uniting art, religion and science. Dublin's Axis Mundi, the River Liffey, flows west to east towards the rising sun. Unlike the Nile, the Liffey has not attracted the same attention, at least to our current knowledge. Our cultural axis has grown in a different direction. Nonetheless, it is a permanent line around which Dublin has negotiated its development. All major cities have at their heart a major river: Paris has the Seine, London has the Thames, Rome has the Tiber and New York has two, the Hudson and East River. Over time these cities have developed various types of crossings to become united and integrated urban centres. It could be argued that without a sufficient number of crossings, permanent or otherwise, an asymmetrical city would emerge, perhaps tied to one side or develop as two cities. In ancient Egypt, the crossing of the river was such a profound event it divided the living (east) from the dead (west). This separation was embodied in their architectural schema. The river gave life and as such it became the symbolic centre of their constructs. It took the Romans – consummate road and bridge builders – to tame river and valley and to construct a model that has been the basis of most western cities. The road and bridge remain the most potent symbols of that empire.

Though millennia separate our world from ancient Egypt and Rome, the fundamental components of city-building remain largely the same. As it was it is now; all cities share common traits but differ in the details, and these details are often a consequence of water. The availability of water is vital to the birth and continuance of urbanism. Dublin, with its wide bay to the east, has been favourably compared to Naples. Its lopsided valley, split by the River Liffey and steeper on the southern approaches, has been home to human habitation long before the official establishment of Baile Átha Cliath (town of the hurdled ford, see below). An ancient way follows the high ground that is now Thomas Street from the west arriving at the highest ridge where Christchurch and the Castle meet. It is no accident that right below this place the Vikings chose to establish their Longphort in 841 at Wood Quay, which has since been home to many subsequent generations, each benefiting from the topography and generous tidal river. The high ground on the southern bank has been adapted largely for its strategic opportunities and later religious purposes. Previous discussions about the built heritage of Dublin has concentrated on the various artefacts, buildings and street facades of the Medieval, Georgian, Victorian and the Modern overshadowing a reading of the river Liffey as divider, unifier, conveyor, purifier and signifier. Its bridges, the footnotes to the city, have long gathered the landscape of the city of Dublin together.

Bridging the river

The earliest archaeological evidence has identified urban settlement in and around Wood Quay in contemporary Temple Bar, but this does not preclude pre-historic settlement elsewhere along the valley. Late Mesolithic fish traps have been found in the vicinity of excavations at Spencer Dock, indicating a wider occupation of the riverine system. Cities tend to continue along the axis of their origin and in Dublin's case the south side has long been favoured over the northern shore. The origins of Dublin support this. Today the asymmetry of the valley is supported by an asymmetry of the city itself with the greater population living south of the Liffey. Water still remains responsible for this characteristic with potable water supplied from reservoirs in the Wicklow

Mountains and Dublin foothills. Though lacking in direct evidence, we can surmise other things about the early city and even suggest that until the construction of Dubhghall's Bridge, located a short distance downstream from what was the ford of the hurdles, sometime prior to 1014 most crossings were taken by ferry. The ford was undoubtedly the key to connecting the two sides of the valley and would appear to have been located just north of Fr. Matthew's Bridge where a confluence of roads that predate Stoneybatter, Bolton Street and Parnell Street met the river.[2] Sea-fishing and trade, especially during the Viking period, was conducted along its east–west axis. But it is the bridges that united the city, making permanent a connection the ford could not secure at high water or winter.

Roads exist because of desires – to connect, communicate, to trade. Once a more permanent crossing is enacted other possibilities come into being, and the landscape is gathered around itself. Evidence of such peripheral settlement can be seen in the remnants of medieval settlements such as St. Mary's Abbey, founded in 1139 and once the wealthiest Cistercian Abbey in Ireland, on the marshy flats of the northern shore. 'Silken' Thomas Fitzgerald started his unsuccessful rebellion in 1534 in the extant Chapter House, hidden off present day Capel Street. With greater activity comes the demand for more crossings, especially practical and secure crossings. The history and evolution of these crossings charts the progress of Dublin as a metropolitan centre. Even without the archaeological record, bridges serve to direct our enquiry. Like the roads and streets that connect them they are amongst the oldest remnants of the city. To underpin their importance several have been re-built time and time again.

Following the first permanent crossing it was another 650 years before a second crossing was established upstream in 1670. Originally called Bloody Bridge, this was renamed Rory O'More Bridge in 1923. Between this bridge and the East Link Bridge, a distance of 4.5 kilometres, there are 17 crossings, at an average interval of 250 metres. Nearer the city's core the interval falls to about 100 metres. The three bridges at the lower end of the river, completed since 1984 (1984, 2005 and 2010) have moving sections to allow for the movement of ships of various draughts upstream as far as the Custom House, completed in 1791. It was prudent to move the Custom House downstream replacing the earlier building from 1701 which was located upstream on Essex Quay.

The Industrial Revolution transformed Dublin into a significant city on the back of its port. From 1755 to 1891 was the busiest period for bridge building with thirteen projects, two of which were rebuilds. Even with this significant expansion of connections, ferry crossings remained an important means of communication, particularly in the lower reaches of the river well into the late twentieth century. Today the last river traffic is the tourist-based Liffey River Cruises. Of the seventeen bridges, seven are over 100 years old and two are over 200 years old. Mellowes Bridge at 243 years is the oldest. Apart from the more iconic examples – the Calatrava twins (Beckett and Joyce), the Millennium and the older Liffey Bridge (halfpenny) – the bridges tend to be invisible to the millions of transits that occur each year; people, bicyclists, cars, taxis, buses and trucks. Stitching together the north and south sides of the city, their role remains the subtext to the river's divisive qualities. Since the 'Emergency' (c.1939-1946), new bridges have made significant contributions to eroding the perceived division between 'northsiders' and 'southsiders'. Great public events such as the Liffey Swim, established in 1920, the St. Patrick's Day Skyfest and the Tall Ships events located around the Liffey, help bring the whole city together. The Point Depot and the IFSC have been recently joined by the National Conference Centre and Grand Canal Theatre, bringing people eastwards towards the sea.

Joining the development of theatre in the seventeenth century and the music hall in the nineteenth century, event-based public entertainment has become a significant factor in late twentieth century urbanism. Further land-scape improvements, such as the boardwalk and the refurbishment of the Campshires, have become the tissue that connects the bridges along the river's axis gathering, as Heidegger wrote, the earth as landscape around the stream.

Both the frequency and the dates of the crossings illustrate how the critical mass of the city has moved steadily downstream from its inception at Wood Quay. The main commercial core from Henry Street to St. Stephen's Green is connected by four bridges, two of which are pedestrian, which support invis-ible desire lines that exist throughout the city. Dublin could not do without these connections as every new crossing attests to the demand. The loss of any one of the road bridges through obstruction, or worse, destruction, would seriously impair the function of the city and would have repercussions as far out as the M50. With nine bridges over 100 years old built in either stone or cast/wrought iron, it is clear that significant investment is required to maintain and repair them.

The river has exacted a toll on the bridges and their foundations. The number of rebuilds attests to this. Where Fr. Mathew Bridge is located at Church Street/Merchants Quay, there have been five bridges constructed since 1000, with intervals ranging from nine to 388 years. These were constructed during a period in which the river was the greatest threat. Today the greatest threat may be the very traffic that they carry. It is the stone bridges that are oldest and most at risk. Stone arches have been used in four bridges while another three are constructed as a stone iron hybrid. Erected long before modern seismic and finite element analysis, we remain fortunate to live in an environment where weather and geological events are relatively benign. We cannot be so confident that that may continue into the future. Serious concerns have emerged in recent years with erosion of some of the stone arches of O'Connell Bridge. In 2008 a section of parapet gave way exposing stress cracks in the structure. At the time it was surmised that rising water levels at high tide was contributing to accelerated erosion.

> It struck me, a belief that has never left me since, that we are just a great machine for looking backward, and that humans are great at self-delusion. Every year that goes by increases my belief in this distortion. – Nassim Taleb[3]

The future

The only thing that can be said about predicting the future is that it will be invariably wrong. In 1985, during a similar period of recession, no one predicted the 'great expansion' of the Celtic Tiger years of 2002–2007, and in 2007 few publicly predicted the rapid deflation of the housing bubble and current deep recession. It is with great trepidation that any talk of the future is undertaken. Nonetheless, based on what we do know, what we can say with a reasonable amount of certainty is that Ireland's population will expand. The 2006 Census measured the population at 4.2 million people and more recent data suggests that it may be as much as 6.5 million by 2060. Just how it will expand is due in part to human agreement and the limits of resources. We can also be reasonably certain that Dublin will be the focus of significant expansion. The main limit to this growth is Dublin's water supply from the south and the complimentary drainage system to the sea. However, the fragility of the situation is not appreciated by its citizens. For instance, the 133 year old Vartry water tunnel that provides for 80 million litres daily represents 25 per cent of the supply to Dublin city and the Greater Dublin Area; the failure of this tunnel would be catastrophic. Even if funds were available for a secure bypass, this would only be available from 2013 at the earliest.[4] Just how Dublin will provide for the future will take a considerable bit of planning and luck, because in spite of ourselves, cities seem to grow under their own steam, even where planning is under-performing.

> The US Economist Herbert Simon points out that an absence of central planning does not necessarily mean that all cities are poorly 'designed'. On the contrary, they are (or at any rate, they once were) often remarkably effective in arranging for goods to be transported, for land to be apportioned between residential, business and manu-facturing districts, and for a lot of activity to be fitted into a small area. – Philp Ball[5]

Recent scientific enquiries have identified planning as having only a partial influence on the resultant urban form. Despite our best efforts it seems that cities behave more like viruses. Maybe then we should not worry so much and place our faith in the 'hive mind'.[6] There are, however, things we do need to plan for. To meet the Kyoto protocols on CO_2 reduction, to improve our energy footprint, and to provide for a more inclusive urban environment, we require a denser urban framework. We need to repopulate the core and provide an integrated transport infrastructure. Not only should the centre provide for new forms of urban entertainment, it must provide for life, make a desirable place to live with larger, family-oriented apartments and family-friendly streets and parks. Since 1945 many cities have been excoriated of their urban core allowing the young to abandon civitas for bucolic suburban fantasies.

Since the 1980s cities have sought to reverse this viral expansion. In order to entice people back water has become a significant draw, and Dublin is following where previously Boston, San Francisco, London, Rotterdam, Amsterdam and more recently Hamburg (Hafencity) have forged new urban identities through waterfront development. In Dublin a suitably attractive contemporary image of urban maritime engagement is attracting businesses and people back to the centre. In Hamburg's Hafencity a strategic decision has been made to include design contingencies to mitigate against climate change flooding. Providing for a complex mix of activities – a university, various business models, entertainment complexes and housing – the plan is attracting a new generation of active citizenry. Most of the significant inward investment seen in Dublin in the last 10 years has been along the lower Liffey corridor with the National Conference Centre, the Grand Canal Theatre, and the O_2 redevelopment along with numerous offices for the banking and legal fraternity.

Preparing for any future will require the preparation of key structures even if invisible to our comings and goings. With only six new bridges built in the last generation (two of which are pedestrian only), the remaining bridges require attention. Only 'making do' with bridges that are over 200 years old is no longer sufficient protection for the future. Vulnerable to the fluctuations of the river, they remain viable, like the Vartry Tunnel, only by the grace of good fortune. At a rate of 2 milimetres per year we might expect that the average sea level around Dublin to rise by 80 milimetres by 2051, but this does not account for any coincidental events such as that of a spring high tide, full moon and an eastwardly storm front such as happened in 2002, and which led to flooding of areas of the northern shoreline.

In February 2002, for example, a low pressure system in the southern Irish Sea coincided with the spring tide, leading to an extreme water level of 2.9 metres above mean sea level. This storm surge led to widespread flooding in Dublin and Belfast and marked coastal erosion between Cork and Belfast.[7]

What were 1 in 1,000 year events are now perhaps 1 in 200 year events, with the possibility that two successive years may see the extremes of 2010 which was bracketed by two harsh winters. Every increase in water level and storm frequency will increase wear and tear on the most vulnerable of these structures. The natural environment is only part of the equation. For instance, man's impact exacts a much greater toll. In 2010 the Dublin City Council's traffic count recorded over 60,000 private cars and nearly 1,000 HGVs entering through the Canal cordon. The report identifies the 5-axle ban and the use of the new port tunnel as making a significant contribution to decreasing the physical impacts to the urban core. Nonetheless, with the progressive impact of this level of use, it is inevitable that the bridges will require ongoing inspection, repair and renewal. The danger of complacency in this regard was

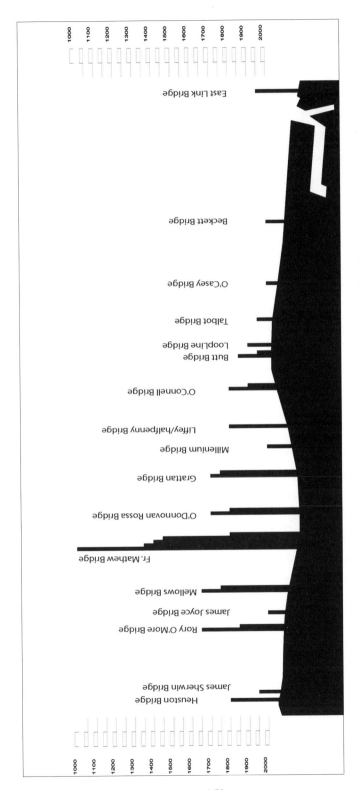

Bridges over the River Liffey. Image courtesy of Noel Brady.

emphasised when the Broadmeadow viaduct collapsed in 2009, shutting down the main Dublin–Belfast rail link. In addition to maintenance new crossings should be considered, in part to supplement the existing, but also to provide for a city that must expand inwards.

The relationship of the bridges to the Liffey is more a relationship between the activities of the city. A city and its bridge are symbiotic. For Dublin the crossings are the musculoskeletal spine of the city and at present there are gaps. The diagram on the previous page illustrates the relative location and number of iterations at each location through time from west to east. Bridge building is equivalent to city building. The synchronicity in developments of the city core and its bridges are self-evident. Further east, the intervals between the bridges stretch along with lower habitation patterns, and as this part of the city intensifies more crossings will be required. In reflecting on this dilemma it should be said that these crossings may in fact take on different dynamics. During the city's Victorian period the Loop Line Bridge was installed without any concern for the Classical ideals of Georgian Dublin. Opting in favour of engineering purity it wrapped around the Custom House, carving through the fabric of Gardiner Street, slicing houses in half. The Loop Line, though vital to both passenger and freight traffic, may be an unwelcome but necessary appendage to the city. Other options are possible, other strategies that will provide for the next generation.

In 1996 the architects NJBA A+U proposed to relocate the Loop Line underground. The proposal to connect the new – then proposed – Barrow Street Station with a new underground Central Rail Terminal at Spencer Dock (the location of the National Conference Centre) would allow the removal of the existing Loop Line Bridge. Pearse Street Station could then be released to Trinity College as a sports hall or art gallery. Similar transfers of land to the city at Tara Street and Gardiner Street would repair the damage done to the visual continuity of the city. The contribution to reclaiming the classical presence of the Custom House would be significant and proposed connections could follow this lead going under the Liffey rather than over. In London's East End, the Greenwich Foot Tunnel built in 1902, connecting the Isle of Dogs to Greenwich, is still actively used by pedestrians and cyclists. Dublin would not require anything as deep or as long to navigate the Liffey. In preparing for the future we should make crossings, lots of them, in as many variations as possible. Only by stitching the city together will we provide for an integrated city attractive to all. Only by preparing for all possibilities can all possibilities be accommodated.

The most recent addition to the city's crossings, the Samuel Beckett Bridge connecting Guild Street (alongside the Grand Canal) and Sir John Rogerson's Quay, opens up a new axis across the city. Through this new structure the immediate landscape of the new National Conference Centre and the Grand Canal Theatre development are brought together. To accommodate shipping access upstream this new structure rotates. This brings to three the number of bridges that move to accommodate east-west river traffic as well as north-south road traffic. Clearly the technology for dealing with an increasingly dynamic city is becoming more commonplace and responsive to changing demands. The next stage is to devise suitable crossings that might connect the South Quays to New Wapping Street or Castleforbes Road. Maybe a causeway bridge link further east completing the often discussed 'Eastern Bypass'? Together these would complete the mesh of streets providing for future densification of the core and open access to desirable water frontage that will persuade people to return to the city. Coupled with this infrastructure will be the necessary tidal protection systems to ensure the survival of the city into the next millennium. The suggested Eastern Bypass may include tidal protection as an integrated function.

A denser core – a living core – will focus more attention on the river itself. The improvements to the quay walls, providing access for people which include the boardwalk development and the Campshires, have made the space of the Liffey more attractive. The introduction of Parisian-like *bateaux mouche* for the Liffey River Tour points in the direction of other dynamic structural possibilities. In 2007, NJBA A+U proposed another development, this time for the Liffey itself. Plurabella (a name inspired by James Joyce's *Ulysses*) was the name chosen for an artificial island at the centre of the Liffey, splitting the river into two channels. Along with this river a number of new pedestrian crossing points were proposed to connect the island to the quays. The proposal for the island was to identify with this ancient Axis Mundi of the city of Dublin creating a cultural island. On this island a number of satellite exhibitions would hold temporary exhibits from all of the main museums and galleries that can be found alongside the Liffey. This island could provide the necessary infrastructure to gather the various drains that still enter the Liffey and treat their contents before returning cleaner water to the current. The island in turn would be an oasis for those who live, work and visit the city. With trees, parks and places for families to visit it would provide a welcome break from what has become a transit zone. It would be a place from which to recognise the role of the river and its bridges and the landscape that is gathered at the heart of the city.

> Histories and societies do not crawl. They make jumps. They go from fracture to fracture, with a few vibrations in between. Yet we (and historians) like to believe in the predictable, small incremental progression. – Naseem Taleb[8]

The benefit of bridges and crossings appears to be self-evident and taken for granted. It is only when lost that we understand their value. The collapse of the Broadmeadow viaduct led to €245,000 in ticket refunds and €4 million in repairs. Whilst only shut down for three months, the incident emphasised how important the physical infrastructure remains even in this digital age. Providing for new infrastructure is bit of a black art. There is a fine balance to be found between the exact amount of investment that will ensure that minimal requirements are met, and at the same time allowing for sufficient expansion, whether designed or not. When Sir Joseph Bazzlegate established the 1,100 mile sewer network for central London (commenced in 1858, opened in 1865), he instructed that the pipework would be double that which was adequate because he said: we're only going to do this once. London has grown on the back of this generosity. Associated amenities such as the Embankment, a direct by-product of the work, has become a defining character of the Thames enjoyed by millions of Londoners and visitors alike. This should not be considered a plea for large scale vanity works un-tethered by cost. It is a plea for sensible generous structures that are truly sustainable in their capacity to deal with a multitude of futures.

Providing for the future of the city is the responsibility of Dublin City Council. In successive five-year development plans it identifies key strategic objectives for the future, and from these objectives it prioritises and commissions works from the public purse. These undertakings are often beyond the means of the council but, because they are of national importance, central funding can be made available. Any work in and around Dublin Port and the Liffey would qualify as work of national importance. This deep-water harbour, sitting close to such a major population centre, is home to petroleum imports, ferry and cruise ship terminals, freight and Ro-Ro operations, as well as bulk goods transfer. Any work that is considered adjoining this facility would have a significant impact on the nation's passenger and trade operations.

More crossings will contribute to making the city functional and efficient, especially a strategic link like the Eastern Bypass. In order to facilitate this later connection a bridge would be necessary to allow shipping unhindered access to Dublin Port. A piled causeway system similar to that of the Florida Keys could provide the necessary connective tissue. The low topographical profile of the bay, though challenging, would be of considerable benefit. It is clear that the city of Dublin alone could not support a massive infrastructural project that had national implications. In addition to the restoration of the older structures, the bill for three new crossings and an Eastern Bypass of combined bridge and causeway would run into the billions of euro. However the return of investment that would be garnered through tolling or some other road pricing system would be considerable.

In 1984 the East Link bridge was completed at a cost of IR£6.1 million (€12.25 mllion at 2011 rates) and currently carries around 22,000 vehicles a day (twice its original prediction). This infrastructure has contributed many times that figure in local contributions and taxes. Though initiated through private finance, it illustrates that public works should remain the domain of the state. The annual profit the bridge garners is by any standards a remarkable return on investment. The return of investment to the state, city and people made by the other city crossings are probably incalculable; their contribution, like their presence, remaining invisible to many. According to Liam Collins:

> The East-Link took in €4.4 million (after appropriations) for the same period (2003) with a profit of €2.6 million to NTR (National Toll Roads) from its share of the bridge.[9]

If one were to look to a suitable comparator it would be the Øresund Bridge (Öresund in Swedish) which connects Denmark to Sweden; this is a combined twin-track railway and dual carriageway bridge-tunnel across the Øresund strait. The cost of the project was about €4 billion but is expected to pay for itself by 2035. It has been credited with instilling a new-found cultural appreciation between the two countries as well as being the impetus for one of the largest and most interesting contemporary urban infrastructure projects in

Denmark, the Øresund quarter south of Copenhagen. If we adopted a similar transgenerational approach to providing for the city of the next generation retaining the benefits for the city and nation, we would have a firmer foundation upon which to deal with the future.

The raising of the necessary funds for any of the works proposed above need not be wholly out of exchequer current spending. Though out of fashion for some time, bridge bonds like war bonds could be floated to pay for the investment, and given what we know about tolling on the East-Link Bridge, it would be a win-win for everyone involved. The 30-year-or-so payback period identified for the Øresund Bridge is nothing in the lifetime of a city over 1,000 years old. In preparing for a future that may require environmental protection against the sea, a combined infrastructure that deals with both may in fact be a highly economical solution.

Preparing for the future with an eye to the past is always dangerous. Nonetheless there are lessons in history that we do well to attend to. The history of cities is one of a history of water, and our relationship to this fundamental element of life. Our transit through, over and under has defined many cities. It has given the world some iconic images, from the Golden Gate Bridge to the Sydney Harbour Bridge, and yet their real value is their consistency of connection, their mute presence a testament to the importance of the city in our lives. The future can never be as certain as the past, but we can prepare for uncertainty. We can provide a reasonable framework for continuity now, rather than waiting for disaster to visit. In the city bridge-building is akin to city-building: it is one of its fundamental building blocks. By gathering to itself the landscape of the city we might have a city united in purpose and ideal.

> There can be little doubt that in many ways the story of bridge-building is the story of civilisation. By it we can readily measure an important part of a people's progress – Franklin D. Roosevelt[10]

Endnotes

[1] Martin Heidegger (1975) 'Poetry Language Thought', in *Building Dwelling Thinking*, Harper & Row, p. 152.

[2] See Hermann Geissel's 'A Road on the Long Ridge' for a discussion and extrapolation of early road systems below the contemporary street pattern of Dublin, CRS Publications (2006).

[3] Nassim Taleb (2007) 'History does not crawl it jumps', p. 12, in *The Black Swan*, Penguin Books.

[4] Information from: http://www.dublincity.ie/WaterWasteEnvironment/waterprojects/pages/waterprojects.aspx

[5] Philip Ball (2005) *The March of Reason*, p. 191, Critical Mass Arrow Books.

[6] The reference to Hive Mind relates to socially intelligent behaviour evident in bee hives and ant colonies where individuals work in concert to achieve a larger goal.

[7] Policy Research Corporation + MRAG EU Commission Maritime Affairs, The economics of climate change adaptation in EU coastal areas, (p.2 Country (Ireland) Overview and Assessment). http://ec.europa.eu/maritimeaffairs/climate_change_en.html. "Were all the ice on Greenland to melt, a process that would likely take many centuries to millennia, sea level would go up by roughly 7 meters"; http://www.climate.org/topics/sea-level/index.htm.

[8] Nassim Taleb, ibid., p. 11.

[9] Liam Collins (2005) *Sunday Independent*, 16 January.

[10] Franklin D. Roosevelt, 18 October 1931.

Biographical note

Noel J. Brady received his diploma in architecture from Dublin Institute of Technology (DipArch, 1985) and a Masters degree from the Massachusetts Institute of Technology (SMArchS, 1989). After a stint in architectural offices in London, the US and Ireland, he established NJBA Architecture and Urbanism. He also is involved with teaching at the School of Architecture and Urban Design at DIT and has written extensively on architectural and urban design matters.

12

Learning from Failure, Building on Success

James Pike
On Housing

In trying to envision where housing and sustainable communities will be in 2050, I will look at what has happened in the last forty years; then I will examine the best of current ideas and policies to learn how to avoid past mistakes and build on successes. I will then describe where housing and communities might be in 2050.

The last forty years

The last forty years have seen a major improvement in housing in the city. In 1974 a film called *Capital City 1974–1975* and sponsored by the Labour Party showed the horrifying extent of dereliction in the city. The availability of the motor car to a wider market meant that the better off were fleeing to the suburbs, leaving the city within the canal ring to council tenants and rooming houses for students and other singles. The population within the canals had shrunk from a peak of 250,000 to 75,000. It proved impossible to attract any private housing back into the city until the late 1980s and then it was the shoe-box sized flat which replaced the rooming house. The construction of all new housing in the centre was left to Dublin Corporation which continued the work started in the 1930s of clearing the slums and re-housing much of the population in new flat developments, or moving them to new terraced housing in Crumlin and elsewhere. In the 1960s the high rise Ballymun development was built on the northern outskirts of Dublin, but the experiment was soon abandoned, and housing on the fringes reverted to vast estates of repetitive two storey family housing.

In the early 1970s a major change took place in city centre local authority housing as a result of a campaign by the Liberties Association; mainly three storey terraces to match existing traditional forms were built, changing to denser duplex developments in the 1990s. After 2000, Part V of the Planning and Development Act meant that most social housing was integrated into private development, much of it high rise. This Part V legislation, which was intended to integrate social and affordable housing into the fabric of new development, has major social benefits, but will need high levels of planning, design and management, and is now under review.

By the 1990s the vast local authority family housing ghettos were generating huge social problems and were in physical decline. Ballymun was the first scheme to be tackled; a new masterplan was in place by 1997 with the high-rise blocks being replaced mainly by three storey housing, designed by many different architects, to a slightly higher density than the high rise. While the social balance is improved, public housing is still in the ratio of about 70:30. After 2000 a start was made on inner city regeneration, with Fatima Mansions being replaced by a public private partnership (PPP) high rise scheme with 50 per cent private housing. Since 2008, the financial crash has led to the collapse of several PPP regeneration projects and the need to find new funding structures. Progress in the regeneration of the inner city is dependent on the redevelopment of the many Dublin City Council housing schemes with their social and physical problems, but the use of the PPP model for redevelopment has unfortunately proved severely flawed.

In the private sector development was concentrated in the suburbs with mostly semi-detached low-density estates. Some apartment developments were built, mainly in the inner suburbs for 'empty nesters'.

The economic boom and population surge of the 1990s generated new ideas for denser private developments, led by the regeneration of the Docklands and a number of city centre and inner suburban schemes. On the urban fringes, masterplans were also prepared for higher density projects, mainly close to rail stations or later the new Luas Lines. Development, however, did not keep up with demand, which led to rapidly rising prices, forcing people further and further afield and helping to create the current situation where the population of Dublin has grown from 720,000 in the 1970s, to 1,200,000 in the conurbation and 1,700,000 in the region in an area as large as Los Angeles.

The spread of the commuter belt did encourage more people to live in the city centre and inner suburbs, and by 2010 the population of the inner city had recovered to 130,000. Families with children returned to the inner suburbs and schools were extended and new schools built. It has been proved that good housing can be provided at higher densities, and Dublin City Council has set much higher space standards. An aspect of urban housing which has grown over the last two decades is infill housing, particularly in mews homes, and the extension and refurbishment of existing houses, much of it designed by architects to a high standard. Some new apartment schemes have been built to a high standard but the general standard is not high enough, and this has been exposed in unfinished estates around the city and country. While a higher proportion of apartments has been built, 68 per cent of the stock are family houses, whereas only 37.5 per cent of households are families with children. It is also apparent across the city that there are many houses in multiple occupation which are a blight to the environment as, for example, gardens are not maintained. There is also the problem of under-occupation, as empty nesters remain in large family homes, causing a declining population in mature suburbs.

These problems are in part due to poor design, but also to poor management structures for high density developments. The Multi Unit Developments Act 2011 has addressed some of the problems. However, the financial structure of most developments, with owner occupiers in a minority as investors rent out most of the units to tenants who have no say in the management of the project and the owners little interest means management remains an issue. Negative equity is now seen across all sectors but particularly in the 'buy to let' investment property sector. Normal ratios of rent-to-value were left far behind in the years to 2008, and indeed land values have been at the core of the property bubble and subsequent bust. The price of land was over 50 per cent of the price of the average dwelling in Dublin at the peak, compared to a 15 per cent average in European cities.

The outer suburbs present similar problems with local authority estates, but also across much private housing as densities are too low to create sustainable communities and lead to considerable car dependency. Regenerating the suburbs is probably an even greater challenge than inner city regeneration.

What are the key issues, and what are the best policies?

Over the last decade two key issues have emerged and were clearly set out in the following quotations. The National Economic and Social Council (NESC) in its 2004 report, *Housing in Ireland, Performance and Policy*, stated in the introduction to its conclusions and recommendations:

> The Council is particularly concerned about two issues: the quality of the neighbourhoods, villages, towns and cities being constructed in Ireland, and the provision of social and affordable housing. Two features of the overall argument should be highlighted at the outset.
>
> First, the instruments that can address these concerns are to be found in the areas of planning, urban design, infrastructural investment, land management and public service delivery, rather than in manipulating tax instruments to alter the supply or demand for land or housing. Second, the Council rejects the idea that a greater quantity of housing must be at the expense of quality development. The Council believes that increased quantity and better quality can be complementary and, indeed, mutually reinforcing. This requires a clear vision of the kind of high quality, integrated, sustainable neighbourhoods that are worth building.
>
> The magnitude of significance of this challenge needs to be recognised. It bears comparison with two other great challenges that Ireland faced and met in the past half century – the opening of the economy in the early 1960s and the creation of a new economy through partnership in the mid-1980s.

In parallel to this statement, Dr. Risteard Mulcahy, the author of *Improving with Age* in an article in *The Irish Times* stated:

> While smoking may be on the wane [through cultural change], we now have a new and serious increase of obesity in the population. . . . To succeed [in tackling obesity] we must understand the fundamental reasons at the basis of the metabolic syndrome. These are

changing eating and physical exercise habits. . . . All has changed over the past 50 years. Most adults have cars; the bicycle is little used; and walking as part of daily life is discouraged by poor urban, suburban and rural planning and by safety and security considerations. Children are particularly disadvantaged by poor walking and cycling facilities in our new suburbs, despite the recommendation in the 1995 report of the Lord Mayor's Commission on Cycling that all new suburbs should be provided with safe cycling tracks. Our suburban sprawl and long commuting distances are serious disincentives to an active life.

The challenges of cultural change and combating obesity emphasise the importance of creating sustainable communities and a city wide environment which encourages everybody to take exercise for sheer enjoyment as well their principal way to get to most activities, thus reducing the car to occasional use. The need to reduce car usage will be reinforced by the emerging oil crises. These are herculean tasks in such a sprawling, low density city, and retrofitting our existing suburbia is particularly challenging. If we follow the goals set out by the Dublin City Architect, Ali Grehan, we might, however, be setting out on the right track:

A perennial challenge facing every city and neighbourhood is fragmentation – social, cultural and physical. Ghettoisation is not just the preserve of the poor; other sectors of society reach out for self-contained 'illusory safe havens'. It is important for the health of the city that, as Jane Jacobs, author of *The Death and Life of Great American Cities* (1961), put it, 'people want the untidiness of houses close to workplaces, shops next to flats and rich next to poor'. Jacob's philosophy succinctly describes [Dublin] City Council's approach to urban renewal today and underpins the Government Policy on Architecture 2009–2015. This policy places an emphasis on sustainable development through good urban design and quality modern architecture that respects architectural heritage in a holistic and integrated manner. The availability of good homes, attractive to families of all sizes and backgrounds, is of fundamental importance in any city and this issue will be a central theme in Dublin's bid to host World Design Capital in 2014.

There is a need to set up criteria for achieving high quality urban development and designing the very diverse range of homes and housing development required. The Department of the Environment has published in recent years several excellent guidance documents, including *Planning Guidelines on Sustainable Residential Development in Urban Areas* (2008), accompanied by an *Urban Design Manual*, which will be followed by *Guidance on Local Area Plans*. These documents now have to be incorporated into all city and county development plans under the Planning and Development Act of 2010.

These documents have covered the external aspects of all housing. The Department have also issued detailed Guidelines and particularly minimum sizes for apartments, and many local authorities including Dublin City Council have adopted their own higher standards for apartments. I would suggest that there is also a strong case for greater investigation of the dwelling itself and apartment buildings, for all urban contexts.

History has proven that there are unlikely to be many new forms of dwelling or building complexes, so we can achieve much by studying existing models, particularly from those countries that enjoy a higher density urban life. New immigrants provide a much higher proportion of the inner urban population than their actual number, and lessons can continue to be learnt there and new development types tried. Buildings are for people and housing is where they will spend a high proportion of their day; these buildings will form a base for their lives whether as families, looser households or individuals. This always needs to be kept in mind when designing housing. Most of the housing we live in is not designed specifically for the actual occupants, and very little consultation or indeed research has been done into the real needs of potential occupants. We either work on a fairly precise set of standards in public housing, or what has been selling well recently in the private sector. The client and their brief is the key element in all building and yet currently in housing we are either faced by a rigid rulebook, or a very arbitrary set of historical precedents. These are further constrained by an expanding body of legislation from town planning to health and safety.

The last body of well researched recommendations on the real needs of families in housing in this part of the world was *Homes for Today and Tomorrow* published by the British Ministry for Housing and Local Government in 1962. While many of its recommendations are still valid, the world has changed dramatically since then. In 1960, 30 per cent of all households were reckoned to be of one or two persons, while recent surveys in London and other European cities have calculated that 75 per cent of households are now in that category.

Consumer satisfaction

The Irish consumer suffers from a severe lack of information when faced with acquiring a dwelling. There is a welter of information on mortgages and finance and tax but there is no reliable information for analysing the performance of the dwelling – how much it will cost to run, how it will adapt to changing household requirements, external costs such as access to jobs, schools, shops, recreation and leisure.

In 2004, the (now defunct) Commission for Architecture and the Built Environment in the UK published a *House Buyers Guide* and such a guide is being prepared here by the Royal Institute of the Architects in Ireland. The UK Guide included a comprehensive range of issues related to the dwelling itself and its location relative to the activities of all household members. The Irish guide needs to build on the UK guide to help households analyse their needs and ambitions and ask all the relevant, functional, financial and aspirational questions.

Finance and management

The best planning and design will not be successful unless we sort out the financial problems related in particular to property development. For example, how do we control volatile land values and property speculation; and how do we find the best models for funding and managing developments to provide affordable housing for all households?

A Site Value Tax (SVT), which is on the agenda for the current Programme for Government (2011), is one measure that would have a huge impact on housing and the provision of all infrastructure, physical and social. SVT would encourage the optimum development of all zoned land, and discourage the zoning of land not ready for development. It has proved successful in controlling land prices and avoiding property bubbles, and its introduction would mean the removal of upfront costs, such as development levies and stamp duty and recover the cost of new infrastructure over at least twenty years. SVT would encourage householders to improve their properties and realise the full potential of sites in well located areas. The alternative property tax, based on the full value of the buildings, would discourage such improvements.

The introduction of SVT as the main source of local government income would mean that local authorities could plan new infrastructure, and sell it to their constituents on the basis of the benefits it will bring. The cost will be borne by the existing residents who benefit as well as the new ones who, at present, carry the whole cost.

A second measure, which would impact on both the financial and social pillars, is Community Land Partnership or Equity Partnership. The current collapse of the housing market and substantial negative equity and mortgage debt of many householders has exposed the faults in our current method of delivering housing to rent. There is a serious need for additional provision of rental accommodation, particularly in Dublin where private apartment rentals are already increasing, and the demand for social and/or affordable housing has grown substantially.

Dublin also needs an alternative to the current freehold sale and mortgage model which drove many people to borrow at unaffordable levels. But the problems with multi-unit developments are not just financial. Investors who buy individual apartments and rent them on short-term leases have little interest in the management of such developments, and their tenants have no say at all. From personal experience I know that owner occupiers are usually the only participants in management companies. The investors have to re-let the dwelling, usually on an annual basis, with potential voids and repairs and maintenance and agents' fees.

Another major problem with public or private developments is their rebuilding or redevelopment when they become obsolete. Currently, each house or apartment is owned freehold, and many local authority estates have been sold to the tenants. I have found over the years that bringing a large number of owners together is an almost impossible task. These developments are facing huge maintenance bills. The current problem with 'ghost estates' and uncompleted developments also need solutions which are difficult to achieve in current financial markets, and finally we need to advance rapidly with regeneration projects for crime-ridden urban areas.

All is not doom and gloom though. There are two alternative solutions which could be used. The first is that a development company be set up to let and manage the development, which can then sell shares to investors rather than individual apartments. The investor would not therefore be involved in the management of the development or re-letting apartments, but would benefit from the rise in market value. The amount that can be invested is flexible, and the sale of shares is simple and cost effective compared to selling individual dwellings. An occupier can also be an investor.

The second alternative is the Equity Partnership. The Equity Partnership or Community Land Partnership (CLP) proposed by Chris Cook of the Nordic Enterprise Trust has been developed by a small group of Irish professionals to fit the Irish situation. It offers an alternative path to property ownership and a stake in the management of developments for all tenants. It also presents a relatively stable and secure development model which should be attractive to pension and other investment funds. It shares some features with current tenant-purchase schemes and rent-to-buy schemes but provides a much more flexible framework. A community land partnership has four key members:

- Custodian – holds the freehold of the land in perpetuity on behalf of the community

- Occupier – the community of individuals which occupy the properties on the land

- Investor – the consortium of individuals and enterprises who invest money and/or money's worth (such as the value of the land) in the CLP

- Developer/Operator – who provides development expertise and manages the CLP once the development is complete.

So, how would these models work? A developer, local authority or Government agency wants to build a housing development on their land. They set up a Community Land Partnership or an Equity Partnership. The custodian body is set up and the land is transferred to this body in perpetuity. Money is borrowed and a contractor appointed to build the development. When the development is completed, a manager is appointed to manage the development, and this manager is responsible to the custodian on behalf of the investors and the subsequent occupiers.

Financially, when the development is complete the occupiers pay an agreed rental to cover the 'capital rental'. The capital rental is charged for the use of the capital that has been invested in the development. The capital is calculated on the current value of the land plus the cost of completing the development. The occupiers also pay an additional annual sum for the provision of maintenance/depreciation and related management/quality control of the development (both necessary for maintaining the capital value of the overall project). If an occupier pays more than the affordable rental he invests automatically in 'equity shares' and thereby acquires a stake in the property in which they live. Once they have acquired 100 per cent, the income which they derive from their investment cancels out the capital rental they are due to pay. The major drivers of the development of housing and communities need to be:

1. The upgrading of our existing stock and high standard for new stock

2. Reducing car usage for energy saving, health and quality of life

3. A closer match of housing to the demographic reality of smaller households

4. Better structures for the management and financing of housing and mixed use development

5. Greater stability of land prices.

If we follow these drivers, then we can achieve major progress in creating much improved housing and sustainable communities by 2050.

The future

Future scenarios for the Dublin region in 2050 range from an incoherent urban sprawl much larger than that of Los Angeles to a set of interconnected urban communities creating a great city region connecting Waterford to Larne, as selected as the best option by the Gateways Study, undertaken by the Futures Academy at Dublin Institute of Technology on the behalf of the Urban Forum. If we adopt the right policies as we rebuild and develop our economy, such a city region would have the potential to compete with the best cities in Europe and the world, on economy and quality of life.

Assuming we aspire towards the optimum goal, the Dublin of 2050 will be the major core of this urban region with a contiguous population approaching two million but occupying an area not much greater than at present, with the city within the canals returning to around 200,000 and the population of the existing townships and suburbs intensifying by 50 per cent to 1.5 million (still a very low density), and the balance coming in contiguous rail-based expansion in Swords, Dunboyne, Leixlip and Bray. Individual communities will be mainly based on existing ones, but all well served by public transport, with new rail-based communities planned on the Adamstown and Clonburris model. There will be a move away from separate industrial and business parks to a greater integration of employment with communities and new and existing town centres, with a much more flexible approach to zoning.

These mixed use communities will mean that at least 50 per cent of employment will be within walking or cycling distance, while all schools, convenience shopping, primary care clinics and other services will also be within walking distance.

Proposed density increases will only raise the average suburban semi-detached housing estate from 8 to 12 to the acre. Such density increases will be easily achieved by redeveloping corner sites and some infill sites to small apartment buildings or shared housing for individuals to balance the community in line with the drop in ratio of families with children to 30 per cent and providing for empty nesters to downsize locally. This has already begun in some suburbs and needs to be encouraged.

If the housing stock is rebalanced towards the current demographic profile, then most construction activity over the next forty years needs to be concentrated on conversion or adaption of existing stock and the building of new stock for the one and two person household, particularly for the significant increase forecast in the numbers of 'empty nesters'.

The completion of the many regeneration projects would provide more housing of a much higher quality in the inner city and encourage the return of more families to the inner core and suburbs and the improvement and extension of much of the existing terraced housing. Even the Georgian core would see a substantial conversion back to housing. There would still be a major requirement for redevelopment of our poorer housing stock, particularly the outer suburbs, but as has been shown, much of the improvement for family housing would be achieved by upgrading and extension of the existing stock.

The adoption of the Equity Partnership model would also encourage greater social involvement and better integration with office and other employment uses into the community. It would also greatly reduce the element of mortgage finance and general indebtedness of householders, and lead to more stable communities which are better managed and maintained.

The introduction of Site Value Tax and other measures would stabilise land prices, and remove a large element of speculation in housing development. This would encourage the trends listed above. The alternative property tax would discourage those trends.

There are still a number of under used or underdeveloped sites, even in the inner suburbs, particularly religious lands. Many existing houses on large plots can be redeveloped or in-filled. Examples of such developments are Mount Saint Anne's in Milltown, 120 Howth Road in Clontarf, or St Anne's, Northbrook Road in Ranelagh, which achieve densities of 75 to 100 dwellings per hectare and provide a greater mix of dwellings types and diverse uses in suburban areas, and will contribute to higher densities overall. (See photographs below and on the following pages.)

The housing group or block

Densities of up to 24 to the acre for family houses can be built to a high standard as can be seen from the inner suburbs, where the terraced house is dominant. This should become the main type of new development and much of the infill. New models of low rise apartment may emerge, but there are many good existing models such as the Dublin City Council two-storey sheltered housing model, and the atrium block with its strong elements of social integration. These dwelling types could be mixed to create balanced groups, with careful design of private open space and shared open space to cater for all ages.

As the use of cars diminishes as the means of access to work, school, and so forth, car-pooling could increase for evening or weekend use. The result will be a public realm not dominated by the car and the creation of the home zone as a safe environment for children.

The dwelling

The development of the dwelling over the next forty years will be gradual and the major changes will be focused on alternatives for the provision for smaller households. Ideas will be developed from student housing with its shared facilities, and the general improvement in the provision of shared facilities for the larger housing schemes. The increasing focus on extension and adaption of existing houses will produce many creative ideas which will be used in new housing. The use of natural daylight to improve the quality of indoor spaces, and solar gain to contribute greater energy saving, will lead to more living space being positioned on upper floors. Bedrooms don't need high daylight levels. Double height spaces and courtyards will also bring light and ventilation to interior spaces in deeper planned dwellings.

Conclusion

I hope I have demonstrated that if we follow policies which are already on the agenda we have every chance of creating a city in 2050 with some of the best housing and communities in the world, particularly if we have learnt from our recent and ongoing market collapse, and avoid the worst of inevitable world financial crises of 2025 and 2043. However my experience as an architect involved in a practice for 47 years has been that we often make the wrong decisions. The failure to bring in the recommendations of the Kenny Report in the 1970s was a key one, as was the adoption of wrong planning policies, particularly in recent years. The decisions we have to make in the immediate future will have a major impact on the long term vision I have set out, in particular the selection of SVT as opposed to an alternative property tax. Society needs to wean itself off the imperative of freehold homeownership and particularly the dependency on the mortgage. We have created great towns and communities in the past, which have been severely damaged by the car. We are beginning to learn how to recreate them, and this presents probably our greatest challenge over the next forty years.

Biographical Note

James Pike was a founder partner in Delany MacVeigh and Pike, which was set up in 1964. This practice evolved into O'Mahony Pike in 1992. He has played a major role over more than forty years in urban planning and housing in Ireland, but has also been involved in major educational, office, retail, hotel and industrial projects, and in projects in the UK and North Africa. He has played a continuing role in the RIAI since the 1960s culminating in the presidency for 2006–2007. He is currently Chairman of the Irish Architecture Foundation and a founding member of the Urban Forum. He contributes to the many urban design projects in the practice, and a number of architectural projects, and has promoted a number of research projects with the Urban Forum and on sustainability issues with DIT and UCD since the 1980s.

120 Howth Road, Clontarf

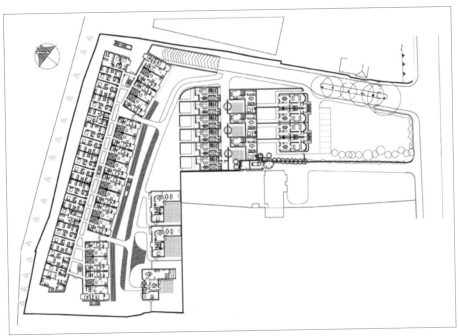

120 Howth Road, Clontarf

St Anne's, Northbrook Road, Ranelagh

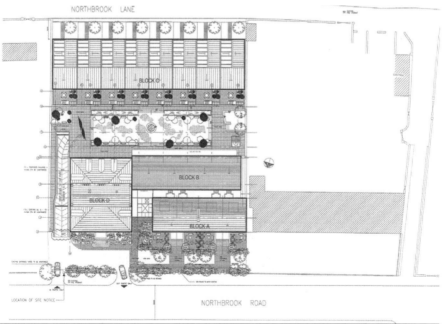

St Anne's, Northbrook Road, Ranelagh

13

Not Written by an Economist

Conor Skehan
On Economy

Preamble

Why is this contribution about the future of Dublin's economy not being written by an economist?

There are two reasons. The first reason is very simple – economists deal with facts and there are no facts about the future. The second reason is that the future comes into being because of alterations in how we respond to changing circumstances. Our responses, based on our ambitions and our fears, change because of how we feel and feelings are changeable and very difficult to predict. Our ambitions and fears, about ourselves and our communities, arise from what we feel to be important – our values.

Values change over time both for society and for individuals. At the foundation of the State, two-thirds of Ireland lived in rural areas and less than one-fifth lived in Dublin; now two-thirds of the population live in urban areas and two-fifths live in the Dublin region. Furthermore, Ireland's wealth[1] has doubled in just the last twenty years. In general, the values of a society change the most when it undergoes transitions from being dominantly rural to being dominantly urban, and also when it becomes wealthier. On the basis of this information alone it is reasonable to assume that Ireland's value systems are changing significantly and rapidly, and that they will do so for another generation, meaning that past or recent trends are likely to be a very poor guide to future values or behaviour.

Economics has, rightly, been compared to meteorology, describing how and why weather changes and using this knowledge to make short-term forecasts based on current trends. But meteorologists only describe and explain the weather – they cannot make it happen. Economics is also a descriptive discipline concerned with explaining the past and the present – with little predictive capacity and no power to either make prosperity happen, nor to prevent calamity. Markets and economies rise and fall on the tide of sentiment that cannot be predicted or controlled.

The long-term prosperity of places only arises when intrinsic geographic endowments are enhanced by the ambition and enterprise of policy or entrepreneurs. Ambition is a 'sentiment' of a sort that can be enabled or retarded by economic instruments but which can never be initiated by them.

Finally, we need to be mindful of how we use words. When we ask, 'has Dublin got a future?', what we mean is whether it is likely to be successful by having a prosperous economy. This contribution is about how Dublin's economy can plan to succeed. Failing to plan is planning to fail.

Writing about the future of Dublin will, therefore, begin by trying to anticipate the values and resultant activities of the city's next generation. This task requires a knowledge of how to accommodate changing future needs, which is the dictionary definition of 'to plan'. We need a holistic picture of what, where, why and how the needs of the next generation of Dubliner's will be met.

For these reasons this survey of the future examines how changing future values (sentiment) may change the future needs of Dubliners, which in turn will change what, where, why and how they do it. A simpler term for Dublin's future, 'what, where, why and how' is the Future Economy of Dublin, and that's what this contribution examines.

No future unless . . .

Dublin has no future unless we start to see and accept two things. First and foremost, Dublin, like all cities, is an economy – a collection of enterprises – not a collection of buildings, because real estate is merely a symptom of economic activity. Secondly, Dublin is rapidly becoming a city region which is an economy. It is no longer a place, no longer a big town.

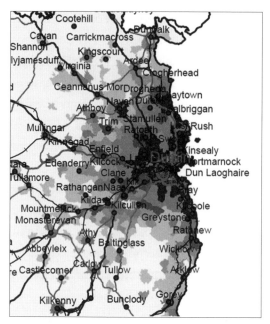

Figure 1: The workforce of Dublin City. In 2006, around 25 per cent of Dublin's workforce of c. 400,000 travelled from an area that stretched from Louth to Wicklow in the east and Cavan to Carlow in the west. The settlements within this area constitute the 'outer city' of the Dublin City region. This is the principle engine of the Irish economy. By 2030 it is estimated that this region will be home to almost two-thirds of the national population. (Source: Central Statistics Office (2009) A Profile of the Working Population of Large Towns)

Dublin is undergoing the transition from being a large town to becoming a regional economy (Figure 1). Some writers[2] refer to this as the Dublin Functional Urban Region (FUR). Completely different opportunities and challenges occur as settlements pass through this threshold of size. The future of Dublin is the future of the region's economy. Only if we make plans to anticipate, accept and accommodate these changes will Dublin's economy have a successful future.

Cities often decline because they fail to notice or adapt to new realities. For instance, some continue to imagine that Dublin is still a city based on an economy of big department stores and offices located near O'Connell Street, while the reality is that the centre of gravity of primary economic activity – in manufacturing, commerce and retail – is already located six kilometres away on either side of the M50.

Planning fails when it prepares for what is believed should happen, instead of preparing for what is most likely to happen. The purpose of this contribution is to draw attention to what is likely to happen to the future economy of Dublin in the hope that adequate and appropriate preparations can be put in place to gain the most opportunities and advantages from these changes – while simultaneously avoiding as many problems as possible.

Most nations have aspirations for their cities to prosper, to increase the wealth of their nation. Ireland, on the other hand, currently fears and seeks to control the growth of Dublin, its main city. The National Spatial Strategy (NSS) wants to ensure that 'a greater share of economic activity takes place outside the Greater Dublin Area', arguing that 'without an NSS, three-quarters of the country's projected population increase of half a million people, or possibly significantly higher than that, over the next twenty years is likely to happen in or near the Greater Dublin Area, making congestion even more difficult to deal with. At the same time, many other parts of the country would remain less developed.'

This contribution will attempt to counter this approach by showing that Dublin's future economic growth and success as a city region will be critical to the future well-being of the entire nation. This growth will first need to be accepted, accommodated and enhanced if all of Ireland's regions are to prosper. This will entail dealing with problems like congestion and housing through effective planning, not trying to avoid it by seeking to suppress the growth in the way that the NSS does.

It is proposed here that Dublin is at a crossroads of its growth and economic development and that it needs to quickly adopt new approaches, especially in relation to governance, if it is to realise its fullest potential. It will also propose that new planning approaches should give priority to the 'soft' topics like equality, convenience, culture and amenity which will be needed to attract and sustain a modern economy for Dublin's future.

The economy of cities

> There are some sorts of industry, even of the lowest kind, which can be carried on nowhere but in a great town. A porter, for example, can find employment and subsistence in no other place. A village is by much too narrow a sphere for him; even an ordinary market-town is scarce large enough to afford him constant occupation. – Adam Smith, *An Inquiry into the Nature and Causes of the Wealth of Nations* (1776)

Cities are the 'engines' of modern national and regional economies, particularly for rapidly growing 'primate cities'[3] such as Dublin that are critical for the whole national economy. The increasing size of cities matter too because they increase income per capita compared to the rest of the nation as they grow. The range of opportunities and the resultant quantity of enterprise and innovation also increase with the size of the settlement and the scale of markets. Furthermore, as earnings increase costs fall because of economies of scale, which means that cities, as wealth creating engines, are very efficient at using energy, capital and natural resources.

Cities attract and sustain economic activity by providing concentrations of opportunity and convenience and, when successfully managed, have higher levels of prosperity that are transferred to the rest of the region. Unsuccessful cities do the opposite and become a burden for other areas. So the future of Dublin's economy is of national significance if it fails or succeeds and, as such, should be a national priority. The economies of cities are relatively fragile and they can fail through neglect, mismanagement, misfortune or a combination of these factors.

For example, in 1950 Detroit had a population similar to that of Dublin today of around 1.8 million; it has now fallen to nearly half that because of the decline of the motor industry in that area. Similar falls have been recorded in many other cities in the US and throughout the EU as a result of a failure to plan for future economic change, growth and renewal. So how do cities avoid failure?

The recipe for failure is easily summarised. Through ignorance or neglect, a once successful city fails to note and adapt to a change of its economic foundation and loses jobs and revenue. This leads to under-provision of physical and social services which gives rise to poverty and dereliction, which in turn leads to dysfunctional services (congestion and pollution), crime and ugliness. These factors combine to make the city unattractive to further re-investment and unable to recover without substantial external assistance.

The recipe for globally successful modern cities is also fairly simple. First the area needs to have amenities, services and opportunities of sufficient standard to provide an internationally distinctive and attractive quality of life. These then retain and attract higher concentrations of well educated and creative people and the institutions that sustain them. In turn, these institutions and people then become the resource that attracts and sustains the best and most successful enterprises – ideally in 'clusters' – which provide and perpetuate the revenue to sustain and further improve these attractive conditions in a virtuous circle.

The amenities required include the range, quality, convenience and affordability of homes, be they apartments or houses; they include the quality of the surroundings of these homes, as measured by safe and convenient access to shops, amenities, schools, recreation and public transport. Services are required to be internationally comparable in standards of health, education and culture for residents – as well as high quality, high capacity global connectivity, intellectual, electronic and personal.

Notice that these attributes prioritise the needs of individuals over corporate economic activities such as manufacturing or business, because the 'raw material' of modern enterprises are the well-educated individuals who are fussy and have choices – international choices – about where they live. Note also that the recipe for success does not include 'job creation': instead it focuses on creating the conditions that will attract and sustain enterprise. In a market economy governments and other public agencies do not create jobs – only entrepreneurs do that.

The 'betterment' of the lives of individuals will, generally, ensure the provision of systems that will deliver the high quality services (communications, power, transportation, waste and water) that are required for enterprise. In a modern economy these can be provided by entrepreneurs drawn by the opportunities presented by urban concentrations of wealth. Once these are in place a proportion of their capacity can be directed in the quantities and to the locations required for economic activity. But first let us survey the patterns of Dublin's economy and examine how that is managed.

The economy of Dublin: employment and income

In 2006, Dublin City's working population, as calculated by the Central Statistics Office, was 442,833, of whom 104,865 travelled into Dublin to work. Business and retail were the biggest employment sectors and Dublin also had the highest percentage of jobs in these sectors of all large towns in Ireland. It is very important to note that outside of 'Dublin City' as defined above there are a further 200,000 jobs in the region. In the same period the entire working population of Cork city was 84,122 people, indicating the importance of learning to view the whole region as Ireland's largest and most important economy.

Currently, about two-thirds of Dublin's jobs are in the private sector such as manufacturing, trade, tourism, financial and other services, while public sector employment accounts for a further third in administration, education, health, social and community services. About a quarter of the city's jobs involve attending to Dublin's health, educational and social needs, while a further 10 per cent of Dublin's public service jobs involve national and government agencies.

Private sectors jobs are the foundation of the national economy, contributing around half of national GDP. The Gross Value Added (GVA) of Dublin is nearly twice as high as the lowest area in Ireland, and is one-third more than the national average. GVA is an important indicator of whether an area is contributing or being subsidised within a larger economy. Dublin also performs very well in comparison with the EU27 where the index of GVA per person is almost twice that of the EU norm.[4]

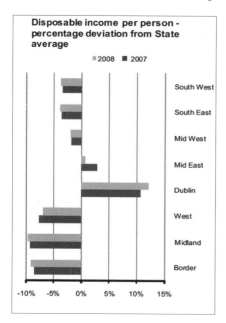

Less than 5 per cent of the workforce serve Dublin's hotel and restaurant sector, used by 60 per cent of all overseas visitors to Ireland (over 3.5 million annual visitors spend over one-third of Ireland's tourism revenue in Dublin). These same workers also provide catering and accommodation to Dublin's working population.

Dublin's status as an internationally popular destination for younger mobile workers has also helped to make it an attractive destination for businesses location in sectors such as financial services, where the majority of the country's 25,000 IFSC employees are located. Other similar sectors are emerging such as the 'cluster' of social networking companies in the south-east of the city centre. The city is also home to numerous individuals and institutions dedicated to many specialist activities in the professions, services, arts, crafts which, like Adam Smith's porter's trade that 'can be carried on nowhere but in a great town ...'.

Table 1: Regional Income Variation. Of the eight regional authorities, the Dublin region had the highest disposable income per person in 2008. At €25,337 per person, this was 12 per cent higher than the state figure of €22,165. The Mid-East was the only other region authority area with an average disposable income higher than the state average.

The economy of Dublin: spatial distribution

Dublin's economic activities have marked spatial patterns (Figure 2): over one-quarter of all jobs in manufacturing, wholesale, transportation and storage are predominantly located to the west and north of the city, while public services, retail and business are located towards the centre. It is noteworthy that public sector employment occupies the most expensive downtown locations, while the productive manufacturing, wholesale and much of the retail occupy the less expensive and less well serviced peripheral areas.

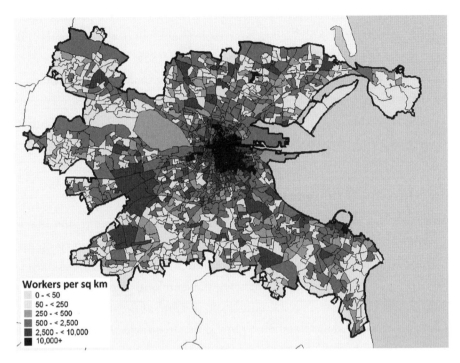

Workers per sq km
- 0 - < 50
- 50 - < 250
- 250 - < 500
- 500 - < 2,500
- 2,500 - < 10,000
- 10,000+

Figure 2: Dublin City's pattern of Employment: Notice the emerging extensive concentrations of new employment in the environs of the M50 to the west of the traditional city centre. Public sector employment is more concentrated in the centre while manufacturing, trade and newer offices (and associated commercial rates) are being attracted to the edges which are less expensive and less congested. (Source: Central Statistics Office (2009) A Profile of the Working Populations of Large Towns)

Dublin is already exhibiting many, but not all, of the ingredients that make a city successful. There is a good mixture of types of enterprise, ranging from high-technology manufacturing, and global software and financial service companies which co-exist with a thriving tourism and conference sector that is beginning to 'cross-sell' with an improving and increasingly cosmopolitan cultural and social milieu.

The economy of Dublin: current economic management

The word 'economy' is derived from the Greek word *oikonomia* – one who manages a household. It is particularly applicable to a city because it too is the management of a particular place, in this instance a collection of households. Dublin clearly has an economy. Despite occupying less than 10 per cent of the national territory it is estimated to contribute about half of the national GDP – yet it is not managed as a single special place. Government departments manage the national economy and the local and regional authorities manage the infrastructure and services of the Dublin region, yet nobody specifically manages this highly localised economy by collecting and redistributing wealth in a planned and coherent way for the betterment of all of the region's citizens.

The economy of Dublin: current planning

Worse yet, the government's planning policy toward Dublin's region is one of containment and reduction of influence, expressed by the National Spatial Strategy, so that 'a greater share of economic activity must take place outside the Greater Dublin Area', and 'enhancing the competitiveness of the Greater Dublin Area (GDA), so that it continues to perform at the international level as a driver of national development'. How is this to be achieved? In Orwellian doublespeak terms the NSS continues by proposing 'physically consolidating the growth of the metropolitan area, i.e., Dublin City and suburbs'. The NSS rationale for this plan – to grow by not growing – is that the growth of Dublin 'created acute pressures in areas like housing supply and traffic congestion', instead of recognising this as a result of a fundamental failure of the planning system to anticipate and provide for adequate housing and transportation.

The economy of Dublin: future management?

This policy vacuum is well recognised, even by official agencies. One of the principle 'Projects' identified by the Dublin Regional Authority's 2009 *Economic Development Action Plan for the Dublin City Region* is to 'lobby for the inclusion of Dublin specific policy and associated funding stream in the National Spatial Strategy and the National Development Plan'. The fact that an official body pleads for the need to plan and fund the engine of national economic growth is, surely, evidence of the need for a radical change of outlook?

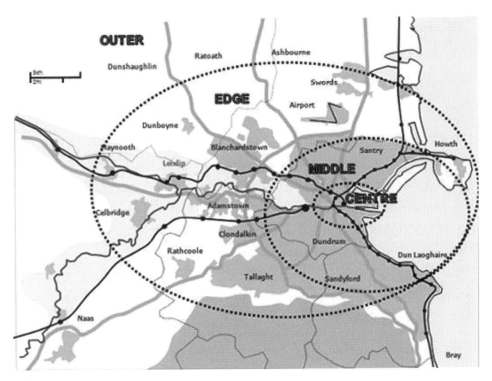

Figure 3. The Four Cities of Dublin are beginning to emerge as the area increasingly behaves as a regional economy instead of a contiguous settlement. The economic centres are concentrated in the Centre City and the Edge City while the Outer City and the Middle City offer a choice of residential amenities. Each of these areas have different needs and different futures. Wise use and management that respects, enables and enhances these differences will significantly improve the opportunities for the prosperity of Dublin's future economy. (Map: Dónall Ó'Ceallaigh, 2011)

Which Dublin?

A marked spatial patterning is emerging as Dublin's economic and social activities cluster into four areas, each of which is a separate type of city, referred to here as the centre, middle, edge and outer cities of Dublin (Figure 3). This contribution will propose that these areas will become more and more distinctive and, if properly managed, can become the foundations of a vision for the future prosperity because it will facilitate appropriate and effective economic structures to meet the needs and realise the opportunities of each area.

1) The Centre City

Even though this area, lying between the canals, contains the largest concentration of protected structures in Ireland, it is also one of the most dynamic and rapidly transforming areas of Dublin. This is largely because its original role as the location of the biggest and most important institutions, shops and offices is now giving way to a zone of high density specialist shops, cultural institutions, administrative headquarters and urban amenities – such as entertainment venues, restaurants and hotels.

2) Middle City

Ireland's largest contiguous housing area lies between the canals and the environs of the M50. This residential fabric is regularly punctuated by large health and education institutions as well as office and shopping areas, resulting in a wealth of employment areas within easy reach of a wide range of house types and neighbourhood centres. These land-uses co-exist with a number of large functioning habitats in the form of a highly varied coastline, three river systems as well as the edge of an extensive upland system. All of these habitats provide significant recreational amenities for the region.

3) Edge City

The west of this area is the constantly advancing edge of the city consisting of areas of industry, housing, office and light industrial parks, as well sporting and leisure facilities. The eastern boundary also changes, more slowly, as the boundary of the Middle City expands in response to the maturing and integration of fully developed areas. The necklace of major planned urban centres along the M50, consisting of Santry/Ballymun, Blanchardstown, Clondalkin, Tallaght, Stillorgan and Cherrywood, all provide stability, identity and urban services to these emerging urban communities. The area is the heart of Ireland's current and future economy because it contains the densest concentration of Ireland's highest quality and highest capacity utilities. It also has the best and biggest transportation links – by air, rail and road – providing the fastest and least congested access to international markets as well as to the country's largest workforce, reaching communities from Clontarf to Carlow within 40 minutes of the M50.

4) Outer City

Figure 1 showed that Dublin's functional economic area is over 150 kilometres long and around 80 kilometres deep, meaning that no part is further than 40 minutes from the M50's economic centre of gravity. It provides opportunities to choose affordable housing in settlements that offer a high quality of life and a sense of identity within smaller communities. They also offer the urban nuclei for those who choose very low density suburban and rural housing. These outer city communities are creating their own sub-catchment economies supplying local demands for convenience goods and especially for local services such as health, education and local administration. Many of these areas are also rapidly developing cultural, recreational and sporting facilities to meet local needs and express local identity. The Outer City is particularly distinctive because it also contains nationally significant concentrations of agricultural resources – including some of Ireland's most productive soils and most valuable and prestigious stud farms.

The future of economies

Modern societies derive most of their wealth from the productivity, innovation and economic efficiencies of large urban areas, which creates a continuing cycle favouring larger urban areas as the location for new economic activity.[5] In turn, modern urban economies are generally understood[6] to derive the majority of this wealth from the knowledge and service sectors. The sources of this competitive advantage are the quality and productivity of the labour force, as measured by their creativity and entrepreneurship.

Urban economies appear to be most robust when they are based on a wide range of sectors, some of which are innovative, specialist and usually high-value; others which may be in a traditional sector but may derive competitive advantage through branding or productivity; while a significant proportion of the economy of all major cities always arises from the need to maintain, feed and operate the city itself.

The future of Dublin's economy

These contributions are exploring Dublin twenty-odd years in the future. In case that seems like a long way off, remember it is only the equivalent of looking back from today to 1990. From our work in DIT's Futures Academy it appears that changes in values and demography create the biggest and deepest changes (Figure 4). Values drive politics, society and as 'market sentiment', they also drive the cycles of the economy, while demographic trends in the numbers, age and location of the population strongly influence both the future opportunities and challenges of areas.

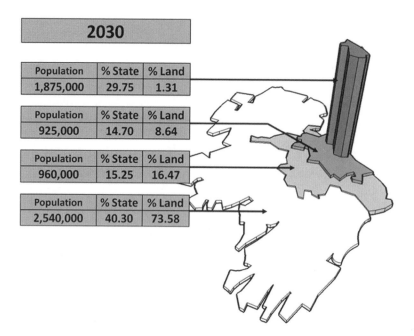

2030		
Population	% State	% Land
1,875,000	29.75	1.31

Population	% State	% Land
925,000	14.70	8.64

Population	% State	% Land
960,000	15.25	16.47

Population	% State	% Land
2,540,000	40.30	73.58

Figure 4: Probable Future Population Distribution. Notice that by 2030 two-thirds of the population will live in the east. The 2011 Census revealed that Leinster already contains over half of Ireland's population (source: Futures Academy DIT (2008) Twice the Size: Imagineering the Future of Irish Gateways)

What do we know about how these two fundamental drivers will affect Dublin's economy? Beginning with demographics, Leinster already contains over half of the State and this pattern will intensify until by 2040 it will contain around three million people or two-thirds of the population. That next generation will have a significantly more urbanised value system than any previous generation of Irish people.

What will the future be like?

The future begins now, in the next minute, hour or day and our ability to know it diminishes as the distance from the present increases. The readily predictable near future is generally a continuation of all existing trends, but the more distant future is shaped by a combination of many unpredictable events with a smaller number of deeper, more slowly changing factors. This makes it difficult to be confident about 'predictions' concerning more than one year ahead. However, the provision of large developments like housing, roads and services takes many years to complete. To overcome this limitation planners, who must try to make provision for society's future needs, employ the use of 'scenarios'.

Scenarios of Dublin in the future

A systematic and practical technique used to characterise future needs is to describe a series of 'scenarios' for the area. These are internally consistent narratives that project how a combination of future events could affect a particular place. The knowledge of the underlying characteristics of a particular area – including its current trends – is used to examine how it would be likely to alter in response to certain 'drivers' of change, such as political, economic or external events. Different types, amounts or combinations of these drivers lead to different future outcomes. These are called 'scenarios' (e.g. a 'high growth scenario' would examine how a small town would cope with the sudden arrival of a large factory requiring many workers and their associated demands). There are many possible scenarios because there are many combinations of drivers: for this reason planners try to make provision to accommodate as many plausibly possible futures as possible. This can present the planner with the dilemma of trying to decide which of the many futures to provide for.

The French *prospectif* approach has been evolved to reduce the range of futures that need to be considered to highlight the best and worst outcomes. This allows policies, plans and projects to be prepared to enable the former and to avoid the latter. Table 2 below illustrates a *prospectif* of the potential future character of each of Dublin's four component areas to provide the context for a subsequent analysis of the future of Dublin's economy.

The likely scenario assumes that changes will be partial,[7] the worst scenario assumes no change, while the best scenario assumes only two significant and major changes:

1. That there will be a recognition of the need to address the issue of Dublin's governance; and
2. That governance will give priority to establishing the highest quality of life for citizens.

The values of this newly urbanised population will drive demands for new services, amenities and systems of governance, all of which will drive profound changes in politics. In twenty years' time, Dublin will need to have an effective regional system of accountable governance that exercises authority over the provision of many public services. The emergence of this system is likely to evolve awkwardly and will involve considerable friction with national institutions – both political and administrative – as they attempt to retain traditional power and structures.

Future Character	Inner City	Middle City	Edge City	Outer City
Likely	Distinctive, Disorganized, Attractive, Expensive, Inconvenient, Uneven, Uncertain, Inefficient	Comfortable, Stable, Dull, Impersonal, Unattractive, Ordinary	Forgettable, Ugly, Busy, Confusing, Cheap, Impersonal, Grimy	Unpredictable, Inefficient, Unconnected, Uneven, Provincial
Best	Memorable, Safe, Prosperous, Desirable, Cultured, Stimulating, Cosmopolitan, Diverse, Beautiful, Exciting, Prestigious, Specialist	Distinctive, Cosy, Comfortable, Secure, Dynamic, Diverse, Attractive, Cultured, Convenient, Confident, Inclusive, Interesting, Fulfilling	Affordable, Practical, Innovative, Specialist, Dynamic, Distinctive, Organised, Efficient, Interesting, Specialist, Prosperous, Funky, Experimental	Innovative, Global, Specialist, Focused, Indigenous, Secure, Distinctive, Branded, Prosperous, Beautiful, Prestigious
Worst	Congested, Unsafe, Inefficient, Unattractive, Expensive, Run-down, Poor, Segregated, Ugly	Mundane, Provincial, Hostile, Inconvenient, Segregated, Divided, Discriminatory	Unsafe, Ugly, Poor, Bleak, Run-down, Polluted, Chaotic, Threatening, Hopeless	Unpredictable Unattractive, Bleak, Disorganised, Wasteful, Chaotic

Table 2. Future Character of the Dublin Region: A prospectif of three scenarios for the region identifies and differentiates the likely characteristics that would emerge in each of Dublin's Four Cities. The best outcome assumes that two critical changes are made. The first recognises that Dublin has changed from being a large town and has become a regional economy that requires management as a regional economy. The second change requires recognition of the need to establish the conditions necessary to attract and sustain the 'raw material' of a modern economy, namely well-educated, creative, ambitious people.

Governance

By 2030 the quality of city governance will be the single most critical determinant of the success or failure of Dublin's and Ireland's economy. Urban governance is a neglected area in Irish public life, unlike mature urbanised societies where the city's prosperity is understood to depend on the vision and energy of the mayor or governor of major cities like Paris, New York or Barcelona. Traditional Irish clientist politics favours the 'light touch' *laissez-faire* approach based on expediency rather than expertise. While this approach may be suitable for rural communities, which are traditionally more self-reliant, this will prove inadequate to the technocratic, outcome-focused approaches that are required to ensure the high quality of urban services and amenities that are needed to establish and sustain a competitive and attractive city region.

Quality of Life

If Dublin is still 'a player' in 2030 it will have succeeded in developing a choice of humanly-scaled neighbourhoods, or 'urban villages', in all four of its areas, each of which will offer levels of convenience, amenity and opportunity which satisfy the quality of life requirements of a well-educated, affluent post-modern community. These attributes will not be mere options. On the contrary, they will be fundamental necessities to attract and retain the internationally mobile workforces that will be the key resource for a future knowledge-based economy. But this alone will not be enough.

High quality residential neighbourhoods will need to be well connected to metropolitan facilities that will offer world-class standards of employment, amenities and services both to cater to the needs of Dublin's residents and to provide confirmation, for both residents and businesses, of international metropolitan status (through culture, events and opportunities).

Why, you may ask, is there so much emphasis on quality of life, amenities and international standards? What about jobs and the economy of this 2030 version of Dublin? What about the industries and offices? The answer is that these 'soft' quality of life characteristics will be the fundamental factors that will attract and sustain the best workforce that, in turn, will attract the economic activities – the next generation of manufacturing, commerce and services. The converse is bleak: no quality, no workers, no jobs, no economy.

The future of Dublin's four cities

It is worth examining in finer detail the future of each of Dublin's spatially defined and very different Four Cities.

1) Centre City

Self-interest usually kills city centres, but if the entrenched local government structures, centralising government departments, monopolising landowners, reactionary residents and vested business interests can be dislodged as power brokers, then Dublin's Centre City is likely to follow the trajectory of most European capitals. If not, then the centre will slowly slip into the dreary 'donut city' pattern of a decayed centre surrounded by a modernising edge.

Successful cities recognise these symptoms and take early action so that the centre becomes a high value, high status area that contains concentrations of national cultural institutions, central clusters of administration, politics and finance as well as enclaves of wealth. However in the most successful examples these relatively small islands of wealth are set within a larger mixed matrix of dense inner city communities that are socially and economically diverse. These centre city communities have expanding populations because they attract both the young and the old, all attracted by convenience and vitality – families will always be tempted by the larger gardens and cultural homogeneity of the Middle City's suburbs. This can increase the proportion of better-educated, professional and 'creatives' near the centre who support and sustain improvements to the public realm which sustains a demand for high quality venues for culture, entertainment and associated cafe/bar areas. This, in turn, intensifies the attractiveness of the centre city as a tourism destination which improves status and the 'brand recognition' of the city making it a more attractive location for investment, thus initiating the self-sustaining cycle required for a successful urban economy.

2) Middle City

If the many residential neighbourhoods of Dublin's Middle City can be given authority and resources within an appropriate organising framework, then this area can become the sustaining bedrock for establishing a city with world-class quality of life. The 'trick' is going to be to create defining, diverse and dynamic neighbourhoods that will have amenities that are convenient both to homes and work places but to do so without allowing this emerging local civic ownership to evolve into the self-limiting NIMBYism[8] that plagues so many maturing cities. Cities like Geneva have shown that it is possible to have a dense and highly mixed fabric of institutions, infrastructure, enterprise and housing so that many citizens can work and live in the same areas – popping home for lunch – and use the amenities of a high quality public realm throughout the week as workers or residents, with parents often mingling with their children as they all walk and cycle home from work. The key to achieving these circumstances is investment in, and commitment to, an enlightened attitude to convenience, connectivity (allowing many mobility options, but favouring the pedestrian), and the quality of the public realm and associated social facilities – especially schools and health care.

3) Edge City

The fate of the region's economy will depend upon the Edge City more than any other part of Dublin's Four Cities because this is where the economic 'heavy lifting' occurs that provides the majority of value addition and the income transfers in Ireland.[9] Success will depend on continuing to endow this area with affordable, reliable and high capacity utilities and mobility. Relatively high turnovers of businesses and premises within this area are likely to continue and high quality and imaginative planning strategies will need to be implemented to sustain and improve the quality that this area has to offer. In the best case scenario many Edge City areas will emulate the successful transition witnessed in Sandyford where an industrial estate has 'evolved' so that the area now consists of high quality land-uses that include apartments, retail, entertainment venues and medical facilities. The economy of this part of the Dublin region is most endangered by poor governance because it lies at the edge of a number of local authority areas. This administrative and political peripherality combined with misapplied 'greenbelt' policies combine to threaten the goal of sustaining and improving the attractiveness of the Edge City as the centre of gravity of the region's economy.

4) Outer City

If the Edge City is the most threatened area, then the Outer City is the most neglected. Indeed, many academic and official commentators[10] continue to regard Ireland's most rapidly growing area as a problem despite evidence to the contrary,[11] such as *The Irish Times's* examination of Leinster's new commuter communities which found that many of those who moved now love their new home because of the accessible schools, affordable housing and good neighbours that were available in these areas. That the market sought out or provided for themselves is a standing rebuke to the failure of the Irish planning system at every level. In a 'best case' scenario this success will be acknowledged and supported by providing investment and ambition for the public domain, as well as cultural, social and community facilities in these areas, because these areas provide another choice of quality of life within the region. Indeed, towns like Kilcullen or Ratoath, for example, are likely to become the seedbed in which the next generation of indigenous economic enterprise are most likely to grow because of affordable and supportive start-up conditions as well ready access to large markets. Such growth, when it happens, will be associated with distinctive places with strong branding potential – particularly when associated with the rich, high quality traditions of agriculture throughout this region. It is very likely that the river valleys within this region will be used as organising themes for communities, branding and intra-regional services.

Dublin's best future economy

The previous section has identified the potential that each part of Dublin's Four Cities have to contribute to the future economic success of the region – and the nation. It also identifies the issues and obstacles to success that may arise and what might be needed to address such issues. Table 3, below, provides a summary of the likely economic characteristics of each part of the region under each of the range of selected scenarios.

Planning to succeed

How can Dublin make this best outcome happen? What concrete steps would a regional government embark on if it were to get the authority and resources to ensure that Ireland will have a globally competitive and successful economy by 2030?

To succeed we will need to have no less an ambition than to emulate Paris which seeks to establish itself 'as a competitive metropolis on a world scale, creating wealth and jobs . . . to become a reality by the year 2030.'[12] The French have used the mechanism of the 'Grand Projet' for centuries to give focus, cohesion and concrete reality to the ambition that has created an economy and a culture that is one of the greatest in Europe. That city's eminent ambition is summarised in just ten projects.

Future Economy	Inner City	Middle City	Edge City	Outer City
Market	International, National	Regional, Local	National, Regional	International, Regional
Likely	Uneven, Uncompetitive, Inefficient, Expensive, Restrictive	Small Scale, Local, Restrictive, Ordinary, Inefficient, Uneven	Low profit, Low cost, Inefficient, Ineffective	Large-scale, Disconnected, Incoherent, Inefficient
Best	International, Specialist, High Value, Affordable, Coordinated, Diverse, Branded, Profitable, Dynamic, Modern, Competitive, Productive	Secure, Innovative, Predictable Distinctive, Dynamic Affordable, Integrated, Efficient, Density	Affordable, Efficient, Innovative, Focused, Specialist, Effective, Profitable, Productive, Dynamic, Modern, Competitive	Large scale, International, Innovative, Distinctive, Branded, Indigenous, Predictable
Worst	Monopolistic, Subsidised, Contracting, Inefficient, Uncompetitive, Expensive, Restrictive,	Anti-business, Stagnant, Slow, Unproductive	Wasteful, Ineffective, Unpredictable, Disorganised	Wasteful, Ineffective, Unpredictable, Expensive, Uncompetitive
Issues	Congested, Restricted, Expensive, Insecure	Restricted, Inconvenient, Dull, Inefficient	Inaccessible Isolated, Insecure, Ugly	Inaccessible, Isolated, Insecure, Ugly, Inefficient
Needs	Mobility, Land, Security	Mobility, Innovation, Opportunity, Density	Integration, Connectivity, Mobility, Diversity	Integration, Services, Connectivity, Mobility, Diversity

Table 3. Future Economic Outcomes for Dublin's Four Cities. Different roles, serving different markets, are emerging for each part of Dublin. Under different scenarios each area is likely to exhibit increasingly different economic characteristics, which will have different needs that will need different approaches.

In another recent example, from Ireland, the National Competitiveness Council (2009) prepared a list of seven initiatives to improve the competitiveness of our cities:

1. Prioritising Investment in Dublin and Our Other Main Cities

2. Improving City Governance

3. Delivering Key Urban Infrastructure Priorities

4. Improving Urban Land Use and Planning Policy

5. Enhancing Social Cohesion

6. Building a City Image

7. Developing a Better Understanding of Our Cities.

But lists are not enough. We need to learn more from the French example: they understand and have successfully implemented many large-scale visionary strategies that have invented and re-invented Paris to sustain it at the economic and cultural forefront of world affairs. It is no accident that the apogee of great cities like Chicago, New York, Paris and Barcelona have all been synonymous with individual mayors and governors who articulated high ambitions. Dublin is still not ambitious enough – it needs ambition at a regional level.

To make the issues raised here more concrete, this contribution concludes with the type of manifesto that might be produced by an aspirant candidate for the position of Governor (or Minister) of Dublin. Eight 'Big Ideas' are proposed to make Dublin's future economy a success by binding the future city network together with a dense web of shared services for transport, water, amenities and education. This is a template for governance as a holistic management of the economy of the region – not just the land-uses and services. For this reason the proposals are set out in terms of priority, costs and benefits – with explicit economic benefits identified in every instance.

Such visions, though concerned with increasing prosperity, pay attention from the outset to the need for social cohesion and the control of poverty. Cities are, and have always been, magnets for joblessness as well as jobs. In civilised cities care is taken that nobody is left behind.

Eight Big Ideas to Optimise Dublin's Future Economy

Cost	Idea	Description of Requirement	Benefits	
			Urban	Economic
	Sectors Benefiting			
€	1. Governance Administration, Manufacturing, Retail & Trade, Transport, Tourism, Financial, Services	A systematic review of how the economy of the Dublin City Region will require a Cabinet Minister for Urban Affairs or Regional Governor with powers to tax and spend and the devolution of control over public services	Integrated, objective-focused management of how public goods and services will provide best possible quality of life and opportunity for citizens of this region	Improve effectiveness and competitiveness, efficiency and effectiveness and increases attractiveness of the region for FDI
€	2. Public Realm[PPP] Residential, Retail & Trade, Transport, Tourism, Financial, Services, Administration, Education, Health	Network of green and grey public spaces stretching from the centre to the outer city provided for the enhancement of the city's culture, amenity and recreation. The Public Realm becomes the facilitator of cultural, sporting, arts, recreation and festive events	Improves distinctiveness, quality of life, equity, social cohesion, security and access to opportunity. Increases indigenous innovation	Increases status, competitiveness, branding effectiveness and attractiveness of the region for FDI
€€	3. Schools[PPP] Residential, Manufacturing, Tourism, Financial, Services, Education	An innovative highest quality free primary and secondary school and system	The education of the citizenry becomes the defining characteristic of the region. Improves equity, social cohesion, quality of life, security and access to opportunity	Improves indigenous innovation, competitiveness and productivity by increasing and improving quality of workforce. Reduces costs of security
€€	4. Landbank[PPP] Residential, Transport, Administration, Education, Health	A large scale reserve of strategic land routes and rights stretching from the centre to the outer city	Increases effectiveness and equity by ensuring availability of affordable housing, amenities, services and public realm projects. Improves quality of life by ensuring connectivity and affordability	Increases competitiveness and effectiveness by reducing future costs by ensuring availability of convenient inexpensive, serviced lands
€€€	5. Water Services Manufacturing, Retail & Trade, Services, Residential	A large-scale regional water supply and treatment system that can be supplied and sustained competitively	High quality, abundant reliability and inexpensive water services are one of the key indicators for the social and economic success of cities	Increases productivity and competitiveness, effectiveness, attractiveness of the region for FDI

Cost	Idea	Description of Requirement	Benefits
€€€	**6. Orbital Routes**[PPP] Manufacturing, Retail & Trade, Transport, Tourism, Financial, Services	Public transport priority orbital routes for multi-modal, integrated mobility throughout the middle, edge and outer city areas	Improves quality of life, equity, convenience, efficiency and attractiveness by increasing connectivity. Creates important opportunity nodes at junctions with radial routes	Improves productivity and efficiency by reducing congestion and ensures easy access from affordable housing. Reduces congestion costs
€€€€	**7. Road Tunnels**[PPP] Manufacturing, Retail & Trade, Transport, Tourism, Financial, Services	3 principle traffic tunnel, one east-west and two north-south to provide convenient access to centre city uses by bus and car from the middle, edge and outer city.	Increases competitiveness and convenience by compensating for inner-city disadvantages of historic street patterns and expensive land. Improves productivity and equity reducing congestion and ensures easy access from affordable housing. Improves distinctiveness and quality of life by retaining access to centre-city amenities and reducing congestion.	Improves productivity, efficiency and affordability. Sustains inner-city retail, business and entertainment. Provides easy access for workers from housing areas. Reduces congestion costs.
€€€€	**8. Rail Extensions** Manufacturing, Retail & Trade, Transport, Tourism, Financial, Services	A surface DART link to Dublin Airport and an underground DART link between Connolly and Heuston combined with the completion of the LUAS network	Increases competitiveness and convenience by compensating for inner-city disadvantages of historic street patterns and expensive land. Improves productivity and equity and improves quality of life by reducing congestion and ensures easy access from affordable housing	Improves productivity, efficiency and affordability. Sustains inner-city retail, business and entertainment. Provides easy access for workers from housing areas. Reduces congestion costs.

PPP = Poverty Proofing Project

Conclusion

Cities are like fruit cakes – they are all made with the same basic ingredients, yet only a few are really successful. The ingredients of ambition, opportunity, wealth, culture and amenities leavened with the problems of congestion, poverty, costs, territorial bureaucrats and greedy businesses are universal. Glittering success, mundane mediocrity or abject failure all result from these same ingredients: the difference is the cook, because the recipe, as we have seen, is well known. The 'cook' ultimately is the prevalent aspirations, ambitions and values of the people of that city – as manifested ultimately by how and who they choose to govern themselves.

At the foundation of the State, Dublin, with 316,693 people, was a big town that could be managed as a collection of businesses and houses by part-time councillors and a few engineers. By 2030 it is likely to be a regional economy ten times bigger serving around three million inhabitants. The quality of the governance of this economy will determine whether it thrives – or merely exists. However it is a sad fact that, in the preparation of this contribution, every single analysis consulted about the future of this region (see the Bibliography) identifies the overwhelming need to reform Dublin's governance as the single most important, most urgent challenge to be addressed. Yet nothing has happened. Nothing is happening.

Beautiful buildings, a distinguished public realm, attractive amenities and a vibrant cultural milieu are at the same time the characteristics and the causes of great modern cities. This means that it is the 'softest' infrastructure that must now be given priority to attract the hard cash generated by new creative urban economies.

Old city management dominated by engineering concerns of water, waste, roads and rails must be replaced. In future, priority, both in sequence and expenditure, needs to be given to equality, culture, distinctiveness and amenity. Pipes, wires and roads will always be needed, it is true, but in future these will serve development with a purpose and not try to lead it. It will not be enough to spend money on projects designed to be the cheapest and fastest. Nor will it be enough to plan to accommodate the continuation of adjoining land uses and emerging trends.

Dublin will need a coherent, planned vision to achieve specific objectives for prosperity, equity, opportunity, amenity and above all else quality. Dublin will need to make specific plans to make the best possible opportunities for specific communities to enjoy the highest quality of life.

By 2030 Dublin will need to be an economy in which the existence and wellbeing of the city as an attractive, vibrant cosmopolitan place will, by its mere existence, summon jobs into being from its many creative citizen-entrepreneurs.

Only Dublin has the potential to be Ireland's key urban centre in a highly competitive global economy: failure is not an option. Dublin needs to plan for economic success. That plan will need to include visions for more opportunities and enterprise; for better amenities and mobility; for greater equality and quality. Such a plan will come to nothing unless there is a co-ordinating authority that has the power and resources to frame and implement a vision on the scale of a city region. The future economy of Dublin can only succeed if the governance structures change radically and quickly. Without this change Dublin's economy has no future.

Epilogue

Writing this contribution about a better future is difficult in 2011 as Ireland enters the middle of a deep recessionary period. At such times it is important to remember that economic cycles are as old as the history of cities. We have learned from history that banking collapses typically result in six year declines – so this one is probably likely to last until 2015 – before the start of the next cycle that will carry us to the 2030s when Dublin will be a city region for three million people. The 'downtime' afforded by recessions is best spent on mending our faults and planning for the future to be a success.

Four years is the perfect amount of time to establish the 'Big Idea' projects outlined above to begin this process. These will change the systems and quality of governance. The quality of life will be ensured by improvements in education, property and public realm that will ensure effectiveness and equity while the transport and water projects will ensure the competitiveness and efficiency of the Dublin region by 2030.

Planning to make a success of Dublin's future economy is a project that will require vision, leadership and great hope – only hope will make this city great. Four years is enough time to make such hope become a habit.

Endnotes

[1] GDP per capita measured at constant prices.

[2] Williams, B., Walsh, C. and Boyle, I. (2010), see bibliography.

[3] A Primate City is significantly larger than any other city in a region or country in terms of population, prosperity and concentration of institutions.

[4] Central Statistics Office (2011), see bibliography.

[5] Morgenroth, E.L.W. (2008), see bibliography.

[6] National Competitiveness Council (2009), see bibliography.

[7] Deric O'Broinn (2009), writing on the likelihood of the reform of governance in the Dublin region, notes, 'the Irish record of significant and radical reform of public institutions, particularly local public institutions, is poor'.

[8] An acronym for the phrase 'Not In My Back Yard' used to describe opponents to new, nearby developments.

[9] CSO (2011).

[10] Williams, B., Walsh, C. and Boyle, I. (2010).

[11] McDonald, F. and Sheridan, K. (2010).

[12] The Grand Paris Project by the French Ministry of Culture and Communication, *Actualité en France n° 15*, April 2009.

Bibliography

Adam Smith (1776) *An Inquiry into the Nature and Causes of the Wealth of Nations.*

Central Statistics Office (2009) *A Profile of the Working Population of Large Towns.* Dublin: Stationery Office.

Central Statistics Office (2011) *County Incomes and Regional GDP 2008*, Dublin: Stationery Office.

Futures Academy (2008) *Twice the Size: Imagineering The Future of Irish Gateways*, DIT, Dublin.

Department of Environment, Community and Local Government (2002) *National Spatial Strategy for Ireland 2002–2020*, Dublin: Stationery Office.

Dublin Local Authorities Managers Co-ordination Group (2009) *Economic Development Action Plan for the Dublin City Region*, Dublin City Council, Dublin.

Dublin Regional Authority (2009) *Economic Development Action Plan for the Dublin City Region*, Dublin.

Hughes, B. (2010) *The Greater Dublin Area – Ireland's potential city-state of the early 21st century*: Unpublished Doctoral Thesis: DIT, Dublin.

McDonald, F. and Sheridan, K. (2010) 'Return to Commuterland', *The Irish Times*, June.

Morgenroth, E.L.W. (2008) *Exploring the Economic Geography of Ireland*, Economic and Social Research Institute (ESRI) Paper WP271.

National Competitiveness Council (2009) *Our Cities: Drivers of National Competitiveness*, National Competitiveness Council, Dublin.

Ó Broin, D. (2010) 'Regional governance and the challenge of managing socio-economic change', Dublin 2026, The Future Urban Environment, Special Issue of the *Journal of Irish Urban Studies*, volumes 7-9, 2008-2010.

Williams, B., Walsh, C. and Boyle, I. (2010) 'The Functional Urban Region of Dublin: Implications for Regional Development Markets and Planning', in *Journal of Irish Urban Studies*, volumes 7-9, pp. 5-30.

Bibliographical note

Conor Skehan is a senior lecturer in Dublin Institute of Technology's School of Spatial Planning. Over the last 25 years, the planning and environmental consultancies that he founded have provided strategic advice to some of the largest new industrial and infrastructure projects in Ireland.

14

The Future of the Past

Gillian O'Brien
On Memory

Streetscapes and statues

In Joyce's *Portrait of the Artist as a Young Man*, Stephen Dedalus remarks that 'History is a nightmare from which I am trying to awake'. Dublin is a city steeped in history. From the names and layout of the streets to the buildings that line them, the city speaks of its past. It was a Viking settlement, an Anglo-Norman centre and, through the eighteenth century, the second city of the British Empire, a city for the colonial not the colonised. Today, Dublin is a multi-layered, increasingly multi-cultural international city, a city of commerce, community, trade and politics.

In many respects, Dublin tells its story through its streetscape. Traditionally, streets were named after geographic traits or associated functions, later they recalled individuals or events that reflected the interests of the authorities. Traces of Viking Dublin can be read in street names such as Fishamble and Winetavern Streets, while Dublin's colonial past can be seen in thoroughfares such as Camden Street, Nassau Street and Waterloo Road. There are probably few who walk down Nassau Street and make the connection with William III and the Dutch house of Orange-Nassau. The same might be said of Camden Street, named in honour of the Lord Lieutenant, the king's representative in Ireland, who was in charge of repressive military measures in 1797 and 1798. Nelson's Pillar, erected in 1808, became a focal point for Dubliners and visitors to the city in the way that the Anna Livia Fountain, which marked the Dublin Millennium in 1988, never did and the Spire has so far failed to do. Despite its connection with British military victories, Dubliners claimed ownership of the monument – it was where the trams terminated, it was where family, friends and lovers met before the advent of Clerys Clock. Although the subject of re-peated discussion about its removal, the figure of Nelson, 121 feet up in the air, had long ceased to have any real significance for most Dubliners by the time the IRA blew it up in 1966. As is often the case, what was commemorated by Nelson's Pillar – the glorification of a British Naval hero – had long since lost its original meaning. How many passing through Dublin city centre know who Sir John Gray was, a man whose statue stands in the middle of O'Connell Street, or notice that the last remaining statue of a British royal, that of Prince Albert, stands at the back of Leinster House?[1] In a hundred years time how familiar will Dubliners be with Phil Lynott or Jim Larkin? Every genera-tion sees a different cityscape. People notice the familiar, the statues of people they've heard of, the street names of their childhood. In 1924 Sackville Street became O'Connell Street despite the objections of many of its residents and traders. For generations the street was often called by its former name. The same process can be seen in the naming of the train stations in the capital. In 1966, as part of the commemoration of the fiftieth anniversary of the 1916 Easter Rising, many of the country's largest stations were renamed to honour the executed leaders. However, for many Dubliners Connolly station will al-ways be Amiens Street while Pearse Station will be forever Westland Row.

The independence of remembrance

Every nation has a need to commemorate, to celebrate a unified past, to tell stories and recount past challenges and glories in an attempt to create a uni-fied present. How we commemorate and how we remember has become in-creasingly important as the number of students studying history declines. In the 1980s, most students took history for their Leaving Certificate but the subject suffered a serious decline in the 1990s and 2000s with only 10,000 taking the exam in 2005, though it appears numbers are on the rise again with over 12,400 sitting the history exam in 2011.[2] Few people read history books on a regular basis and most of our knowledge of Irish history is based on dimly remembered lessons from primary school and television programmes, films, fictional accounts, family stories, ballads and poems. Very often accuracy is lost for the sake of a good rhyme, a twist in the tale or the need to fit in advertising breaks.

There are a variety of reasons why individuals and events are commemorated, the primary one being a genuine belief that permanent note must be taken of an event or an individual. The prospect of generating income, of increasing tourism, also frequently features in the decision-making process. Marking territory can also be a motivation, though this is often done by private groups or individuals rather than by the state – this form of commemoration is perhaps most obviously seen in nationalist and unionist areas of Belfast where wall murals clearly define segregated areas. Opportunity is another factor, particularly in politically motivated commemorations. As different political organisations take control of the civic purse strings they sometimes promote the recollection of their own glorious past and advance individuals and events that show their idealised past in its best light, or commemorations of past events are often hijacked to promote a current preoccupation. To avoid this it is important that an independent body is established to oversee commemorations, to ensure that historic sites are not prostituted to whatever political agenda is current at the time. The means by which decisions that dictate the form of commemoration are taken must be transparent. Neither the Office of Public Works (OPW) nor Dublin City Council are independent bodies and so neither can be entirely objective. Decisions taken by both can be interpreted as politically motivated, and it is imperative that an independent board of assessors is established to report on decisions made by both Dublin City Council and the OPW, particularly on contentious issues such as the commemoration of the centenary of the 1916 Easter Rising.

The art of commemoration

When looking to the future of recalling the past in Dublin it is informative to look at commemorations that took place in the recent past. In 1998 the bicentenary of the 1798 Rebellion was commemorated. The Irish government, with some assistance from its British counterpart, funded and supported many commemorative events. Several stages of the Tour de France took place in Dublin and Wexford, ostensibly to mark the links between the United Irishmen and the French Revolutionaries of the 1790s. Politicians made ready and simplistic comparisons between the Peace Process, the Good Friday Agreement and the ideals of the United Irishmen. The then Taoiseach, Bertie Ahern, went so far as to claim that 'it is precisely because of its enduring relevance that

1798 has never truly passed out of politics and into history'.[3] A safe and somewhat sanitised version of the 1798 Rebellion was offered for public consumption.[4] Much was made of the inclusive nature of the United Irishmen, little was made of the often sectarian reality of the 1798 Rebellion. This marked a significant change from the celebrations that had greeted the centenary of the 1798 Rebellion. In 1898 the 1798 Rebellion was celebrated as a 'faith and fatherland' rebellion which conveniently overlooked the fact that most of the United Irish leaders were protestant, that the Catholic Church had very limited involvement in the Rebellion and that the objective had never been to create a Catholic state.

Plaque commemorating Thomas Clarke opposite no. 16 Moore Street, Dublin

There was, therefore, one 1798 Rebellion for 1898, another for 1998. This latter year also saw the opening of the Island of Ireland Peace Park at Messines in Belgium. This park honours all Irishmen of all political and religious beliefs who fought on the side of the Allies during the First World War and is in many ways an attempt to reclaim a controversial and, until the late 1990s, often ignored chapter of our past. As President Mary McAleese observed at the opening of the Messines Peace Park on 11th November 1998: 'Those whom we commemorate here were doubly tragic. They fell victim to a war against oppression in Europe. Their memory too fell victim to a war for independence at home in Ireland'. It is not insignificant to note that the official opening of the monument took place in the same year as the Good Friday Agreement – a year when tales of a united history were endlessly told. In many respects we learn as much about the present as we do about the past when we examine the motives behind commemorations. The recent visit of Queen Elizabeth II to Dublin was laden with symbolism, nowhere more so than in the laying of wreaths both at the Garden of Remembrance to honour those who died fighting to free Ireland from British rule, and at the National War Memorial to honour the Irish soldiers who had died during the First World War.

A plethora of centenary commemorations will shortly be upon us. In 2013 Dublin will mark the anniversary of the Lock-out of 1913. In 2014 we will see the centenary of the beginning of the First World War. In 2016 it will be the centenary of the Easter Rising, swiftly followed by the centenary of the War of Independence beginning in 2019 and the Civil War beginning in 2022. How these events will be commemorated in Dublin is of increasing interest.

For a number of years tentative plans were made to move the Abbey Theatre into the General Post Office (GPO) in time to mark the centenary of the events of 1916. In the 'Renewed Programme for Government' of late 2009 the Fianna Fáil-led coalition committed itself to completing 'a detailed assessment of the GPO complex with a view to locating the Abbey Theatre there in time for the centenary of the 1916 Rising.'[5] In October 2010, Mary Hanafin, then Minister for Arts, Sports and Tourism, admitted that almost €400,000 had been spent by her department on the Abbey/GPO project.[6] In hindsight this seems an enormous waste of money. Aside from the difficulties involved in attempting to shoehorn a theatre (or two) into a post-office building, why link Patrick Pearse and W.B. Yeats together in perpetuity when the men themselves had little time for each other while Pearse was alive? In 1899 Pearse referred derogatively to Yeats as 'a mere English poet of the third or fourth rank'. While in Easter 1916 Yeats admitted that he had frequently met Pearse and his fellow conspirators and had:

> lingered awhile and said
> polite meaningless words,
> and thought before I had done
> of a mocking tale or a gibe
> to please a companion
> around the fire at the club,
> being certain that they and I
> but lived where motley is worn.[7]

When Fine Gael and Labour entered government together in March 2011 it was interesting to note that their Programme for Government made no mention of either the Abbey Theatre or the GPO, though it declared the Government committed to developing a 'cultural plan for future commemorative events such as the Centenary of the Easter Rising in 2016'.[8] It came as little surprise to learn in July 2011 that the idea of moving the Abbey to the GPO had been scrapped and a new scheme proposed.

The GPO and Spire on Dublin's O'Connell Street

The future of commemoration

The new government plan as proposed by Minister of Arts, Heritage and the Gaeltacht, Jimmy Deenihan TD, would take the former Parliament Building at College Green from the Bank of Ireland and return it to state ownership. In many respects this is an excellent idea; however the current plan as outlined by *The Irish Times* on 9 July 2011 is deeply problematic.[9] The proposal suggests turning the Bank of Ireland, the old parliament building, into Dublin's 'Smithsonian'. Quite what this means is unclear – the Smithsonian in Washington DC is an agglomeration of nineteen museums and galleries, a zoo and nine research facilities.[10] To try to replicate this in one building under the proposed title of the 'O'Connell Centre for the Arts' makes little sense and would seem to dilute collections until they formed little more than a taster of Irish history, literature and heritage. Any future plans for commemoration need to be careful not to rob Peter to pay Paul. The National Library, National Archives and the National Museum are grossly underfunded and there needs to be a cohesive policy that safeguards and enhances the position of these three vital resources before attempting to create additional repositories of documents and artefacts. The proposal also envisages transforming College Green into one of the great squares of the world – citing St Mark's in Venice, St Peter's in Rome, Trafalgar Square and Covent Garden in London, and Times Square in New York as examples. It may be that these iconic locations were chosen simply as recognisable place names as the squares have little in common with each other – one crammed with tourists, another the central public space in a city-state, another overflowing with traffic and museums, another a shrine to commercialism flanked by some cultural attractions, and the final square a homage to flashing billboards. The combined scheme has great potential but at this stage (at least based on the information provided by *The Irish Times*) it lacks real cohesion. To take the former Parliament Building and transform it into a literary centre and a museum dedicated to the 1916 Rising and call it the 'O'Connell Centre for the Arts' makes as much sense as taking the Tower of London and transforming it into the 'Alfred the Great Centre for the Study of Dickens and Cromwell'.

The departmental document seen by *The Irish Times* identifies a rejuvenated College Green as 'a national gravitational point on the verge of Europe', and while this might be overstating the attraction of the site somewhat, it is

The former Parliament building on College Green (photograph Arco Ardon)

certainly true that College Green and its associated buildings are very significant. In 1757 the Wide Streets Commission (Europe's first official urban planning body) was established and it created much of the layout of the city centre as we know it today. The Commission was responsible for developing the area around College Green – D'Olier Street, Westmorland Street and Dame Street – streets which were intended to rival the great boulevards of Paris. Alongside these fine boulevards the grand buildings of the eighteenth century such as the Parliament Building, the Four Courts and the Custom House were designed to equal and better anything London could offer. As the second city of the British Empire, Dublin was determined to be seen as the match of London and visitors frequently noted the similarities between the two cities, both with fine Georgian Squares and exquisite civic buildings. One commentator observed that he was 'forcibly struck with the strong likeness [Dublin] bears to London, of which it is a beautiful copy – more beautiful in truth, in miniature than in the gigantic original'.[11]

There is no narrative arc apparent in the proposal to use the former parliament building to house an exhibition about the 1916 Rising, parts of the

The work of the Wide Streets Commission – d'Olier Street and Westmoreland Street

national art collection, a genealogical centre, a literary centre, a digital media lab and an archive of significant papers. This appears to be a mish-mash, an attempt to be all things to all people. Perhaps a more coherent idea would be to use the former parliament building to create a centre for the study of Dublin – its history, literature, architecture, culture and heritage. This would provide a clear narrative arc – an opportunity to tell the history of the city from its Viking origins through to its period as a colonial capital where it was the second city of the British Empire. From there the centre could focus on the turbulent nineteenth century where it might examine the impact of the famine and the rise of tenement living in Dublin. This would be a great opportunity to rescue some interesting artefacts from the out-dated 'Dublin City Hall: The Story of the Capital' exhibition tucked away in the vaults of the City Hall. It would be entirely appropriate to have a centre focussed on Dublin in the old parliament building, a building that housed the Irish parliament from 1729 until 1800, a building that was designed by three of the most significant architects working in Ireland in the eighteenth and nineteenth centuries – Edward Lovett Pierce, James Gandon and Francis Johnston. Further, discussion of the campaigns led by Daniel O'Connell and Charles Stewart Parnell to restore a parliament to Dublin would sit very comfortably within the old parliament building. Within the framework of the Museum of Dublin, it would also be fitting to include a substantial discussion of the 1916 Rising, the War of Independence and the Civil War in this centre. Additionally, given Dublin's recent designation as a UNESCO City of Literature (alongside Melbourne, Edinburgh and Iowa City), it would make sense to examine Dublin's rich literary heritage and as 'The Historic City of Dublin' is currently on a tentative list for consideration by UNESCO for World Heritage Status it would surely bolster the application if the city of Dublin had a museum and cultural centre dedicated to the study of the history, literature and architecture of the city. As Lorcan Sirr has argued in his introduction to this book, it is time that Dublin, as the capital city, and the city with the greatest future population growth forecast, was given adequate recognition by government and relevant state agencies. For too long we have focussed on natural attractions and ancient monument when promoting Ireland abroad; perhaps we should now and in the future turn our attention to the capital city and commemorate and celebrate its story with all its attendant complexities and contradictions.

Clearly it would be insufficient to simply tag commemoration of the 1916 Rising onto a huge cultural centre and museum project, so civic authorities need to consider carefully how specific events will be organised to mark the centenary of the Rising. For years it seemed that the commemoration of the 1916 Rising was owned by extreme republicanism, by men wearing balaclavas. It is vital that the centenary commemorations give ownership of the Rising to all. It is imperative that the full story of our past is told for, as James Loewen has observed in *Lies Across America: What our Historic Sites get Wrong*, 'omissions . . . can be hard to detect especially for visitors who come to a site to learn a little history without bringing some knowledge of the site with them. People don't usually think about images that aren't there'.[12] In commemorating our past we need to examine all of our past, not just the uncontested parts of it.

The government, and city council, might consider transforming 16 Moore Street (and adjoining buildings, see following page) into a centre for the study of the 1916 Rising and associated events, and also a centre for the global study of Irish nationalism and republicanism from the eighteenth century to the present day. The Taoiseach Enda Kenny referred to the area surrounding Moore Street and the General Post Office as 'the laneways of history', while the Sinn Féin Deputy Leader and TD Mary Lou McDonald called for the area around

16 Moore Street to be designated a 'revolutionary quarter'.[13] This would make sense
from a number of different
perspectives: the area around
Moore Street was, during
Celtic Tiger times, intended
to form part of an extensive
commercial development.[14]
The project is unlikely to
take place in the current economic climate and the government may well find itself
as the owners of properties
on Moore Street bought at
a fraction of the price these
properties commanded at
the height of the boom. In
addition to providing a vital
resource for the study and
explanation of the 1916 Rising, the establishment of a
cultural and heritage centre

No. 16 Moore Street, Dublin 1

in Moore Street would help regenerate an area of the city that is currently in
decline. Fianna Fáil Senator Mark Daly recently suggested a very American
form of commemoration when he proposed the raising and lowering of a
new national flag every day at the GPO and sending the flag to a school until
each primary and secondary school had a flag that had flown at the General
Post Office.[15] Given the triumphalism associated with flag waving in Northern Ireland, this sort of flag-waving nationalism seems inappropriate.

Fear of the past

It is vital that the City Council and the government take independent advice
on how best to commemorate the 1916 Rising, the War of Independence, the
First World War and the Civil War. It isn't necessary to have a comfortable
consensus about the history of Irish republicanism, nationalism and unionism,

but it is important to tell all the truths, not just the easy truth. It is important not to colour the commemorations by seeing them only through the prism of today. Civic authorities need to be brave, they need to be far-sighted and they need to be objective. Dublin has not always got it right when it comes to preservation, commemoration and celebration. What we value of our past changes rapidly. In the 1960s there was a rush to demolish significant sections of Georgian Dublin, partly in a belated attempt to create a modern European city, partly to erase reminders of two painful periods of Irish history – that when Ireland was part of the British Empire and, later, when many Georgian houses became tenements. Dublin once boasted the longest Georgian street-scape in the world – nearly three-quarters of a mile from Holles Street Hospital to Leeson Street Bridge. In the mid-1960s, the Electricity Supply Board (ESB) demolished sixteen of them to build their headquarters. Despite public protests and objections from Dublin Corporation, Neil Blaney, Fianna Fáil Minister for Local Government, signed an order granting permission to demolish them in September 1964, the day before the publication of a new planning act that would have protected the buildings. The *Dublin City Development Plan 2011-2017* now states as policy that it will 'promote the reinstatement of the Georgian façade of the sixteen Georgian houses on Fitzwilliam Street Lower which were demolished in 1965'.[16] In April 2011 a building design was approved by the ESB but it remains unclear as to whether the new building will ever transfer from plans to building.

In 1969 and 1970 protests were held to try to prevent the destruction of Georgian buildings in Hume Street. Despite a six-month sit-in that included UCD architecture students Marian Finucane and Ruairí Quinn, the protest was in itself unsuccessful as the buildings were demolished, though mock-Georgian facades were incorporated into the new plans. However, the protest succeeded in raising public awareness of the destruction of valuable heritage in the city and the Georgian streetscape was increasingly valued both by the public but also by the civic authorities. Having been a symbol of oppression and poverty, the Georgian houses and squares now provide iconic images of Dublin. Few tourists leave the city without dispatching cards around the world festooned with the images of Georgian Dublin.

The Wood Quay debacle of the 1970s would, one would hope, not happen today. In 1968 Dublin Corporation[17] held a competition to design civic offices on land it owned beside Christchurch Cathedral. When digging began significant Viking material was found, sparking a campaign led by the Friends of Medieval Dublin to halt the Corporation's plans and to focus instead on preserving the remains of Viking Dublin. Professor F.X. Martin of University College Dublin and chair of the Friends of Medieval Dublin took the case to court where he attempted to have the site declared a national monument. He was successful but even this designation and public protests of up to 20,000 people failed to halt plans for a building on the site and the first phase of the civic offices were completed in 1986.

In many ways we have been afraid of the past. In the decades following the establishment of the Irish Free State many politicians and civil servants alike were fearful of looking to the past, particularly a nationalist or republican past. From a tourism perspective it was safer to look to a more ancient past – the Ireland of saints and scholars – than to consider one that might touch on the raw nerve that was the memory of the civil war. Kilmainham Gaol was, and is, steeped in Irish nationalist and republican history. The prison opened just prior to the 1798 Rebellion and closed its doors in 1924 shortly after the end of the Civil War. The prison walls told the story of British repression and brutality, of heroism and martyrdom, and of the bitterness of civil war. There was no political will to engage with the jail and certainly not as a tourist attraction. Disused, the buildings fell into disrepair until the early 1960s when the jail was rescued from dereliction and restored by volunteer members of the 'Kilmainham Gaol Restoration Society'.[18] The State, under the auspices of the OPW, finally took control of the jail in 1986 amidst recurring fears that tours of the prison were inspiring young men and women to rush into the arms of the IRA.

The city of the imagination

The imagined city has been commemorated in Dublin in plaques, statues, street names and bridges. There are statues to James Joyce, Brendan Behan, Oscar Wilde, Patrick Kavanagh, Oliver Goldsmith and Edmund Burke, amongst others, while there are bridges named after Joyce, Samuel Beckett, Sean O'Casey and Austin Clarke. As Eileen Battersby noted in an article in July 2010, 'most cities are built of stone and brick, but Dublin . . . is firmly planted on a bedrock of words'.[19] To a large extent Battersby is correct. Dublin has always been more comfortable commemorating writers than revolutionaries. Through the nineteenth century a largely nationalist Dublin Corporation erected a statue to only one revolutionary (William Smith O'Brien) but unveiled many to writers. The association of Dublin with literature has been given international status with the designation of the city as a UNESCO City of Literature.[20] The fictional city is easy to negotiate. The city of Joyce (or indeed Leopold Bloom), of Flann O'Brien, of Roddy Doyle, of James Plunkett and of Sean O'Casey is a city of the imagination. The fictional Dublin is idealised, sentimentalised, romanticised and brutalised. The fictional Dublin is complex, controversial but in many respects safer than the real Dublin – a Dublin that can be described in fiction in a way that no museum could ever get away with.

The citizens of Dublin are encouraged to see the city through fiction. Dublin City Council runs a 'One City, One Book' scheme where every April people of the city are encouraged to read a book chosen for them by the Dublin City Public Libraries. The book this year was Joseph O'Connor's *Ghost Light*. Previous books have been *Gulliver's Travels*, *At Swim Two Birds*, *A Long, Long Way*, *Dracula*, and *The Picture of Dorian Gray*. The selection so far has been a mixture of books by authors from (or associated with) Dublin and books set in Dublin. As we approach the series of centenaries associated with the city it will be interesting to see if books that relate to historical events are chosen.

More than one truth

In *Ill Fares the Land*, published in 2010 just before his death, Tony Judt noted that the historian's job is 'to tell what is almost always an uncomfortable story and explain why the discomfort is part of the truth we need to live well and live properly. A well-organised society is one in which we know the truth about ourselves collectively, not one in which we tell pleasant lies about ourselves'. But we do tell lies about ourselves. It's what makes our past palatable, it's what allows us to perpetuate myths and grow legends. Without such lies the past becomes like the present, full of contradictions and uncertainties. Do we want our heroes to have feet of clay? Do Irish Republicans really want to be reminded that Theobald Wolfe Tone, 'the father of Irish republicanism', as a young man wrote to the British Prime Minister suggesting the expansion of the British Empire for trade purposes and volunteered to lead the posse to take the Sandwich Islands? Do Unionists really want to recall the fact that many of the first Irish Republicans were Presbyterian or that the Ulster Unionists fought alongside Irish Nationalists during the battle of the Somme in 1916?

True history is awkward and uncomfortable; sanitised versions are comforting, safe, uncontroversial and, frequently, profitable.

But is there one truth? In much the same way as there is no one future, there is also no one truth. In some ways the historian can know more than the participants for the historian has a bird's eye view in a way the participant did not. But the historian cannot know what each individual thought. The historian is reliant on incomplete records, written or otherwise. Many words are lost or were never recorded. The conscientious diary writer of the past may well have written him or herself into the present, and perhaps the future. Perhaps those who were out doing, rather than scribbling notes about what they had done, or observed being done, are more deserving of our consideration, but can we consider what we cannot know?

It is remarkable that few of the leaders of the 1916 Rising are commemorated by statues in Dublin. There is a statue of James Connolly close to Liberty Hall, a bust of Michael Collins in Merrion Square and a plaque to Patrick and William Pearse on Pearse Street but little else. There is no statue to Collins, Pearse or Éamon de Valera. Elected politicians are rarely commemorated, Henry Grattan being one of the few to be marked by a statue. There are no statues to any of the presidents of Ireland, nor of any of the Taoisigh. It is true that permanent art may not be the best way to remember. Dublin City Council appears reluctant to rush to commemorate through sculpture and notes in its 'Policies and Strategies for Managing Public Art' that 'there is need to respect and understand the nature of Dublin as a city. . . . The need to remember and note the contribution [of] a person or group of people can be addressed in many ways and permanent art is not necessarily the best way to do this.'[21] There is undoubtedly a need to remember those who fought in the 1916 Rising, but their memories might be better served through heritage centres, museums, and exhibitions rather than a series of sculptures lining the streets.

Stephen Dedalus wanted to escape the nightmare that was history. We shouldn't try to escape our history; rather we should embrace it and commemorate it in a truthful, objective and non-sentimental manner. As Dublin moves towards an uncertain future it is important that the city examines the past honestly. It is only by accepting our contested past, by shining a light into the darkest recesses of a divided and divisive history, that we can ensure that our history ceases to be a nightmare.

Endnotes

[1] Sir John Gray was a medical doctor, owner of the *Freeman's Journal* and politician from the 1840s to the 1870s. His statue was erected in recognition of his work in bringing a clean water supply to Dublin.

[2] *The Irish Times*, 16 June 2011.

[3] Speech by An Taoiseach, Bertie Ahern T.D. at the unveiling ceremony at the Memorial Garden of the Croppies Acre in Collins Barracks, 22 November 1998. Kevin Whelan, reiterating, though not acknowledging, Roseberry maintained 'the rebellion never passed into history, because it never passed out of politics'. Whelan, K. (1996) *The Tree of Liberty. Radicalism, Catholicism and the Construction of Irish Identity 1760-1830*, Cork, p. 133.

[4] R.F. Foster (2001) 'Remembering 1798', in *The Irish Story: Telling Tales and Making it up in Ireland*, London, pp. 225-6.

[5] Renewed Programme for Government, 10 October 2009, p. 37, http://www.taoiseach.gov.ie/eng/Publications/Publications_2009/Renewed_Programme_for_Government,_October_2009.pdf, accessed 20 July 2011.

[6] Mary Hanafin, Dáil Debate, 14 October 2010, http://debates.oireachtas.ie/dail/2010/10/14/00017.asp, accessed 19 July 2011.

[7] Patrick Pearse, Letter to the Editor, An Claidheamh Soluis, 20th May 1899, quoted in Kiberd, D. (2005) *The Irish Writer and the World*, Cambridge: Cambridge University Press, p. 52. Yeats wrote 'Easter 1916' between May and September 1916.

[8] 'Art Culture and Sport' section, Programme for Government, 2011.

[9] Paul Cullen, 'College Green to become "Great Square"', *The Irish Times*, 9 July 2011.

[10] Smithsonian website, http://www.si.edu/About, accessed 19 July 2011.

[11] John Gamble (1810) *Sketches of History, Politics and Manners in Dublin and the North of Ireland*, p. 22.

[12] James W. Loewen (1999) *Lies Across America: What Our Historic Sites Got Wrong*, 4.

[13] Taoiseach Enda Kenny (FG), Mary Lou McDonald TD (SF), Dáil Debates, 7 June 2011, http://debates.oireachtas.ie/dail/2011/06/07/00004.asp#N22, accessed 19 July 2011

[14] 'Park in the Sky' at the heart of €1bn O'Connell Street Plan, Paul Melia, *Irish Independent*, 22 April 2008.

[15] Mark Daly, Seanad Éireann, 26 January 2011, http://www.kildarestreet.com/sendebates/?id=2011-01-26.166.0, accessed 4 July 2011.

[16] Dublin City Council (2010) *Dublin City Development Plan 2011-2017*, Interim Document, Chapter 4: 'Shaping the City'.

[17] Now Dublin City Council.

[18] Eric Zuelow (2004) 'Enshrining Ireland's Nationalist History Inside Prison Walls: the Restoration of Kilmainham Jail', *Éire-Ireland*, 39, 3 & 4, Fall/Winter, pp 180-202.

[19] Eileen Battersby, 'Firmly Planting Dublin on a Bedrock of Words', *The Irish Times*, 27 July 2010.

[20] See Peter Sirr's chapter in this volume for further reference to this designation and literature and the city.

[21] Dublin City Council (n.d., prob 2009) 'Policies and Strategies for Managing Public Art', Public Art Advisory Group Report, 6.3 Commemorations and Memorials, p. 6.

Biographical note

Gillian O'Brien is a historian. She has lived and worked in Dublin, London, Liverpool and Chicago which may explain her interest in urban history. She is also interested in the history of Irish Republicanism, commemoration and newspaper history. At the moment she is engrossed in a study of a sensational murder which involves police corruption, embezzlement, freak shows and journalistic fraud. The book based on this study, The Murder of Dr Patrick Cronin, *will be published in 2013.*

15

Texting the City

Peter Sirr
On Literature

If cities could speak

Text flies through the city, rushing from fingertips to the towers and masts of the phone networks and back into the eyes of the messaged, or from keyboards to mail servers, flitting from domain to domain before being retrieved, consumed, forgotten. The endlessly updated social networks multiply, virtual events and friends insist on recognition, acknowledgement, reply. The city is built on words; the self is carved from words and expressed in text. We are all fingers and thumbs, words have abandoned our mouths and crouch under the skin of our fingertips, giddy, heady with the scent of new freedoms, anonymities, disguises and possibilities. I think again of those pink neon phrases from Joyce hung on the city's buildings by two artists in the nineties, how already the gesture seems to belong to another age. It was conceived as a kind of radical proclamation of privacy, invented privacy, the bedroom thoughts of Joyce's Molly Bloom sitting on top of the city's public buildings. What if we could tap into the river of text that flows ceaselessly through the city, or what if we could find a way for people in the ordinary course of their lives to write the city, to convert it into words that would be available for others to read, not to write about the city, but to write with it, from inside it? What if part of a city's art was this attempt to get the city in some way to write itself?

The practice of the German artist Jochen Gerz is all about finding new ways for art to interact with the city. His current project in Ballymun, *Amaptocare*, was commissioned by Dublin City Council for the Civic Plaza. Gerz invites the local residents to donate a tree for Ballymun. The site and the species can be chosen. Each donor is asked the question, 'If this tree could speak, what should it say for you?' The donors' responses are published on a lectern beside their tree.

> I donate this tree in order to say thank you to this community. I want to give back a little thing. Even if this cedar will be big, it is a little thing compared to all the love and contentment that I have found there. (May Harvey)

> This tree symbolises our arrival here and our attempt to set up a new home. It has not been easy but with time we grow and change, building a new house where we can welcome other people too: like a tree that gives shelter for strangers. (Eya Ofuka, who moved to Ireland some years ago from Nigeria).

The names of the donors are to be engraved on the Civic Plaza and at the centre of the granite pavement covered with names, a glass map of the new Ballymun will be installed, surrounded by the first of each of the fifteen donated species. The map will be illuminated by a series of bright lights, each marking the site of a donated tree.

A project like that, with its community participation and its tangible end products, is easy to grasp. But what if the results were less quantifiable and the process more complex, even life-altering? What if you could take people out of their current environment and offer them a new experience, a new life, and if that new life and the consequences that flowed from it were themselves the art project? *2/3 Streets* began with an ad on property websites, in daily papers and cultural journals in Germany's Ruhr area, advertising a year's free rent to participants who agreed to come and live in renovated flats in Dortmund, Duisburg and Mülheim an der Ruhr. Nearly 1,500 candidates from thirty countries responded to the ad. The project offered sixty flats and about seventy-eight people took part. In return for their year's rent the participants lived a normal life in the community, and the only artistic requirement imposed on them was to contribute to a collaborative book, an ongoing river of text that was simply the sum of everyone's writing; there were no constraints, no guidelines. The writing includes journals, random jottings, fiction, poetry, even recipes. Not only the participants but their visitors and the permanent residents of the neighbourhoods were invited to contribute, and participants were also encouraged to develop projects which brought them into contact with the existing community. Some baulked at this element of social control and insisted on staying in their flats and producing their quota of civic text. Reporting on the project for *The Irish Times*, Aidan Dunne noted some resistance:

> There have been rows, disagreements and disaffections. Several younger participants reportedly restrict their co-operation to contributing to the ongoing text. This doesn't mean that the project is not going to plan, because there is no plan. One participant noted that, at one of the initial group meetings, Gerz became annoyed when asked what his expectations of the project were. 'It doesn't matter what my expectations might be,' he is said to have responded. 'The project has the meaning that you give to it.'

Gerz might not have had a plan, but he has no doubt that the function of art is to introduce change. This is why the project is limited to only a couple of streets in each of the designated cities. The interaction of new and established tenants will be more evident packed into a couple of streets than dispersed across the cities. This interaction, this deliberate cultivation of change is one of the desired outcomes, the book is another. The book itself sounds like the last great modernist project, a three-hundredfold *Ulysses*, a year in the life of the inhabitants of several cities, composed of text submitted anonymously:

> A YEAR (a text neither consciously desired nor prevented by its authors) is, incidentally, picking up the trail of modernism following Joyce, Pound, the écriture automatique, Holz, Burroughs, Schmidt, Kerouac and many others. It tests the opportunities offered by contemporary tools of production for society as an author, rather than an audience at large.

Dailiness is thus converted into art, neighbourhoods are given the means to express themselves in text, and the boundaries between art and the life it springs from are blurred.

Artist and audience merge in a workaday alliance that removes both from the orbit of art. There is no exhibition to see, no value for money municipal output, but for the life of the project it was possible to visit designated sites to add text to the ongoing book. Still, though, some things remain stubbornly the same. If the social interactions that are one of the intended outputs belong to the community, the creation of the text, for all the impersonal operations of the technology and the anonymised ultimate production, is still internal, private, a cursor blinking in solitude. And this contrast between the sphere of the communal and neighbourly and the isolation of creativity is the paradox of Gerz's project. Even in the context of a collective enterprise, society doesn't in fact become an author; the technology may be a liberation, but it is a liberation into privacy, into the individual response.

Yet Gerz has hit on something essential; in his focus on urban experience and his choice of language as the medium of expression he allows us to step outside the traditional framework for thinking about the relationship between city and art. His 'textibition' frees us from thinking about collections of artefacts or static commodities in strategic municipal locations, and it finds a way for large groups of people not necessarily interested in being artists to be fully involved in an artistic creation. I don't think it's just a sentimental egalitarianism that makes me feel there's something very attractive in its subversion of the normal pattern of consumption, and the often awkward attempts to make an explicit link between a city and its creativity.

Cities, writers, Chicken McNuggets

Literature is probably the most difficult art for a city to incorporate into its sense of itself. Novels, stories, poems are crafted and designed to be consumed in solitude. Performances at readings, launches and festivals are really public acknowledgements of that private relationship. Once the writers have left the podium we are alone with their books again, maybe even relieved at their absence. Given the privacy of the contract, can there ever, in fact, be a meaningful connection between a city and its literature? Are the two sides of the equation too abstract to really touch other? Can a city be ever said to own its literature as it owns its architecture or its music if it has conservatories, orchestras, concert halls and composers?

There's also the fact, troubling to tourism executives, that writers' relationships with their cities are often adversarial or otherwise critical; they may, like Joyce and Beckett, abandon them altogether and settle down elsewhere, or they may stay and subject it to satire like Karl Kraus or Flann O' Brien or Swift.

They may have difficult or unpleasant things to say, may well be offensive to a large portion of the city's population. How then does the city engage with them? In Dublin, it's usually after the fact, and usually by attempting to domesticate them, to make them amenable to civic consumption, erecting statues to them, calling bridges after them, organising tourist trails and otherwise claiming them as exploitable products. The Dublin Writers Museum offers the personal effects of writers – typewriters, trousers, glasses, pens – on the canny assumption that the life is easier to package and digest than the work.

There are some municipal initiatives that engage directly with the world of writing. One of these is the One City, One Book campaign, where the Dublin City Libraries takes it on itself to persuade its citizens to read the same book during the month of April each year through a campaign of posters, hoardings, exhibitions and events. Literature here means fiction; there's no appetite yet for poetry or non-fiction. The first choice was Flann O'Brien's classic *At Swim Two Birds* and this was followed by a contemporary novel, Sebastian Barry's *A Long Long Way*. The idea seems to be to balance established classics with contemporary voices. After Sebastian Barry there was a run of what you might call heritage titles: Jonathan Swift's *Gulliver's Travels*, Bram Stoker's *Dracula* and Oscar Wilde's *The Picture of Dorian Gray* before another contemporary choice, Joseph O'Connor's *Ghost Light*.

On the surface One City, One Book seems like a great idea; it has the virtue of simplicity. The citywide promotion of a single title is an uncomplicated concept, easy to market; it incorporates literature into the street life of the city, its only area of potential controversy is the choice of the contemporary texts, where the city runs the danger of becoming simply an extension of a commercial marketing campaign. But is there any particular reason for a focus on a single book? What if you don't feel like reading *Gulliver's Travel*, *Dracula* or *Ghost Light*? The campaign's title has a whiff of the hortatory, a teacherly recommendation, as if the city has been assigned homework for the month, or as if the whole city has been converted into a reading group. Except that it doesn't get to report on the book, just as it doesn't have a say in the choice. What, though, if half the city should rise up and reject the offered book and maybe propose another? When the scheme, which started in the US in Seattle, was brought to New York, the city's mandarins lined up to denounce it on the basis that its sophisticated inhabitants didn't need to be told what to read. 'I don't like these mass reading bees,' Harold Bloom told *The New York Times*. 'It is rather like the idea that we are all going to pop out and eat Chicken McNuggets or something else horrid at once.' After six months of wrangling the committee of educators, publishers and librarians entrusted with making the controversial decision finally narrowed the list down to two finalists: Chang-rae Lee's *Native Speaker*, a novel about a Korean-American in New York, and *The Color of Water*, a memoir by James Mc-Bride about a family with a Jewish mother and black father. Some of the committee apparently fretted that Hasidic Jews would take offence at passages in McBride's book; others worried that Asian-Americans would be upset by Lee's novel. In the end, the committee fell apart, leaving one faction, the New York Women's Agenda, to proceed on their own with *The Color of Water*. Many were unsurprised at the fiasco; after all, how could you expect a city as diverse and fragmented as New York to row in behind a single title? In a way, its arguments and shambolic collapse are more interesting than Dublin's apparent consensus. Literature should be fought over, should provoke passions in way that a display of hoardings will never manage. How much do we really care about that brand of perfume, that breakfast cereal, that magnified book cover?

The problem with campaigns is that we become immune to them; they reach our eyes but don't much engage us. Dublin is now a UNESCO-designated City of Literature, one of four such cities. The others are Iowa City, Edinburgh and Melbourne, so for now at least UNESCO seems to see literature as an Anglophone affair. The event to announce it took place in the shiny new Grand Canal Plaza, in the shadow of the Liebeskind-designed Grand Canal Theatre. There were speeches by the Minister of Arts, the Lord Mayor and a representative of Dublin City Libraries, which was the prime mover in the initiative. There was an atmosphere of general good feeling and a sense that whatever may or may not happen in the future the accolade was the least the city deserves given its rich tradition of writers. This note was struck again and again, in the comments from writers, in press release and in the press reaction. The editorial in *The Irish Times* was in no doubt about the literary importance of the city:

> The submission to Unesco goes straight to the point when it states that 'Dublin's chief credentials as a City of Literature lie in the historical body of work that has come from its writers over the centuries and from the equally acclaimed contemporary output of writers native to, or living within, the city's confines'.

But it does go on to acknowledge that relations between the writers and their city, or the country whose capital it is, were not always cordial, and gives a list of escapees: Richard Brinsley Sheridan, Bram Stoker, Oscar Wilde, Shaw, O'Casey, Beckett and Joyce. It also offers a compensatory list of those who stayed – Mangan, Yeats, Behan, Flann O'Brien, Kinsella and Austin Clarke – and refers to the many writers who migrated to the city and 'enriched its literary DNA', like John McGahern from Leitrim, Brendan Kennelly from Kerry, Seamus Heaney from Derry. Yet all of this, and indeed the event in the Grand Canal Plaza, left me a little queasy for reasons I couldn't quite articulate. When asked by a reporter what I felt about the designation I mumbled something about not being sure what it meant but that if it resulted in practical initiatives that promoted literature then it would be a good thing. But even as I spoke the words I felt I felt as if I had taken a mouthful of corporate chewing gum. It was as if the weight of official approval, of municipal and ministerial good cheer, was somehow too much. Maybe it was the implicit notion that writing was a kind of collective enterprise, an industry directed towards good, or economically quantifiable, ends. There was a sense that writing represents a moral good, an alternative to venality. 'Dublin is being seen as a literary city as opposed to the very crass city as it was during the boom. It's a reassertion of literary values,' one novelist commented, though another, the author of the satirical Ross O'Carroll-Kelly books, disagreed. 'Having made my living from the crassness of the Celtic Tiger, I'm afraid it's all over for me. Now, it's all about values.'

I suppose I resist the idea that writing shines like a beacon of good in a nasty world, or that writers, of their nature, add an exploitable lustre to a place. It was almost a relief to read in a follow-up article that hardly any tourists in Dublin were aware of its literary mightiness, past or present.

> Neither father nor son, Frank and Thomas Seidl, from Graz, Austria, can come up with the name of a single Irish writer or book. When asked what they'd expect from a Unesco City of Literature, Frank suggests, 'To be able to visit birthplaces of writers. And to have more big libraries like this one,' he says, indicating the Long Room behind him.

Maybe another element in my resistance was the emphasis on prizes and awards: the Nobel winners, the contemporary prize-winning novelists. All of these prizes are awarded outside of the country because, in fact, as a nation we don't go in much for prizes and awards, and in most cases the rewarded writers are published in London and New York rather than Dublin. We still depend on validation from abroad, it seems, even in the midst of this celebration of cultural prowess. The emphasis on prizes by the various speakers is actually an indication of just how difficult it is to incorporate writers into the municipal self-image. It might be difficult to celebrate amorphous concepts like writing or literature, but everyone can identify with success, and success is what the city badly wants in this low economic ebb. Rock stars, athletes, Nobel and Booker prize winners are what it wants. Not every writer, though, will be a medal winner, and some may not even want to enter the race. Some will be happy to choose invisibility or opposition; 'writing', after all, means nothing in itself, everything depends on the particular product of a single imagination working alone and not necessarily for anyone's benefit.

'Inquire for me in Baggot Street'

So what, then, is the proper relation between a writer and a city? As I walk back along the canal I think of the many writers who got on with their work near this stretch of urban water. This is one definition: a place where writers live and work, where literature happens. The city offers inviting physical evidence of creative habitation: within minutes I find myself glancing up towards the shining curve of the new stadium to salute the shade of John Berryman in Jack Ryan's in Beggars Bush. Berryman wasn't drawn to Dublin by its beauty or its literary tradition; he chose it because it was cheap and English-speaking, as good a place as any to disappear into his own head, let the 'Dream Songs' combust and converse with the major Irish stroller in his mental neighbourhood, Yeats. Although he met many writers and gave a famous reading, he didn't really engage with the place or its writers – 'are there any Irish poets of interest?', a diary note wonders. A troubled, ferociously intelligent, brilliant poet, he reminds us, maybe, that relations between writers and places can often be ghostly, that a writer can inhabit a place without being inhabited by it.

A little later, still alongside the canal, I'm outside 15 Herbert Place, looking up at the window of Elizabeth Bowen's childhood nursery with its watery light from the canal, and picturing, downstairs, the 'shapely Sheraton chairs, tables, cupboards, mirrors and sideboards that had been the work of Cork cabinet-makers in the eighteenth century'. Cork inside, and a cut-down Dublin outside, a micro-city, all rich 'red roads' and Ascendancy politics.

She spent her first seven winters in that house – spring and summer were for Bowen's Court when 'Dublin seemed to be rolled up and put away' – and gives an account of the period in her memoir *Seven Winters*.

Evidence, I'm thinking, maps, plaques, proof of the print of imagination. Here is Shaw as a toddler in Synge Street. Here are Wilde, Kinsella, Behan, here's Mary Lavin hunched over a story in the National Library, here's Máirtín Ó Cadhain correcting the proofs of *Cré na Cille*, and here, where fact and fiction intersect, is the house where Leopold Bloom lived 'in the imagination of James Joyce'. Here are 'Nightwalker', 'Mnemosyne Lay in Dust', 'My Love, My Umbrella'. Here is the molecular transference by which posterior and bicycle saddle are united. It's getting crowded . . .

All of this adds welcome layers to the city; a city, after all, is as much a mental as a physical space. It becomes a map of achievement, and everybody is free to construct their own version of it. All the more free since, in a sense, a literary city doesn't exist, any more than a composer's city or a visual artist's city. Writers and painters and composers and playwrights and makers of video installations exist. The literary pub crawl is a crawl through writers' heads, the clickable map is a virtual reality. And there's no absolute literature, no one version of literary truth.

For some writers, though, the city does have, or did have, absolutist functions, as an arbiter of taste, a seal of approval, offering itself as a kind of club, a collegiate conviviality, a beacon of the imaginative life drawing the best to itself, and a place, ultimately, where the hierarchies were settled: the minor, the lesser, the pretender and the king slugging it out in The Palace, The Pearl, McDaid's, The Bailey. Here's Kavanagh trying to get McGahern to go across the road to fetch him cigarettes like an errand boy, here's Behan frightening the life out of Kavanagh. Here are the famous remark, the ultimate put-down, the libel trial. A map of a particular kind of competitive maleness. The literary Dublin of the posters and the brochures was a male kind of city, hard-drinking and cordially vicious.

> I am so at home in Dublin, more so than in any other city, that I feel it has always been familiar to me. It took me years to see through its soft charm to its bitter prickly kernel – which I quite like too.

This observation by Louis MacNeice features on a bookmark for the literary website *Dublin Review of Books*, chosen, maybe, because it perfectly catches the familiar strangeness of the place and reminds us that a city can hold a mind even if it won't 'have me alive or dead'.

'It honours the city, it promises life'

For many writers the city is an irrelevance; it may provide them with jobs or sustenance but *la vraie vie* is elsewhere, on the Aran Islands, in a Connemara graveyard, on the streets of Boston or the villages of Maine. A literary city doesn't always feature in the list of characters. It may become familiar and comfortable enough to disappear from the attention span. But for others the place itself is always part of the story, the city's print on the imagination is heavy and the writing unimaginable without it. And the visible presence of writers themselves can also lend an extra dimension. In her biography of Kavanagh, Antoinette Quinn quotes the diary of a young engineer-cum-poet who lived in an apartment in Pembroke Road with his wife. He had missed the presence of the poet in the street when Kavanagh was on one of his doomed expeditions to London and had written to him when he returned to tell him he was glad to have him back. Why was it so good to have him back? She quotes his diary: 'it honours the city, it promises life'. A city, in other words, is enhanced, in ways hard to articulate precisely yet easy to appreciate instinctively, by the presence in it of creative artists. It adds to the currents of energy that make up a city, and by the same token a city in which artists can't live, for whatever reason, is impoverished.

Yet in some respects I realise that the way I think about Dublin is conditioned by the present reality of the place, and that nearly all my thinking is aesthetic, focussed on the imaginative resonance, the imaginative capital of the place, not just because those forces are powerful but also because the real cultural agencies are often situated elsewhere. The Irish writers celebrated by the city are not published here but in London or New York. Their success bears the stamp of the approval of the powerful English-speaking cultures whose prestige, money and marketing muscle place their work in the global Anglophone stream of writing, and at the same time allow the writers make a living from it. And yet as you attend book launches in the city and listen to English publishers and agents you realise that the city, and indeed the country, are peripheral, they are simply small scale local manifestations of a larger market. Irish literature is to some extent a local resource determined, developed, packaged and sold by external agents. There are of course local publishers, but they are generally small operations with a local reach. Children's literature, poetry and much nonfiction wouldn't exist without them, and their activity, even if limited by scale and resources, remind us how crucial it is to have a place for these voices to be taken up, to be dispersed where they can resonate. If we think of publishing or other kinds of cultural transmission as bus routes, these are the routes that the big companies don't want to operate. But our City of Literature is only left with these awkward and unprofitable routes. Does this matter, and will it matter in the future? Surely it's the writers who are important, regardless of who publishes them? It's complicated, but when I think about the future, I realise how much more I want than is currently available. There will be writers fifty or a hundred years from now, just as there are today. Their works will appear in many different forms, beamed at a keystroke or an inclination of the head into any number of micro devices. But beamed from where? A truly self-confident city would have its own secure cultural channels rather than relying wholly on the signals from beyond its boundaries; it would articulate itself rather than be articulated by forces beyond its control. It would entertain the marginal as well as the obviously commercial, its antennae would be attuned to the local peculiarities, the particular blend of noises this isle produces.

This isn't an argument for naïve sovereignty in a world where that concept has long lost its meaning, nor a plea for patriotic narrowness. The Dublin and the Ireland of the future will be very diverse, and its cultural infrastructure will reflect that diversity. But could Dublin, along with its festivals and its poets and writers, not also be home to great, far-reaching, internationalist publishing houses? Why should it not be a player in this as in other cultural industries? Why should we allow ourselves to forever be imprisoned in the hegemony of the English language, determined by our very success to be eternal provincials in the suburbs of the big decisions? Literature in Irish is a different matter; it will survive much as it does today, as a micro-culture within the city, insulated from the powers that marginalise it. It will continue to have its own dedicated writers and readers and its own public events, like today's lively and imaginative Imram festival and year-round events. The audience will probably not grow substantially, but Dublin will still be a centre for writers and readers in Irish, and the institutions that support the language – the universities, Foras na Gaeilge, An Gúm, the journal *Comhar* – will still be based in the capital.

I look around and see the enterprising magazine culture: *The Dublin Review*, *Dublin Review of Books*, *The Stinging Fly*, *Poetry Ireland Review*, *Cyphers*, *Comhar* and others, and realise that I want all that ambition and enterprise magnified by the gods of the future. And selfishly, unreasonably, I want more even than that. I want Dublin to be a creative city in the real meaning of that term, a city which values creativity for itself, and which puts it at the heart of everything that matters: education, planning, cultural policy. Artists have a role to play in the city beyond their individual artistic output, but there are very few outlets for their contributions. The Campaign for the Arts, with artists organised on a constituency basis as an effective lobbying group, demonstrated what artists could achieve as a vocal group dedicated to the improvement of their own sphere. It shouldn't be too utopian to want to see artists stitched into the fabric of the city so that all municipal policy incorporates their contribution and all citizens can benefit from the presence of art as an organic element of the city's life. Then we'll have a truly creative city.

Future shocks

And what about the marvellous, book-cancelling technologies of the future, are you not going to mention them? Surely we'll be well on the way to realising the dream of Jochen Gerz's *2/3 Streets*, surely the city will have found new, possibly author-less ways to tell itself to itself? I sit surrounded by technology – laptop, desktop, ebook reader, tablet computer – and use all of it happily, yet I don't feel any on it really impinges on the core experience of literature. It makes no difference to me how I am reading a book, once I am reading it: print, eInk, pixels may operate differently on the eye but the reading experience is the same. Literature has always depended on technology, but it has been its good fortune to be paired with enduring inventions – papyrus, paper, the printing press – each of which achieved such a plateau of seeming permanence as to become invisible, so the readers could get on with reading. The point of modern electronic technology is that it is short-lived, driven by intense marketing, and once it achieves the desired saturation, the technology will be replaced. I remember my first encounter with serious technology – my first typewriter, saved up for and bought in a shop in Pearse Street, used for years, brown nicotine stains on the top from my habit of resting a cigarette on it. Since that machine finally gave up the ghost how many computers have I been through, each proclaiming itself loudly and expensively as the last word in perfection?

How many hard drives, floppy discs, external drives, thumb-drives, CDs and DVDs? How many lost poems and essays? The average lifespan of data is five years or next week, whichever comes first, or nothing exists unless it exists in three places simultaneously. The future will in all likelihood be as technologically unstable as the present, locked into repetitive cycles of commoditised innovation, which is one reason it will remain essentially irrelevant to literature. Literature is the eternal vinyl, as constantly returned to as its demise is constantly proclaimed. The coders of e-books and web pages still struggle to represent the individual lines of poetry, maybe itself an emblem of poetry's commercial marginalisation. But poetry probably doesn't care too much – it's used to it. Literary forms are remarkably resistant and resilient. Virgil and Catullus could feel reasonably at home in twenty-first century Irish poetry. They might not like it, but they will at the very least recognise the continuity of the impulse, the hunger to force language into forms that codify and ramify.

The city of the novelists of the future will have changed out of recognition, but the novels themselves in their forms, impulses and narrative strategies won't have altered that much. Despite those who pronounce that every shift in the technology should be met with an answering aesthetic shift, art doesn't function as a linear progression and doesn't answer to the demands of the minute. People can have too much faith in gadgetry, imagining, as in one article I read recently, the children of the future walking around with the equivalent of the Library of Alexandria in their satchels. Apart from the fact that that library's existence could prove as precarious as the original, the essential component of any library or any literary experience is not technology, but time. The future of literature in Dublin as everywhere will depend a good deal on how much time its citizens carve out to produce and enjoy it. And on the things that no technology can predict or prescribe: the hunger, fire and talent of individual artists.

Biographical note

Peter Sirr lives in Dublin where he works as a freelance writer and translator. His most recent collection of poems is The Thing Is, *published by Gallery Press in 2009, which won the 2011 Michael Hartnett Poetry Award. He is a member of Aosdána.*

16

City Green

Deirdre Black
On Landscape

Introduction

Lucky is the citizenship that truly inhabits their city – that knows how to play in the city, learn, dance, eat, drink, work, make a home in the city, get around, make babies and grow older in the city, with no small sprinkling of panache and enjoyment. The good city is playful and nurturing, permitting self-realisation, a life freely constructed. People do not come to the city to experience nature, but are drawn by the opportunities of a kind of human habitat where roles are not quite fixed, where power and influence can be fluid. The great city holds the centres of command, but also enables revolution, protest and sedition, allowing sparks of change to ignite and urban processes to evolve over time. Dublin's streets, while not paved with gold, certainly twinkle where the original quartzy granite remains.

As human beings, other human beings are what interest us most in the cityscape. It is the richness of human variation that gives vitality and colour to the streets, squares, shopping centres and parks. What Jane Jacobs famously called the 'ballet of the street' is the great draw and the great engine of city life. Dublin is, however, a largely suburban city, even what may be called a rural city, for much of its extent. This sets up interesting possibilities for the future, some of which will be explored in this chapter.

The purpose of 'the green bits' in the city is primarily to support the well-being of the populace. It does this in a number of ways, but primarily by fulfilling biophilic urges, biophilia being what Edward O. Wilson defined as 'the innate affinity with nature' and a 'tendency to focus on life and lifelike processes'. A city plaza does not need to be green, but an open space with nothing living can become oppressive. A cycle route does not need to be a green route, but the experience can be more enjoyable if undertaken in natural surroundings. A street does not need trees to succeed, but they can contribute to sense of place, a humanised scale and comfort.

In more recent times, cities have begun exploring the practical uses of their green bits for flood control, sustainable drainage, improving air quality, energy use reduction in buildings, micro-climate modification, food production, transport, habitat linking and therapy. But in reality, if all the green in the city were to disappear tomorrow – no trees, no parks, no gardens, no beaches – the city would survive, albeit in a fairly miserable state. Not formally recognised as an illness (yet), Nature-Deficit Disorder is a term coined by Richard Louv in 2005 to describe an alienation from natural processes, which has particularly disastrous consequences for children.

While the green bits are not essential for cities to function, getting them right elevates a city from bearable to enjoyable. Getting the green bits wrong (wrong place, wrong scale) can create obstacles to a full life in the city. The green bits add structure to the city, providing edge and canopy, focal point, backdrop, wallpaper, corridor, barrier as well as bringing movement, seasonal change and beauty. City green, well-executed, provides opportunities for recreation, sport, meditation, and facilitates human interaction and celebration. More often than not, the green bits in our cities, including Dublin, are accidental, an afterthought, a by-product. And this is not always a bad thing. The discovery of a hidden green bit in the city (at the scale of a flower or an abandoned industrial site) is a revelatory pleasure. The current quasi-legal and dangerous practice of 'urban exploration' or urbex, where organised groups of people access forgotten or normally off-limits buildings and spaces of the city, exemplifies how the hidden or accidental parts of our day-to-day-worlds will always entice.

This chapter is about how we might, could, should and most likely will define, make, maintain, adapt, destroy, use, and pay for the green bits in Dublin. The city green, as I define it, is found in and around streets, plazas, pedestrian areas, footpaths, squares, roof gardens, parks, cycle-ways, play spaces, derelict lots, woodlands, cemeteries, allotments, community gardens, sports-fields, churchyards, urban farms, rivers, canals, beaches, agricultural land and, last but not least, in the extensive network of private gardens throughout the city. In this chapter, I take Dublin to mean the Dublin Metropolitan Area as defined by the Dublin and Mid-East Regional Authorities. This extends from Donabate to Greystones and inland to encompass Maynooth and Celbridge. The Greater Dublin Area, as defined by the Regional Authorities, incorporates all the counties of Meath, Kildare and Wicklow.

To put some structure on this visioning exercise, I have devised an equation that summarises the main variables in relation to future of the city green. It will be used as a mind funnel to distil the possible impacts of changing contexts. The variables of Baseline, Grey Bits, Fashion, Policy, Resources and Climate are factors that will determine the future evolution of the city green. See the following formula:

$$(\text{baseline} - \text{grey bits}^3) + \frac{(\text{fashion} + \text{policy})}{\text{resources}} \times \text{climate} = \text{the green bits}$$

The fist variable is the Baseline, or what the land wants to be. This largely concealed theoretical Baseline changes over time, and according to soil quality, climate, succession stage and whatever vegetation, seed banks and animals are in the vicinity. The contents of thousands of Dublin gardens set free would result in woodlands of unknown future structure and variation. It is not impossible to imagine great eucalyptus forests, rhododendron scrublands or sumac savannah, given the right conditions.

The next variable, the Grey Bits, encompasses what has been built, above and below ground: buildings, roads, paths, culverts, river walls, tunnels, pipes. Influencing the Baseline and the Grey Bits are Fashion, Policy and Resources. Fashion in this sense encapsulates the style of the day, the ideas of the generation, the wants of the populace, the zeitgeist, the 'now'. Policy is the official fashion of the day, tempered by the motivations of power structures, and encompassing the legal, and what is at any moment in time 'in the interest of proper planning and development'. Fashion often makes its way into Policy, but is also made manifest by individuals and communities.

Modifying all the fore-listed aspects are the Resources of the day, including money, skills and technology. Finally, the green bits are ultimately steered by Climate, macro and micro, climactic factors not just in Dublin but globally. The future may hold climate events in Ireland or beyond that would radically alter the make-up, structure and function of the green bits in Dublin city.

Previous centuries in Dublin have seen the taming and buffeting of the rivers and sea shores, the draining of the marshes, the layering of Modern over Victorian over Georgian over Medieval over Viking, with more recent overlays of suburban, new urbanism, town and village absorption and urban generated rural housing. Dublin also has to deal with the unstoppable green-ness of itself, a verdancy only really appreciated when one travels to cities with green that needs to be copiously watered and coaxed into existence. What we are left with is a city region with a huge variety of green spaces and features. But in this mélange, a curious homogeneity prevails, as if pseudo-Victoriana and a watered-down Garden City got married. And walls, lots of walls, as if the west of Ireland field-maker deep in our collective psyche still needs to clear the land of stones and mark out a territory.

Recent interventions have brought an approach to landscape design and maintenance that prioritises habitat protection, creation and linking, mainly arising from EU Directives, County Biodiversity Plans and the more recent Green City Guidelines. Some showcase spaces of contemporary design have also been constructed (to varying degrees of success) which broadened the understanding of how the city green can manifest itself: see, for example, O'Connell Street, Grand Canal Plaza, Fr. Collin's Park and the open spaces as-sociated with many of the new residential and institutional developments. The green in the city will most likely continue to evolve in accordance with these two broad churches – Biodiversity Protection and Clever Design for People.

Dublin is progressing from a long adolescence, essentially functioning as a large town, to the exciting grown up challenges of a modern city. As this evolu-tion unfolds, attitudes to the green bits will change from the rural concept of the green bits as 'setting' – productive field, uninterrupted view, more is better, heritage, tamed – to a more urban approach to green bits as social, nature experience, less-is-more, mutable, accessible, activity space.

If Dublin does densify and achieve acceptable levels of population to gen-erate a larger amount of strong urban areas, the services currently provided by the private green (gardens) will become demanded of the public green. People will be less likely to expect a private garden in the city. The parks and streets will be required to provide the green to satisfy a multi-generational city population.

The Baseline – *Sous les pavés, la plage*

$$(\textbf{baseline} - \text{grey bits}^3) + \frac{(\text{fashion} + \text{policy})}{\text{resources}} \times \text{climate} = \text{the green bits}$$

I keep an old postcard from Paris on my desk. On it, a 1968 protester throws a paving stone to the rallying cry *Sous les pavés, la plage!*, translated somewhat more clunkily into English as, 'beneath the paving stones, the beach!'. This quip was one of the many aphorisms put about by les '68ers who noticed a sandy foundation as they liberated the paving setts for throwing at les gendarmes. Sand is, of course, exactly what you would expect to find as a base for setts in a historic city, but the symbolism of a natural world trapped beneath the streetscape was of interest to the 1968 spirit of revolution and old order overhaul. The existence of another imagined city lay beyond what was obvious in contemporary social and political organisation.

'Sous les plage' postcard. (photograph Deirdre Black)

Fittingly, Paris was one of the first cities to create an actual urban beach with deckchairs, games and bars and has done every year since 2002. Now taking place on both sides of the Seine, Paris-plages roll out from July every year and provide welcome relief to overheating Parisians. Dublin has had its own urban beach, a pleasant, if compact beach-like experience on an island in George's Dock in 2008 attracting over 45,000 visitors, according to the Dublin Docklands Development Authority. One could argue that a city with real beaches with real sand

and the added benefit of real sea doesn't need an artificial one, and the Dublin plage wasn't repeated.

Making the most of the amenity potential of Dublin's natural landscape features – the visible Baseline within the city – is something the future Dublin will most likely grasp with sticky ice-cream fingers. The location and extent of the beaches will shift according to tidal diktats and future flood protection measures, and human use may be subject to habitat protection regulations, but the proximity of the water's edge will come to be seen as one of the city's Unique Selling Points when it comes to competing globally on quality of life charts.

The wider Baseline is what the city's land wants to be if left to its own devices. In Dublin's case this is probably a mixture of marsh, sand bank, woodland, scrub and bog. Short of a major accident at Sellafield or some other such catastrophe, and the subsequent abandonment of the city, it is difficult to predict exactly what ecosystems may emerge from the mixture of native and exotic plants and animals (including pets and the contents of the zoo) if we all packed up, left and turned off the lights. But what is certain is that nature would gorge on the dead city. The sight of a brazen sycamore shoot breaking through asphalt, or buddleia growing seemingly out of brick reminds us that nature is no shrinking violet. Rivers and streams would re-emerge, currently flowing unloved beneath the city. Beyond the contiguous city, and into the fields of grass, cows, horses and houses, the Baseline is also suppressed due to the suitability of the soils for raising cattle, horses and more lately, negative equity. Here a Baseline of high, dense oak woodland would most probably dominate with some areas of heath and bog.

We can see the beginnings of Baseline emerging in the forgotten places with seed banks of long memory, the long vacant sites in the city, at the new piece of land forming at the sand spit at Booterstown (virgin land formed from the sea, free to anyone to claim, I wonder, if one were to stake a claim, spike a flag, Neil Armstrong style), or at the salt marshes of Bull Island, naturalised riverbanks, pockets of woodland, overgrown gardens.

The future will more than likely take more heed of the Baseline. Legal protection of habitats and species will demand restoration, creation and linking of habitats in the city. The resurgence of what-the-land-wants-to-be will form part of long-term Green Infrastructure strategies arising from the current Greater Dublin Area Regional Planning Guidelines (see Policy section below). Increasingly urbanised generations will desire a natural complement to urban life: contained, accessible wildernesses, farm experiences, accessible and serviced beaches and swimming areas. Urban woodlands may become more acceptable, the key for success being the clever design of access points, edges, activities and throughways. This desire for *rus in urbe* will go hand in hand with the rise of a new aesthetic, let's call it the Berlin aesthetic, because that is where you find it in full sail, where what was previously described as 'messy' or 'abandoned' becomes redefined as 'natural' and 'pure'.

Oscar Wilde bemoaned 'nature's lack of design, her curious crudities, her extraordinary monotony, her absolutely unfinished condition'. These aspects will be integrated into city design, and may inspire new approaches to planning that follow nature's 'unfinished condition'. They may permit evolving rather than prescribed building use, which values adaptation and process management over large scale master planning and design.

Humanity's relationship with nature is by no means fixed, and there's nothing to suggest that it won't change from its current eco-idealisation to a more malevolent relationship as possibly cataclysmic natural events unfold. The identification of Ireland as a lifeboat nation (carrying refugees from other more climate change affected parts of the world) may in fact cause a desire for nature to be subjected, boxed, controlled. However, in the medium term it is probably safe to assume that our benign relationship with the Baseline in the city will continue.

The Grey Bits – The buildings between space

$$(\text{baseline} - \textbf{grey bits}^3) + \frac{(\text{fashion} + \text{policy})}{\text{resources}} \times \text{climate} = \text{the green bits}$$

The form of city green is, to a large degree, determined by the grey bits, where they exist, on, below and above the ground; the roads, footpaths, buildings and underground infrastructure. The space between buildings is a phase often used to bring awareness to the form and detail of the external 'voids' in the cityscape, and away from an analysis based on structures alone. This section looks at the buildings between space – what impact will the grey bits have on the green bits?

Many approaches to urban design which result in safe, lively streets and vibrant urban villages require no real green to work. David Sucher in *City Comforts: How to Build an Urban Village* (2003) proposes the following design principles as a simple prescription for a pleasant urban experience:

1. Build to the footpath (i.e. the property line)
2. Make building fronts permeable, i.e. no blank walls
3. Prohibit parking in front of buildings.

A general consensus is emerging of the benefits of laying out a city to favour the pedestrian. As Gordon Price, a former city councillor in Vancouver, said, lay out the city 'to be experienced at three miles per hour'. This advice ensures that the fine grain and pedestrian comfort of a city is respected, again, no real requirement for green.

The psychogeographer of the Situationist International and Baudelaire's *flânuer* share a love of experiencing the city afoot, wandering where one is drawn as opposed to what may be called utility walking, directly from A to B. The measured integration of the grey and the green is the key to supporting such simple urban entertainment. Street trees can bring beauty to the scene, but can also be an unnecessary intrusion to the delicate proportions of a vibrant street. Long lines of trees of the wrong proportion can bring monotony, but a single one in the right place can provide a visual pivot or focus. Sometimes the green and the grey combine in a less obvious manner. Many parts of the city benefit from the visual pleasure afforded by florist shops, flower stalls, garden centres and flower markets. The commercial green of the city is a simple, small scale tool to green a part of a street.

Dublin's buildings, roads and infrastructure have followed various different approaches to integrating grey and green. The intact medieval and Georgian streets in the city take no real heed of green for most of their extent. The green bits were concentrated in formal parks such as Merrion Square, Mountjoy Square and Fitzwilliam Square. These city parks have followed different paths in recent times, with a general trend of increasing activity and planned attractions: a major playground in Mountjoy Square; a calendar of events in Merrion Square. Further out from the centre, Victorian suburbs also concentrate green in small squares. Rarely a week goes by in the People's Park in Dun Laoghaire without an event, festival or market. Even the famously inward-looking Fitzwilliam Square has begun hosting markets and fairs. These parks are reflecting what is required of the changing city – an increasingly urbanised populace requiring activities, festivals and demanding more than benches and floral displays from their green spaces.

The suburban developments of the twentieth century often included green for ameliorative effect, but, when wrongly designed, located, scaled or used, the green bits can blight a neighbourhood. Too wide, too extensive green space, results in off-putting distances between buildings, people, and activities and stifles good city living. The term Subtopia was coined by Ian Nairn in the *Architectural Review* as early as 1955 to describe a landscape degraded by badly designed suburban sprawl. He described Subtopia as 'the annihilation of the site, the steamrollering of all individuality of place to one uniform and medio-cre pattern'.

In the future, the suburb will be retrofitted or die. This landscape retro-fitting will be carried out either by councils or by people taking things into their own hands. Suburbs will be made denser. Designs that support walking and cycling will become more important as issues of public health and energy use become more and more problematic. The western world diseases of the twenty-first century will be diabetes, obesity, asthma, and depression and these can be moderated by how we design the human environment, primarily by reducing car use for day-to-day activities.

Changes to suburban layouts are, however, often staunchly resisted, as sta-sis is the very thing that attracts people to the suburbs in the first place. But time will show that the scale of suburban development in and around Dublin is not sustainable in its current form. Approaches to retrofitting will vary. Dave Chiras and Dan Wann, in their 2003 book *Superbia!*, describe retrofit steps to a New Suburbanism which includes clustering parking, merging private green spaces to form better communal green spaces, introduction of local shops and offices – essentially turning a suburb into a village. More dramatic retrofit-ting is recommended by those in the Transition Town movement, as part of a shift to local resilience in the face of a predicted energy crisis, described in Rob Hopkin's *The Transition Handbook*. Each suburb will find its own way in updating what is undoubtedly an anachronistic housing layout.

In the future, the implementation of Green Infrastructure strategies will result in cities with more defined green spaces with specific functions. Barcelona famously embarked on a 'Spaces and Sculptures' programme at the end of the twentieth century – a series of projects which created 160 small public spaces. The spaces bore the strong stamp of their authors, a risk it was felt worth taking rather than maintaining what the mayor Pasqual Maragall called 'environmental mediocrity'. Oriol Bohigas, the instigator of the scheme, summed up the approach: 'Public space is the city, the space of collective life must not be a residual space, but a planned and meaningful space, designed in detail.' Dublin embarked on a similar, if smaller scale, project in the 1990s with a number of small spaces around the city receiving an overhaul. It is a policy of Dublin City Council in the current Development Plan to identify areas deficient in public space in order to identify appropriate locations for pocket parks. Such low key projects will continue as the city evolves with more attention to the fine grain.

The current architectural fascination with roof gardens and green walls, while certainly of benefit, is a piecemeal solution to a problem that requires

Killiney Woodland (photograph Deirdre Black)

a more extensive approach to facilitating green within the city region. However, if Dublin intensifies and grows taller, as some predictions would have us believe, we may find ourselves looking to other dense cities for advice on how to integrate the green and the grey. Osaka Station City is a new multi-use development at the city's main train station. The scheme includes 'Farm in the Sky' (*Tenku no Noen*) on the roof of one of Japan's busiest commuter stations. The farm contains 1,500 square metres of rice paddies and vegetable patches, and willing salary men swap suits for boots to tend their patches on the way home from work. The farm produces quinces, cherries, apricots, persimmons, oranges, chestnuts, kumquats, blueberries, rice, tomatoes and tea.

Historically, many of the world's cities practiced forms of urban agriculture, and while current urban farms primarily provide agri-therapy to city dwellers along with a home-grown supplement to their weekly food requirements, such projects may become more important in the future if fuel shortages or conflict disrupt food supply.

Fashion – We the citizens

$$(baseline - grey\ bits^3) + \frac{(\textbf{fashion} + policy)}{resources} \times climate = the\ green\ bits$$

Coco Chanel, who might be considered an expert on the subject, said: 'fashion is not something that exists in dresses only. Fashion is in the sky, in the street, fashion has to do with ideas, the way we live, what is happening'. In this section, the word fashion is defined to mean popular trends; bottom up demands; the zeitgeist; what seems appropriate at any given time. People of previous ages, who were perfectly nice apart from their large slave ownership or questionable attitudes towards women, are often excused because they were 'of their time'. This section will investigate what is 'of our time', and what might be 'of tomorrow'.

While some future prophets of the mid-twentieth century would have us all by now travelling in flying cars and wearing tin foil suits as we commute to the moon, the current future is looking a little more subtle. Ubiquitous technology is becoming more discreet and wireless than seemed possible. Tolerance, diversity and choice have become the values of the post-modern age. The green of the city is subject to its own fashions and to the fore, at the moment, it is that of the edible landscape.

If this fashion for Grow Your Own survives the recession, the demands on green spaces would radically alter the look of Dublin. The extent of land required for real urban food production is massive and the extent of urban space given over to traditional agriculture would ironically further disperse population with attendant problems for good urban living. New technologies are exploring high rise agriculture, hydroponic agriculture and living walls in order to close the gap between food source and food eater. In the near future, a real sustainable food supply system needs to be based on having shops with fresh produce for sale within five minutes walking distance of your house. Farmer's markets can fulfil a similar service. Dublin is lucky to have large areas of very productive land in its near vicinity, and in the event of series of food supply crises, these would most likely be utilised. In Spring 2011, Portland, Oregon enacted new planning regulations to protect over 100,000 hectares of farmland close to the city centre – might urban farmland protection be the new habitat protection?

A more urbane citizenship will demand access to nature within reasonable proximity. In Dublin this will mean more coastal recreation, more access and use of the mountains, and green infrastructure linking the city core to the suburbs and on to the agricultural lands surrounding the city. Cycle ways, bridleways, running tracks, mountain biking routes, hiking routes, rock climbing, marine sports – all will proliferate as Dublin flexes its muscles. Issues surrounding access to private lands will eventually be solved through meaningful inclusion of all relevant parties in recreation and land use planning, leading to consensus and win-win solutions,

In her new multi-platform project, Biophilia, Icelandic singer/artist Bjork plays with the boundaries of where nature, music and technology meet and overlap. The work includes music, apps, live shows, a documentary, a website and games and is concerned with Nature with a capital N, from cosmic to atomic. In the voiceover to the introductory downloadable app, David Attenborough's trusted tones lead us through a taster of the project:

> With Biophilia comes a restless curiosity, an urge to investigate and
> discover the elusive places where we meet nature, where she plays
> on our senses with colours and forms, perfumes and smells, the taste

and touch of salty wind on the tongue . . . we are on the brink of revolution that will reunite humans with nature through new technological innovation.

The project is a forerunner in terms of technology use, but also in terms of exploring a new interface between humans and nature. The barrage of discoveries currently taking place about the nature of nature, the astonishing achievements of physicists, biologists and astronomers, will, as scientific worldviews generally do, filter down into how society thinks of itself, and therefore, how we construct our places. While we can't be quite sure yet what this will be, it won't, I think, be boring.

Policy – Official fashion and the fashion police

$$\text{(baseline − grey bits}^3\text{)} + \frac{\text{(fashion} + \mathbf{policy)} \times \text{climate}}{\text{resources}} = \text{the green bits}$$

On 12 July 2011, armed police accompanied Meath County Council staff to dismantle an unofficial playground and pet farm that had been constructed by local residents in Churchfield's Estate, Kentstown, outside Navan. Pet animals such as rabbits and ducks were first taken away by the Council, and then later handed back to residents. According to local residents, the development (a shelter, picnic tables, play equipment, some fencing and a pet farm) had been funded by a whip around and built by the residents' association. There were complications around ownership and planning permission, and the whole lot had to come down. The scene represents an often repeated scenario, where policy and individual action fail to meet in the middle. The widespread print and radio time the event garnered proved how attracted we are to this clash of local bravado against 'the man'. It represents a long-standing (and often justified) distrust of planning processes in Ireland.

However, one would like to hope that the planning tribunals and the physical manifestation of bad or corrupt planning decisions have lanced this particular boil. Current policy in relation to the green bits of the Dublin region can be divided into two discrete approaches – any particular policy will find itself somewhere on a spectrum between one and the other. The first approach is determined by Deep Ecology – a branch of environmental ethics that confers value on the environment considered independent of its effects on its human inhabitants. The second is steered by Biophilia, which emphasises the importance of the human inhabitants' viewpoint and the ultimate dependence of human happiness on nature. The terms used in policy often reveal the underlying approaches, and where 'protect', 'preserve', or 'conserve' are used, the leaning is usually toward Deep Ecology. Where 'manage', 'evolve', or 'access' crop up, a more Biophilic approach is most likely.

One of the most powerful tools in the planning canon is 'access by proximity', and if we are to discuss green bits in the city, we must always discuss the human aspect. In Hamburg, nearly all of the city's residents are within 300 metres of a park and more green corridors are being made. Over the next seven years Copenhagen is planning to establish 14 pocket parks on disused land and plant 3,000 trees to create green streets. Dense architecture will be weaved with spaces to meet in and play. It's important to remember why people like to live in cities – interaction with other people and options for social life. Places should promote easy and natural interaction. In some ways, nature is in the city by way of invitation and must play by our rules. The concept of Sociotope mapping, progressed primarily in Sweden, is a process of looking at how spaces are used by humans in order to understand the meaning of the space, and in order to design the city green in a way that provides appropriate habitat for the human species.

The Regional Planning Guidelines for the Greater Dublin Area 2010-2022, published in June 2010, set out official policy for the immediate future. The document gives us some indication of the trends in high level planning policy. While the Metropolitan Area is defined as an area stretching from Donabate to Greystones and incorporating Celbridge and Maynooth (the 230m OD line denotes the southern extent of the metropolitan boundary), the Greater Dublin Area includes all of counties Meath, Kildare and Wicklow.

The Dublin and Mid-East Regional Authorities has an administrative influence on approximately 1.7 million souls. This still makes up less than 50 per cent of the population, but it is likely that the population of the Greater Dublin Area will push above the 50 per cent mark in the future, with interesting consequences for governance and self-perception of the city. Portland, Oregon tackled its own sprawl issues with the emergence of a regional government – Metro. A common urban problem is that the scale of political institutions is smaller than the scale of the actual region that needs to be planned. Ultimately, it is probably only a matter of time and population growth before the citizenship of Dublin demands truly urban governance for an urban area.

The concept of Green Infrastructure referred to extensively in the planning guidelines will help planners and designers look holistically at the areas of habitat protection, agricultural land maintenance, play and recreational needs and linkages to and between centres of population. Green Infrastructure is defined as including 'pasture lands, croplands, woodlands, heath, bog and scrubland, quarries, parks, formal and informal green spaces at varying scales, active and passive spaces, areas around domestic and nondomestic buildings, brownfield areas, waterways and water bodies, wetlands, coastal areas, and community/institutional lands such as hospitals, schools, graveyards, allotments and community gardens'. Really, what the concept does is put the green on a level par with what is elsewhere in the document called 'physical infrastructure' (as if the green were somehow imaginary).

The Guidelines recommend that Green Infrastructure is 'integrated, enhanced, managed and/or protected as part of the ongoing changes taking place regarding settlement and population, land use, planning, transport, economic activity, rural development, lifestyles, and ecology'. The inhabitants of a city do not have the time or inclination to spend their days traversing continuous green corridors, but love to flit between the green and the grey, the good city providing a pleasing interplay of both. These issues will need to be dealt with skillfully in Development Plans, Local Area Plans and in detailed design.

This approach extends to the 'Blue bits' with a specific policy recommending that 'the concept of coastal parks is considered in future planning as a means of enhancing coastal habitats, marine protection and sustainable marine-based tourism and of integrating coastal (blue) infrastructure with green infrastructure'. The ambitious goal of a coastal path for the entire greater Dublin area (feasibly from Balbriggan to Greystones) is mentioned in the Guidelines, part of which would include the Sutton to Sandycove promenade and cycle route which has been developed to preliminary design stage. The success of such a route will hang on the treatment of access points and links to the centres of population and transport nodes.

The National Landscape Strategy, which has been developed to a draft stage by the Department of Environment, Community and Local Government, and which currently awaits cardiac revival, will provide a welcome na-tional-level steer to the future of Dublin and Ireland's landscapes. It includes strategies for awareness raising, training and education, landscape identifica-tion and assessment and implementation. The use of fairly blunt instruments of prohibition such as Special Amenity Area Orders will probably die out in favour of more process-orientated approaches to landscape, as recommended by the European Landscape Convention (which Ireland ratified in 2002) where multi-stakeholder charters are entered into, management plans devised and action plans developed.

Taking all of this into account, we need to be careful in the future of the danger of too much open space in the city. In her seminal 1961 book, *The Death and Life of Great American Cities*, Jane Jacobs describes the misjudged application of More Open Space to solve society's ills. Her question posed of Manhattan in the 1960s may well apply to Dublin now or in the future, 'why are there so often no people where the parks are and no parks where the people are?'

Resources – You can't always get what you want

$$(\text{baseline} - \text{grey bits}^3) + \frac{(\text{fashion} + \text{policy})}{\text{resources}} \times \text{climate} = \text{the green bits}$$

In 2003, Berlin's mayor famously described the city as 'poor but sexy'. The quip found its way onto tourism brochures and t-shirts and enticed creatives from around the planet to live the modern Berlin life, one which revolves around intensely and freely inhabiting the city, embracing creative use of spaces and an assumption that city life should be seriously fun. Berlin balances a tragic historic legacy with the freedom that comes with the knowledge that it has been to the brink and back. It has swimming pools and paddleboats in the river, artificial beaches with bars, party parks, graffiti everywhere, barbeque areas, and an aesthetic that accommodates messy and calls it biodiverse, and puts on Sunday afternoon Karaoke in Mauerpark, a park made from the old Death Strip along the Berlin Wall. There can be problems, but the spaces don't get blamed, the people who cause the trouble are blamed. The lesson to learn is that good design usually costs the same as bad design. And when money is short and people have time on their hands, good open space design, or rede-sign, or retrofitting is infinitely possible.

The future is not what it used to be – the technological march does not necessarily stomp in the one direction. While we seem to be hurtling towards ubiquitous technology, with wi-fi everything at our fingertips, all the time, anywhere, there is always a possibility that the future will be less technological than the past. Fuel crises, electricity shortages, a forced move to self-sufficiency, climate change, catastrophic war, all could cause a retreat from technological progress. History, if nothing else, usually repeats itself, and if the Dark Ages happened once, who's to argue they may not happen again, but on a potentially more dramatic scale considering the dependence of so many and so much on electronics, mass media, consumer culture, food imports and oil.

Dublin has the capacity to remain liveable even when times are tough. A certain lo-fi styling always suited Dublin. It did not wear well the glitzy tack of the brief turn of the century boom. Clever things like the city bike scheme suit Dublin, funky ramshackle places like Shebeen Chic on George's Street and the Dice Bar on Benburb Street suit Dublin. The equivalent green lo-fi experi-ence is difficult to identify in Dublin, and perhaps this is what's next in the evolution of the city green. The recession has seen an upsurge in community gardens, where process and participation is valued over aesthetic perfection – in the future these places may need to be formalised in terms of management and funding. Less is often more when it comes to the green bits – one big tree, properly planted, in the right place can have more impact than a swathe of fiddly planting, or 'those little cartoons of the countryside', as described by James Howard Kunstler.

The future will favour cleverness over showiness, the accommodation of process and change in the city over the construction of sterile and 'finished' spaces, which is just as well, as there doesn't appear to be any money to finish them anyway.

Climate – Rain drops keep fallin'

$$(\text{baseline} - \text{grey bits}^3) + \frac{(\text{fashion} + \text{policy})}{\text{resources}} \times \mathbf{climate} = \text{the green bits}$$

The final variable, Climate, is a constantly changing factor, particularly on any particular day in Dublin. The trend towards global warming will, according to current forecasts by Met Éireann, affect Ireland in two distinct ways – drier, warmer summers and wetter winters. It is anticipated that the type of variability we experience now will still be a feature in the future. We may still have four seasons in one day, but when heatwaves occur, these are likely to be record-breaking.

Climate change may not have a huge effect on Dublin's green bits, short of a need to avoid schemes requiring extensive irrigation and to rethink plant and tree species. What might have a greater impact on the green of Dublin would be an influx of climate change refugees, with a new set of expectations as to what the green bits are for. Another consequence could be a large influx of seasonal tourists attracted by the relatively mild summers (compared to that perhaps experienced by southern Europe). This could result in a celebration of our relatively sodden climate, with opportunities provided for people to be happily rained on in public spaces.

Wetter winters are a thing no Dubliner would welcome, but the fact is that Dublin is drier than generally lamented. The average number of wet days (days with more than 1 milimetre of rain) is currently about 150 days a year along the east coast. That makes up less than half of the year, with many fewer days in summer than during the rest of the year. Average hourly rainfall amounts during any of those days are quite low, ranging from 1 to 2 milimetres. As a professional pedestrian, I have come to appreciate the effectiveness of shelter provided by certain trees when navigating the city. Selective sheltering of some routes for utility walkers may become more of a requirement if future climate predictions are fulfilled.

Conclusion – Tomorrow life will reside in poetry

$$(\text{baseline} - \text{grey bits}^3) + \frac{(\text{fashion} + \text{policy})}{\text{resources}} \times \text{climate} = \textbf{the green bits}$$

The variables discussed in this chapter will come together in different combinations to produce city green of varying character, function and style as the centuries roll along. The wide-spreading Dublin Region may come to resemble something like what architect Will Alsop has called the rural city, or what Kevin Lynch has called the urban countryside:

> 'Imagine an urban countryside, a highly varied but humanised landscape, it is neither urban nor rural in the old sense, since houses, workplaces and places of assembly are set among trees, farms and streams. Within that extensive countryside, there is a network of small intensive urban centres. This countryside is as functionally intricate and interdependent as any contemporary city'.

Another possibility is the development of an American-style 'doughnut city', with an increasingly derelict and desperate centre surrounded by more affluent suburbs. Each generation abandons a new ring, to colonise a wider untarnished piece of Greenfield sub-suburbia with all its promise of 'the best of the city and the countryside'. The city eventually becomes unnecessary, as people retreat to the private sphere for entertainment and technological communication. The draw of the coast may make this option less realistic, as proximity to the sea is always a bonus in the city – bar, of course, catastrophic sea level rise.

Dublin could go the way of Vancouver – much of a similar baseline is there, sea, mountains, fresh air, youth. A concentration in the core and an application of impeccable green policies could transform Dublin into a world ranking work/play city. However, while nature is currently seen as a benign element to be welcomed into the city, the occurrence of natural disasters, climate upheavals or new diseases spread by wild animals could tarnish humanity's current love affair with the natural. We could come to curse nature and seek to exclude it from our living spaces as much as feasible.

The still fresh font of agricultural expertise in the Dublin region could fuel a successful commercial scale urban food industry. There would be less need to rely on the clever approaches more built-up cities need to utilise – roof farms, hydroponic growing, permaculture, etc. – although these would certainly need to form part of the plan. Dublin has land resources such as the Pheonix Park, the vast field-like spaces of the suburbs, mountain pasture, productive market garden and agricultural areas and the sea, all of which combined could set a world standard in city-region food self-sufficiency. The aspirational 100-mile diet, where only food grown within one hundred miles is consumed, is a possibility for Dublin citizens.

Yet another possibility is a radical change to our aesthetic sensibilities. This may evolve naturally, as has happened since aesthetic sensibilities began, or occur as a reaction to some unknown event in the future. A recent surge in the amount of books, art, film and photography concerned with types of landscape variously termed 'Edgeland' (Marion Shoard), 'Drossscape' (Alan Berger), or 'Unofficial Countryside' (Richard Mabey), could be the start of a general aesthetic appreciation of apparently meaningless spaces in the urban fabric, in-between spaces with little function, abandoned gaps in the urban/rural interface. The photographer Paul Seawright has explored the impact of such spaces in his work, as well as the poets Paul Farley and Michael Symmons Roberts in their 2011 book *Edgelands*. A film festival was held in the UK this summer to celebrate the 'liminal' and 'urban outskirts'. Ever popular with adventurous children, attracted to an unsupervised wilderness, and surprisingly biodiverse, they could become the protected lands of the future.

Biographical note

Deirdre Black works as a landscape architect and writer in Dublin. She is a past president of the Irish Landscape Institute and has taught in UCD and DIT. She lives in a fairly urban part of the city near the sea, with her family, and considers herself a bit of a flâneuse.

17

To Thine Own Self Be True

Gregory Bracken
On the View from Without

Being outside

'Neither a borrower nor a lender be.' Polonius's advice to his son Laertes would perhaps seem to sum up the smug and somewhat head-shaking incredulity of some of the wealthier nations of Europe at the seeming folly of their spendthrift smaller neighbours. As this is a book about the future of Dublin, and this chapter is to try to provide a view from the outside, it might be a good idea to try to take into account what has been happening to Ireland in recent years to explain the perceptions of these events from the outside. Outside the country, that is, not merely the city of Dublin.

The notion of being outside is an interesting one. One that is part and parcel of Ireland's somewhat insular perspective – a forgivable and not inappropriate foible given the country's island status. It might also be useful to explain a little about who I am, and which particular bit of the outside I inhabit. Actually, I was brought up in County Kildare and studied architecture at Bolton Street College of Technology (since 1992, Dublin Institute of Technology), starting in the mid-eighties. I now live in Amsterdam and teach architecture at the Technical University of Delft. I am also a research fellow in Leiden University's International Institute for Asian Studies. My work at both universities combines the practical experience of having worked as an architect in Asia (in Bangkok and Singapore) and the theoretical research I have been doing while studying in the Netherlands.

This essay will look at Dublin from the point of being outside of it, and will also try to place the city within its wider context vis-à-vis the rest of the world. It might be instructive to begin with something that happened to me while I was on a visit to Dublin about ten years ago. I was home from Singapore and had stopped for a coffee in Bewley's. It was a wet Friday afternoon so the place was packed. My telephone rang. It was a friend from Singapore who wanted to know if I was going out for a drink later on. I said I couldn't as I was home in Ireland. 'Where?' came the puzzled reply. 'Ireland,' I repeated, a little louder. 'I come from Ireland,' I added by way of explanation. Now, I have to point out that my friend was very far from being stupid, but he came from a rural part of Peninsular Malaysia and had not attained what could be called a particularly high level of education. '*Where* are you?' he persisted. I kept repeating the word 'Ireland' until I was at last obliged to say, to the considerable bemusement of those at neighbouring tables, 'it's a small country near England'. 'Oh,' said my friend. He didn't sound exactly sure where this exotic location might be. 'OK lah, I'll see you when you get back,' and he hung up.

While this may seem a somewhat startling anecdote to those who have always lived in Ireland – the notion that our entire country may not even exist in the consciousness of someone on the other side of the planet – it remains a sobering thought. It also goes to the heart of what it means to be outside. The Dutch word for 'foreigner' is *buitenlander*, someone who is from the *buitenland* (literally the 'outer lands'). In Chinese it's *wei ren* ('outside person') from *wei guo* (again, 'outer lands'). This would seem to reinforce a nation's consciousness of being at the centre of the world, a place where everything else is, by definition, peripheral.

The title 'The View from Outside' was suggested to me by this book's editor and I thought it an appropriate one. Perhaps it's the result of the genetic memory of all those centuries of emigration, but Oscar Wilde's comment about exile being for the Irish what captivity was for the Jews still holds true (at least for the Irish – the Jewish side is sadly out of date in a post-Holocaust world). The view from outside is an important one, not only for the millions who have been forced to leave the country, but also for those who have been privileged to stay at home. The notion of Ireland as home, as a place where there will always be a candle in the window, has become increasingly important once again. For a few years it seemed as if economic success would banish the spectre of emigration for ever, but then something, sadly, went wrong. It wasn't any one thing in particular, rather a series of inter-related incidents that plunged an entire country, and of course its capital city, into the bad old days of gloom and despair – at least that's what seems to be the case from the outside. Perceptions of course depend on perspective, and perspectives can be temporal as well as spatial. This essay will take a somewhat *longue durée* view of what has been happening to Ireland in recent years, but will begin by taking a brief look at the perceptions of what exactly this is.

Old models and new

The Celtic Tiger which roared its way through the nineties and the early years of the twenty-first century was a time when the candle in the window was replaced by winking neon over a door that was always open for business. The country, to use the old saying, was on the pig's back. All this new-found wealth and confidence was particularly obvious in Dublin, with new buildings, new restaurants, new cars and new clothes. The new confidence was built on a seemingly safe sense of fiscal security. What could possibly go wrong when all that money was tied up in something as solid as bricks and mortar? Everyone's investments seemed, literally, as safe as houses.

Sadly, western capitalism, and particularly perhaps its most recent incarnation, neoliberalism, is premised on a cycle of boom and bust. It is of course obvious when a system collapses or, as in Ireland's case, undergoes a severe correction, that the boom-and-bust cycle may not after all be the best way of doing things. But even when things are going well there are dangers. Sudden wealth can be as devastating to a city, and its people, as any natural disaster. This has been the case in the boomtowns of East Asia over the past few decades. The waves of neoliberal capital that washed over Ireland had their worst effects on its cities, particularly Dublin because of its size and dominant position in the country. Indeed, it was in Dublin that some of the worst excesses of the property market were perpetrated.

Cities are crucibles of change and development. All those glittering new buildings were like the cathedrals of a new religion: Money (with the ATM being the road-side shrine). New buildings may have raised the average height of Dublin's skyline, but sadly, they probably also lowered the quality of life for its inhabitants. All that noise and dust; the arid new 'public' spaces; the people who had been forced to move from their homes as their neighbourhoods were earmarked for redevelopment – and the impatience with anyone who seemed less than willing to join in this new economic miracle. And then came the crash: 2008 saw the banks' dangerous practices exposed for what they were – which was hardly limited to Ireland, but in Ireland's case this was followed by a devastating collapse of the inflated property market, particularly in a Dublin which had seen the worst of the overvaluation. The overvaluing of property is easy to spot in hindsight, and there have been similar crashes – London in 1989, southeast Asia in 1997 – but in an Ireland marooned on a threadbare patch of now, what can be done to improve the chances of having a brighter future? Perhaps this is where the view from outside can be helpful. If we look at the years of neoliberal capitalism for what they were – an invasion – we may then be able to see them as a valuable lesson, a warning to be more circumspect about what models we choose to import in the future.

Ireland has traditionally embraced its invaders. Danes, Normans, Elizabethans all tended to 'go native' after a generation or three, and the evidence of their invasions is still to be seen in the landscape: Palladian country houses, Norman castles, round towers, and of course that most influential invasion of them all, the Roman Catholic one. Even that most Christian of symbols, the cross, was subsumed into native Irish culture, becoming a hybrid of orthodox cross and pagan moon to form the Celtic cross. Catholic churches still spike the skyline while the remains of the once powerful monasteries pepper the countryside. Some of these became picturesque ruins, but others made the successful segue into elite educational establishments. The Palladian country house was a particularly clever import. The houses themselves may have represented what Michel Foucault calls an invading aristocracy and were resented by a native population who saw them as impositions from England, rightly so, as they clearly represented the new ascendant class of Protestant landowners, but the model itself wasn't English at all – it was Italian. Andrea Palladio had rediscovered and reinvented the classical Roman precedents and applied them creatively to design effective working farms. Which is probably why they worked so well in Ireland (and England). These houses weren't simply gaudy status symbols, they were social relations writ in stone. They represented an agrarian way of life, one that was laid out in all its hierarchical simplicity with a great house at the centre and a great estate surrounding it. They may indeed have represented an inequitable system, one that was eventually overthrown, but for a time, and a very long one at that, they worked.

Sadly, the twentieth century saw the import of other less successful models, one of which also came from the south of Europe: the Spanish bungalow (most of which were about as Spanish as Santa's Grotto). Not all models will work when they are transplanted from place to place. Another notoriously unsuccessful model – and one with special relevance for Dublin – is the Modernist tower block used for social housing. In places like Ballymun, Le Corbusier's utopian dream of towers dotted across a park turned into a dystopian nightmare of discarded dreams and broken promises. There were streets in the sky that nobody wanted to visit, and there may have been parks but they were car parks full of rusting trucks and rubbish. The once beautiful (and fertile) landscape that surrounded these towers was assaulted and left to die. It is now generally accepted that the Modernist social housing model was a failure, certainly in the West, but it enjoyed considerable success in Asia, in cities like Singapore and Hong Kong. We can conclude, therefore, that it is not necessarily the model that is at fault, rather how it is applied.

Ireland's most recent wave of invasion, neoliberal capitalism (something that was wholeheartedly embraced by the country), has also left its mark in the form of the ghost estate. Karl Marx was wrong when he said all that was solid melts into air. In Ireland, where nearly everything that was sacred had indeed been profaned, we need to start thinking carefully about what models we choose to accept. Maybe it's time to start looking for new ones?

The Dutch word for debt is the same as 'guilt'

I mentioned earlier that what has been happening recently in Ireland is not unique. There was the collapse of the London property bubble in 1989, and the disastrous crash that rocked southeast Asia in 1997. There was also, of course, the infamous Wall Street Crash of 1929, the South Sea Bubble, Tulip Fever, and so on. The list is a long one. Every society has had its setbacks, it's how they deal with them that shows what they are made of.

There is, in fact, a lot of sympathy for what is happening in Ireland, even a degree of understanding. Long poor, the country suddenly became rich. It even went a little mad. Why not? People tend to lose their heads when that sort of money starts rolling in – sadly, it's the sort of sympathy reserved for lottery winners who drink themselves to death. What is alarming is that no one in Europe is questioning the system that led to this situation, the one-size-fits-all mentality that led Ireland and Portugal, Greece and Spain to this sorry pass. But that is not what this essay is about. Besides, there are better qualified people than I to examine these issues.

I opened this essay with the famous quotation from *Hamlet*. 'Neither a borrower nor a lender be.' This is followed by, 'For loan oft loses both itself and friend/And borrowing dulleth edge of husbandry', which is not to say that I am against borrowing per se, or lending for that matter. I am perfectly aware that life as we know it would not be possible without such transactions. Even so vast and, for a time, successful an entity as the British Empire was only made possible by creative debt financing (something which the crafty Dutch invented and England embraced along with Protestant William of Orange). England's brilliant move was to always pay on time, something which lulled their lenders into being less concerned about the sheer size of the loans. And this is what Ireland is doing, diligently paying back what is owed. This is important to a watchful union of nations who take debts (and their repayments) very seriously. Indeed, the Dutch word for 'debt', *schuld*, is the same as 'guilt', something that tells us a lot about their attitude to money. Of course the twenty-first century has more sophisticated financial markets than those that operated at the time the British Empire began to put out its imperial feelers. This is an era when ratings agencies can, and do, create self-fulfilling prophesies. Ireland is not in a position, like Malaysia in the 1997 crisis, to opt out of a system that has brought it to such a sorry pass. (Malaysia, with its oil reserves, was simply able to ignore the International Monetary Fund when it felt its interests were not being served.)

I mentioned the old phrase 'on the pig's back' to describe the good old days of the nineties and early years of this century. The Chinese have a similar saying – on the tiger's back – and like many a Chinese saying, it is very similar to those of the west, yet subtler. When your ride a pig's back you can simply hop off when the jaunt is over (you even have the option of eating the pig). A tiger, however, is a much more dangerous beast, one that is far more likely to want to devour you. The Celtic Tiger turned on its rider with a vengeance in 2008 and it is interesting that a Chinese saying should so neatly capture what happened to a country so far away.

In fact, there are more similarities between the Chinese and the Irish than you might think. We both have clan systems, both have ancient family names (many of which are interchangeable, such as Long, Low, Hoey, etc.). There is a rural ethos permeating both nations' identities, as well as a profound respect for the rural way of life. Both countries have ancient and unbroken cultures stretching back millennia, and there is an acute awareness of history in daily life. Events from centuries past are perceived as having an immediate relevance to the present day in a way that Americans, for example, would never understand (a country where if you want to dismiss something as irrelevant you simply call it 'history'). And both China and Ireland have national diets that revolve around pork – although admittedly the Chinese have the edge there. The only real difference is size. Occupying opposite ends of the Eurasian landmass, Ireland is a small island, whereas China is a vast empire (roughly the size of America).

The past is part of who you are, it makes you into the nation you are today. Where you come from also determines where you're going. The Irish are good in a crisis, sometimes they even seem to thrive on them. It's their inability to handle success that has caused the recent problems. If we take the *longue durée* view, however, you will see that recovery will follow, it always does. The nineteenth century was one of decline for Dublin, the first half of the twentieth century also. Then growth began to occur, but unfortunately it was the wrong sort of growth, in that it followed the American model of urbanism. City planners privileged the car and developed endless suburbs, ripping out what had been one of the world's most efficient public transport systems in the process – Dublin had five mainline railway stations, two depot stations and fifteen tram lines (not to mention the one that linked Terenure to Blessington) at the outbreak of World War I. All of this was replaced in a post-independence Dublin by the Brave New World of American planning which led to the 'doughnut model' of rings of homogenised housing encircling a decrepit and decaying city centre.

I first moved to Dublin as a student in the mid-eighties, a low point for the city, but one from which it was about to miraculously emerge (although nobody could see it at the time). All we knew was a damp smoggy city, with the dereliction around Bolton Street, once one of the most fashionable parts of the city, being particularly depressing. Ruined mansions overlooked vast rubble-strewn car parks taking up whole city blocks. Street fronts snarled at you like so many gap-toothed thugs. Then came the miracle. The city revived, almost by magic. Temple Bar took off and the gaps in the rest of the city slowly filled up. Derelict blocks were developed. The money that poured into the city during this time has done no end of good. It may have caused some problems as it was happening, something I referred to at the opening of this essay, but its overall effects were good. The city fabric has been repaired, streets have been rebuilt and tramlines reinstated. New bridges span the Liffey and new motorways link the city to its hinterland. This reconstructive surgery has changed the face of Dublin, and while it may be unsettling at first to see an old friend with a facelift, you soon get used to it (especially when it's an improvement). What was done during the Celtic Tiger years was done well and will stand the city in good stead in the future.

Take for example the docklands. This was actually an exemplary piece of urban regeneration. Unlike many such gentrification efforts in the cities of East Asia, the Dublin docklands ensured a good social mix, at an appropriate scale with good connectivity. All of which will ensure its success as a new and potentially vibrant district for the city for years to come. The Dublin Docklands Development Authority clearly modelled their interventions on similar schemes in the United Kingdom, but they were also (perhaps even unwittingly) following a pattern that was being widely seen across Europe at the time, in port cities like Hamburg and Amsterdam especially. And this is what has made it so successful. The docklands redevelopment model is one that works well both in Europe and the Anglo-American world. Certainly it was better than the exclusively American models that had been employed in Dublin in the twentieth century.

Just because a model works in one place does not mean it can be applied everywhere. We saw how disastrous the Modernist tower block and the Spanish bungalow have been in their Irish settings. Yet the Palladian town and country houses did work. We need to be more circumspect about what we choose to import, and we need to stop slavishly following Anglo-American trends (which is not to say we can't use them if they're good – sadly, they so seldom are). We can't help sitting like a gooseberry in the middle of the 'special relationship', but it need not fool us into thinking we have more in common with Americans (or the English) than we actually have. Ireland has often been seen as a handy stopping off point for American politicians on their way to the larger arenas of Europe, but we need to break out of this false sense of similarity. Of course we feel comfortable with the American way of life, so many Americans claim Irish descent (even the unlikeliest of presidents), but this *does not* work both ways. Then of course there are the films, the music, the technology and the food. There's even the so-called democratic values and, perhaps most confounding of all, our sharing of a common language (which in our case is nothing more than a stepmother tongue). Do not be fooled, however; we are not the fifty-first state, we are in fact closer to Europe than most people realise (as any Irish person living in Paris or Berlin or Amsterdam will tell you).

There is one particularly striking example of the Europeaness of the Irish that is apparent in Dublin: the café. Dublin has always had a distinctly European-style café society. Something that London never had – the closest they got was the Lyons Corner House and even they didn't stay the course. Dublin has always been home to Bewley's – the grim little London caff is hardly the same species. There was always something luxuriously Middle-European about Bewley's panelling, its stained-glass windows and its crackling grates. Not to mention the mugs of milky coffee (a European decoction if ever there was one). Even in the bad old days of the seventies and eighties, Dublin had this most European of institutions. Perhaps we should now be looking again to Europe for other institutional models instead of following the easier English-speaking path?

Go East!

Rousseau tells us that 'houses may make a town, while only citizens can make a city'. After all my years of study, virtually all I have learned can be summed up in one simple phrase: a city is its people. A sobering thought for any architect or urbanist. Of course without the buildings, and the spaces between them, people wouldn't be able to make proper use of a city, but anyone can design buildings, and anyone can plan cities; we've been doing it for millennia. But for a city to be successful there has to be something else, something that is ineffable, something, for want of a better word, 'magical' about how people get together and form a place they call a city. Marguerite Yourcenar tells us that, 'Plumber and mason, engineer and architect preside at the births of cities; [but] the operation also requires certain magical gifts'. Dublin without Dubliners would be nothing; worse, it would be unthinkable.

Dublin has produced writers, artists and wits, scientists and statesmen. In terms of culture the city has always punched above its weight. The city has a profile that is internationally known and respected. People all over the world know who we are (ill-educated Malays notwithstanding), a fact that has leant our plight in recent years more sympathy than some of our neighbours (who have signally failed to give so much intellectual pleasure). Culture is rightly understood to be important to the Irish. We are, after all, the only country in the world to have a musical instrument for its emblem (instead of the more usual eagles, lions and unicorns). Whether it's the novels of James Joyce or Maeve Binchy; the music of U2, Enya or Westlife; the plays of Beckett, Shaw or Wilde; the poetry of Heaney, Kinsella or Yeats; even the sainted Irish bar everywhere to be seen throughout the world, the Irish are known and appreciated, admired and respected. Even a city like Shanghai, whose immense size and wealth has made it an excellent place for the harnessing of the hardware that makes for global greatness, would love to be seen in the same light as Dublin, at least in cultural terms. The Shanghainese may have built any number of state-of-the-art museums, concert halls and libraries, but this hasn't placed them on the cultural map for the simple reason that culture is a very delicate flower, one that can only thrive in the most fertile of soils. It is not something that can be imposed from above, and it does not automatically follow as the result of good city planning. Culture can only develop naturally, and only if the conditions are right. The conditions are right in Dublin, and always have been. Ireland's history may be one of sadness and regret yet the Irish people's ability to make the best of things is reflected in this culture. This enviable ability to produce so much bald-faced talent – in music, in literature and in the arts – will stand the country in good stead and is something to bear in mind for the future, not just in the heritage sense, but as something practical yet beautiful to sell to the rest of the world. It could be one of the building blocks on which to build a brighter future.

There is something very democratic about the future. It really is everyone's to do with what they like. What Dublin does now will affect its future for generations to come. And if the past is anything to go by, the future will be bright. Ireland's millennial view of things (the *longue durée*) means that the city will survive, it will even thrive. What Dublin needs to do is stop following the tired old transatlantic tropes that have failed to serve it in the past. Look to Europe and choose from what is best for a medium-sized port city facing onto one of the world's richest regions. The smaller European countries have to make better models for a small island like Ireland than the homogenising vastness of America. Look at the cities of the Netherlands, or Finland or Denmark. Places like Amsterdam, Helsinki and Copenhagen all have a cosmopolitanism that resonates with a Dublin that is home to places like Bewley's rather than the bleak blandness of its suburban office parks (interestingly, the very places where American companies feel most at home).

Ireland may be English-speaking, but never forget that it is in fact a bilingual culture (increasingly so, it seems, every time I visit). Dublin's openness to Europe can only be helped by this enviable ability to think in two languages and more people need to start learning the languages of our European neighbours. We should be more like the Dutch, a tiny trading nation where everyone can speak three or four languages. And Dublin need not limit its scope to Europe. It can afford to look further afield, to the cities of Asia perhaps, places like Singapore and Hong Kong, and the cities of China. We've already seen the affinities between the Chinese and the Irish; Dubliners could do worse than follow Rem Koolhaas's advice and Go East! The Irish could even go one better than the Dutch (who tend to concentrate on English, French and German, the languages of their nearest neighbours). We should be learning *Putonghua* (Mandarin Chinese), Arabic and Hindi.

Ireland also has something that the Dutch, for all their hard work and diligence will never enjoy, which is a beautiful landscape. This is apparent even in a city like Dublin because it sits on a bay that has been compared to Naples for beauty, and from almost every point in the city the Dublin Mountains can be seen hovering in the distance. One of the most fascinating features of the Irish landscape, as we saw earlier, is that it is so full of ruins, the time-worn evidence of so many invasions. Ghost estates and empty office blocks are just the latest in this poignant series. In time, these too will fade and come to occupy their proper place in Ireland's story. Ireland has survived through the centuries because it was able to overcome these previous waves of invasions. The country even managed, for a time, to enjoy spectacular success. Even if it didn't last, it could well happen again, why not? And next time we'll be ready for it.

A city like Dublin has rich resources, culturally, socially, geographically. It should start thinking about building its recovery on that. Stress the quality of life in the city when attempting to attract new business and tourists. Stress the fun that can be had here, and the beauty of its surroundings. Make the city a source of envy, safe envy, as there's nothing you can do about where you happen to be born. And there is the added advantage of speaking English, a fact which makes Dublin more open to the world, but would make it even more so by learning to speak more of the world's languages, particularly the up-and-coming Asian nations.

Look to the success of the cities in Asia at generating economic growth. See how the Chinese have made clever use of imported models – the most clever about it being their ability to adapt them to their needs. Communist China has embraced western capitalism, but has imbued it with 'Chinese characteristics' (and don't forget, China was one of the few countries to remain unaffected by the crisis of 2008). The Chinese are brilliant at taking what they want from the west and making it their own. They don't swallow ideas whole, as we did with Modernist tower blocks and neoliberal principles. We could learn a lot from that (and from our own ancestors who so artfully combined the new Christian symbolism with the existing pagan ones to produce the famous Celtic cross). Dublin should cast its net wider over the globalised world but should be more careful about what it hauls in, and should not be afraid of making it its own. Which brings us rather neatly back to Polonius and his warning to his son about the dangers of borrowing and lending, because he then goes on to say perhaps the most profound thing in the entire play: 'This above all: to thine ownself be true.'

Biographical note

Dr. Gregory Bracken is a studio master at the Technical University of Delft's Architecture Faculty, and also a Research Fellow at the International Institute for Asian Studies at Leiden University. He did a BScArch and Dip.Arch in Bolton Street College of Technology (graduating with distinction in thesis in 1992) and then worked as an architect in Bangkok and Singapore before doing an MScArch, with a specialisation in urbanism, at TU Delft (graduating cum laude in 2004). He followed this with a PhD at Delft, which he successfully defended in 2009. He lives in Amsterdam.

18

A Small Island Off the East Coast of Trinidad

Lorcan Sirr
Conclusion

Dublin's future will most likely not be an amalgamation of the previous 17 chapters. It will most likely not even be the total realisation of one of the preceding chapters. Logic would lead one to presume that Dublin's future will be the realisation of some elements of some of the visions set out in this book – a fraction of a fraction; hope would lead one to think that someone with influence and conviction will read and be courageous enough to run with some of these ideas. Instead, the future of Dublin will be so dependent on myriad actions, inactions and events, some within our control, some without, that it is only the foolhardy who might specify with absolute certainty what Dublin will be like, as the only thing that is certain is uncertainty. But likewise, only the foolhardy would give up whatever opportunities come their way to influence the future of their capital city for the greater good; however, there is little point talking of visions unless there are means to achieve them, and increasingly opportunities to exercise this influence are at once becoming easier and more difficult.

On the one hand, methods of mass communication through social media have to a large extent democratised the dissemination of opinion and the ability to comment. Huge numbers of people now have some way to air their views through various electronic means: online discussion groups, Facebook,

Twitter, and so on. Immediately, news and government scandal and gossip and local policies and issues can be analysed and debated, picked apart and put back together again: politicians and cities can be demolished and rebuilt via a keyboard. Communities can be motivated to protest, to get together, to advise, to party, to assess, to respond, to form action groups and other communities and specialist sub-communities. Even national newspapers carry online comment sections – aside from the letters pages – so their readers can contribute their ha'penny's worth on the journalists' ha'penny's worth. The greatest asset of the internet is that anybody can contribute; it is also, frequently, its greatest liability, as straightforward debates and questions descend into fractious and personal mud-slinging contests over the most innocuous of issues. Often lost in the online 'debate' of course are the real issues which raised the questions in the first instance. What government or local authority needs to worry about reaction to their initiatives when any meaningful discussion disappears in the first twenty comments? It sometimes seems that the potential power of the internet is often wasted as the technology is subsumed under the weight of human personalities. Democracy can often be its own worst enemy.

The democratic achievement of any vision is also now often subject to the influence of what might loosely be termed 'management'. This involves the rise of what used to be – and still should be in local and central government – support functions, to a situation where offices like 'administration', 'finance' and the Orwellian 'human resources' are now regarded as initiators and arbiters of policy and initiatives.[1] So for a vision to be realised it not only has to pass the professional test – is it a good idea?; will it work?; how will it work?; will it be beneficial? – it also has to pass a set of tests set by generalist, administrative, invisible, unaccountable non-experts who will determine its viability based on how much money it will cost (not the long-term benefits), and how will it be staffed. The closure of public toilets in Dublin and the removal of pedestrian (pelican) crossings both appear to have occurred without debate or inquiry, and belie a lack of any sort of urban ethos or empathy. These managers have an unquestioned and suffocating influence on much of the world these days, and a brave, forward-looking and transparent city would only engage them as what they should be – support – not as determiners of policy, action and democratic will. The will of the people to realise their vision in and for a city should not be shot down by unaccountable bean-counters and health and safety paranoiacs.

Although democratic opportunity to comment or influence in cities is increasingly (through provision of faster broadband, for example), it is also being taken away equally fast, the dilution of the Freedom of Information Act being an example: in addition, hiding the release of public information under the phrase 'commercial sensitivity' has no place in a well-run public sector, as without transparency there can be no real trust. So, if there is no democratic aspect to the realisation of personal and professional visions then what results is the realisation of the will of power – essentially political will – which is mostly locally-focussed, short-term and unimaginative. That's if the politicians generate ideas themselves; if they don't, they will leave it to civil servants and in Ireland this will merely be an economic vision. In either case, on evidence to date, Dublin will not be at the core of any vision.

For years now, Ireland's economic rationale has been at best befuddled in its direction, as politicians, lacking in personal ideas and ideology leave policy development and implementation to the civil service. Conveniently, this creates distance between policy and responsibility, as politicians blame other bodies who are, again conveniently, both anonymous and unaccountable; this is one reason for the lack of political resignations in Ireland for below-par conduct or performance. But leaving strategy to the civil service or public sector means that, in general, economic necessities dominate, ironically without recognising the importance of Dublin; however, to have any vision realised based mainly on economic rationale would (and indeed might) be disastrous. Ireland still knows not whether it sits to the left or the right of the economic ideological spectrum (if it isn't all a blur by now), perhaps because we never really had a guiding philosophy or set of principles to begin with. Or even a vision. Maybe we are right-wing socialists, but in reality we have tried to sit on the fence and have it all ways. We are free-marketeers, apparently, or at least until there is a crisis when we suddenly discover our socialist DNA and feel the government money should be used to bail out those most affected by the economic crisis. Having no guiding principles, we get this upside-down and rescue the archi-tects of the disaster, the free-market bankers.

In the United Kingdom, the privatisation of what were formerly public services provided by local authorities has continued apace in cities as part of a free-market ideology started by Thatcher, seized on by New Labour, especially in their latter years, and continued by the Conservatives. Housing, transport, waste collection, benefits administration and many other services are now in the hands of the private sector, which is naturally enough, purely profit-driven. If Dublin appears to be heading towards any ideological position it would appear to be this one, unfortunately. But British governments and local authorities are learning the cost of such outsourcing – it is ultimately very expensive and not citizen-centred. An urban ideology driven purely by short-term economics is not a positive thing.

The point here is not to make an economic criticism, but to say that the realisation of a consistent, liveable, positive Dublin, one which supports Ireland effectively, is difficult to do in the absence of any guiding philosophy, principles, ideas or vision – democratic visions, not merely administrative or economic or management ones (indeed, it has been argued that our political system has created a situation where there is no room for new ideas). This applies first at a national level, but Irish politics are notoriously ideologically barren, a fact that doesn't inspire hope. But for Dublin, without a vision to guide and direct, without leaders with urban sentiment or ethos, the city is left with reactive or short-term policies. A city without visions such as those of Gillian, Dermot, James, Gregory, Helen, Katrina, Patrick, Catherine and the others set out in this book, is essentially a city that doesn't know where it's going, is a city adrift. It is the absence of an urban ideology that has Dublin the way it is, deftly tended to and defended carefully by a few doing their best (some planners, architects, businesspeople, community activists, academics, citizens, etc.) against what is essentially an anti-city mentality from those with real power, government politicians, administrators and policymakers (see the National Spatial Strategy for example).

So, what would I suggest? My vision for a future Dublin encompasses the following:

1. That Ireland, north and south, east and west, acknowledges the importance of Dublin in its future

2. That current and future successive governments recognise and support Dublin in their planning, economic, and social policies, and do not attempt to divert investment, development and income away from the capital city

3. That successive Dublin city managers are people with a proven urban ethos and sentiment, who understand from long experience how cities operate, and that they may be appointed from without the local government system and from outside Ireland

4. That there is increased transparency and accountability in the operations of the local and central powers who determine policy for Dublin; integrated targets are set and collective remuneration related to achieving these targets, and

5. That Ireland learns to celebrate, not denigrate, our capital city – Dublin belongs to everybody in Ireland and, treated properly, will maintain and sustain us well; treated badly, it will cost us dearly.

Ireland wants to be a successful global country but other such countries recognise their greatest assets are their cities and unless and until Ireland recognises that cities are the future – in our case, Dublin – then it is forever destined to remain, not just physically, but economically, sociologically, and ideologically a small island off the east coast of Trinidad.

Endnote

[1] See the late Professor Peter Mair's excellent paper to the McGill Summer School in 2010, 'Paradoxes and problems of modern Irish politics', in which he discusses this phenomenon amongst other interesting aspects of Irish politics.

Biographical note

Lorcan Sirr is a lecturer in the School of Real Estate and Construction Economics at the Dublin Institute of Technology. He has an MA in Literature from the Katholieke Universiteit Leuven in Belgium, and an MA and PhD from the School of Architecture and School of Planning and Landscape respectively, both at the University of Manchester in the UK. He has written for The Irish Times and Sunday Tribune, various journals and magazines, and provided commentary on housing, planning and related issues for RTÉ, the BBC, and CBC in Canada.